SEVEN GRAMMARS OF THE DIALECTS AND SUBDIALECTS OF THE BIHÁRÍ LANGUAGE

SEVEN

GRAMMARS

OF THE DIALECTS AND SUBDIALECTS
OF THE

BIHÁRÍ LANGUAGE

SPOKEN IN THE PROVINCE OF BIHÁR, IN THE EASTERN PORTION OF THE NORTH-WESTERN PROVINCES, AND IN THE NORTHERN PORTION OF THE CENTRAL PROVINCES

(Volume-3 in Three Parts)

Part-6. South Maithil-Mágadhí Dialect
Part-7. South Maithilí-Bangálí Dialect
Part-8. Maithil Bengálí Dialect

George A. Grierson, BC.S.

Publications

KALPAZ PUBLICATIONS

DELHI-110 052

Seven Grammars of the Dialects and Subdialects of the Bihárí Language

ISBN : 81-7835-451-9 (Set)
ISBN : 81-7835-454-3 (Vol. 3)

Published in 2005 in India by
Kalpaz Publications,
C-30, Satyawati Nagar,
Delhi-110 052
E-mail : kalpaz@hotmail.com

Laser Typesetting at: Tact Computer Graphics, Delhi
Printed at: Salasar Imaging Systems, Delhi

SEVEN

GRAMMARS

OF THE DIALECTS AND SUBDIALECTS OF THE

BIHÁRÍ LANGUAGE.

SPOKEN IN THE PROVINCE OF BIHÁR, IN THE EASTERN PORTION OF THE NORTH-WESTERN PROVINCES, AND IN THE NORTHERN PORTION OF THE CENTRAL PROVINCES.

PART VI.

SOUTH MAITHIL-MÁGADHÍ DIALECT

OF SOUTH MUNGER AND THE BÁRH SUBDIVISION OF PATNA.

Compiled under orders of the Government of Bengal,

By GEORGE A. GRIERSON, B.C.S.,

JOINT-MAGISTRATE OF PATNA.

CALCUTTA:

PRINTED AT THE BENGAL SECRETARIAT PRESS.

1886.

CONTENTS.

Section. Page.

CHAPTER VI.—THE REGULAR ACTIVE VERB.

CHAPTER VII.—THE REGULAR NEUTER VERB.

CHAPTER VIII.—VOCALIC ROOTS.

CHAPTER IX.—IRREGULAR VERBS.

CHAPTER X.—THE PASSIVE VERB.

CHAPTER XI.—CAUSAL VERBS.

CHAPTER XII.—COMPOUND VERBS.

DIVISION III.

INDECLINABLES.

APPENDIX.

SELECTIONS IN THE SOUTH MAITHIL-MÁGADHÍ DIALECT.

INTRODUCTION.

§ 1. The following grammar treats of an impure variety of the South Maithilí dialect, spoken in South Munger and in the Báṛh subdivision of Patna. This dialect is founded on the much more archaic North Maithilí dialect spoken in North Darbhangá and the Supaul subdivision of Bhagalpúr. A grammar and reading-book of Northern Maithilí has been published by the Asiatic Society of Bengal.* In Báṛh, and in the Jamuí subdivision, the language more nearly resembles the Mágadhí dialect than in the rest of South Munger.

§ 2. The alphabet and rules for spelling will be found in the General Introduction to this series of grammars, and the remarks therein found are not repeated here.

---

* Introduction to the Maithilí Language of North Bihár. By G. A. Grierson.

	Rs.	A.	P.
Part I, Grammar (extra number, J. A. S. B., 1880)	2	0	0
Part II, Chrestomathy and Vocabulary (extra number, J. A. S. B., 1882)	4	0	0

DIVISION I.

DECLENSION.

CHAPTER I.

NOUNS.

§ 3. For general remarks, see the General Introduction, § 38 and ff.

The following are the post-positions used in declining the noun in this dialect :—

		Power.
Nom.	*Wanting.*	
Acc.	*Wanting* or कऽ *ka*, के *ke*, or कौँ *kaŭ*.	
Instr.	सऽ *sa* or से *se*.	'By.'
Dat.	कऽ *ka*, के *ke*, or (rare in South Munger) कौँ *kaŭ*.	'To.'
	ला *lá*, ले *le*, लेल *lel*, लागी *lági*, or खातिर *khátir*.	'For.'
Abl.	सऽ *sa* or से *se*.	'From.'
Gen.	कऽ *ka*, के *kĕ*, or केर *ker*.	'Of.'
Loc.	मैँ *mē*.	'In.'
Voc.	*Wanting.*	

All these post-positions will only be used in one example, that of घोड़ा *ghoṛá*, 'a horse;' but they can all be used with all nouns.

Except that for the genitive, they can be used with all pronouns. In the genitive singular many pronouns do not take these post-positions, but have other forms subject to special rules.

The following are examples of declension.

§ 4. (a) Masculine Tadbhavas in आ *á*.

Example of the declension of a *tadbhava** masculine noun in आ *á* :—

घोड़ा *ghoṛá*, 'a horse.'

Short form, { Weak, घोड़ *ghoṛ*. Strong, घोड़ा *ghoṛá*. } Long form,* घोड़वा *ghŏṛ'wá*. Redundant form,† घोड़ौवा *ghŏṛauwá*.

Singular.

Nom.	घोड़ा[1] *ghoṛá*,	'a horse.'
Acc.	घोड़ा *ghoṛá* or घोड़ा कऽ *ghoṛá ka*, के *ke*, or कौँ *kaũ*,	'a horse.'
Instr.	घोड़ा सऽ *ghoṛá sa* or से *se*,	'by a horse.'
Dat.	घोड़ा कऽ *ghoṛá ka*, के *ke*, or कौँ *kaũ*,	'to a horse.'
	घोड़ा ला *ghoṛá lá*, लेल *lel*, लागी *lágí*, or खातिर *khátir*,	'for a horse.'
Abl.	घोड़ा सऽ, *ghoṛá sa*, से *se*,	'from a horse.'
Gen.	घोड़ा कऽ *ghoṛá ka*, घोड़ा के[2] *ghoṛá kĕ*, or घोड़ा केर *ghoṛá ker*,	'of a horse.'
Loc.	घोड़ा मेँ *ghoṛá mẽ*,	'in a horse.'
Voc.	ए घोड़ा *e ghoṛá !*	'O horse!'

[1] Or घोड़ *ghoṛ*, घोड़वा *ghŏṛ'wá*, or घोड़ौवा *ghŏṛauwá*, and so throughout.

[2] The genitival affixes remain unchanged before all genders and cases. Sometimes the genitive affix केरी *kerí* is borrowed from Mágadhí, and should be used only before feminine nouns, but this distinction is very little adhered to.

Plural.

Nom.	घोड़वनि *ghŏṛ'wani*,	'horses.'
Acc.	घोड़वनि कऽ *ghŏṛ'wani ka*, *&c.*,	'horses.'
Instr.	घोड़वनि सऽ *ghŏṛ'wani sa*, *&c.*,	'by horses.'
Dat.	घोड़वनि कऽ *ghŏṛ'wani ka*, *&c.*,	'to horses.'
	घोड़वनि ला *ghŏṛ'wani lá*, *&c.*,	'for horses.'
Abl.	घोड़वनि सऽ *ghŏṛ'wani sa*, *&c.*,	'from horses.'
Gen.	घोड़वनि कऽ *ghŏṛ'wani ka*, *&c.*,	'of horses.'
Loc.	घोड़वनि मेँ *ghŏṛ'wani mẽ*, *&c.*,	'in horses.'
Voc.	ए घोड़वनि *e ghŏṛ'wani*, *&c.*,	'O horses.'

This plural is not used in Jamuí, the periphrastic plural (§ 12) being used instead.

* See General Introduction, § 12.

† See General Introduction, §§ 12, 38, and ff.

DIVISION I.

DECLENSION.

CHAPTER I.

NOUNS.

§ 3. For general remarks, see the General Introduction, § 38 and ff.

The following are the post-positions used in declining the noun in this dialect :—

		Power.
Nom.	*Wanting.*	
Acc.	*Wanting* or कऽ *ka*, के *ke*, or कौँ *kaũ*.	
Instr.	सऽ *sa* or से *se*.	'By.'
Dat.	कऽ *ka*, के *ke*, or (rare in South Munger) कौँ *kaũ*.	'To.'
	ला *lá*, ले *le*, लेल *lel*, लागी *lági*, or खातिर *khátir*.	'For.'
Abl.	सऽ *sa* or से *se*.	'From.'
Gen.	कऽ *ka*, के *kĕ*, or केर *ker*.	'Of.'
Loc.	मेँ *mẽ*.	'In.'
Voc.	*Wanting.*	

All these post-positions will only be used in one example, that of घोड़ा *ghoṛá*, 'a horse;' but they can all be used with all nouns.

Except that for the genitive, they can be used with all pronouns. In the genitive singular many pronouns do not take these post-positions, but have other forms subject to special rules.

The following are examples of declension.

§ 4. (a) Masculine Tadbhavas in आ *á*.

Example of the declension of a *tadbhava* * masculine noun in आ *á* :—

घोड़ा *ghoṛá*, 'a horse.'

Short form, { Weak, घोड़ *ghoṛ*. Strong, घोड़ा *ghoṛá*. } Long form,* घोड़वा *ghŏṛ'wá*. Redundant form,† घोड़ौवा *ghŏṛauwá*.

Singular.

Nom.	घोड़ा [1] *ghoṛá*,	'a horse.'
Acc.	घोड़ा *ghoṛá* or घोड़ा कऽ *ghoṛá ka*, के *ke*, or कौँ *kaũ*,	'a horse.'
Instr.	घोड़ा सऽ *ghoṛá sa* or से *se*,	'by a horse.'
Dat.	घोड़ा कऽ *ghoṛá ka*, के *ke*, or कौँ *kaũ*,	'to a horse.'
	घोड़ा ला *ghoṛá lá*, लेल *lel*, लागी *lágí*, or खातिर *khátir*,	'for a horse.'
Abl.	घोड़ा सऽ, *ghoṛá sa*, से *se*,	'from a horse.'
Gen.	घोड़ा कऽ *ghoṛá ka*, घोड़ा के[2] *ghoṛá kĕ*, or घोड़ा केर *ghoṛá ker*,	'of a horse.'
Loc.	घोड़ा मेँ *ghoṛá mẽ*,	'in a horse.'
Voc.	ए घोड़ा *e ghoṛá !*	'O horse!'

[1] Or घोड़ *ghoṛ*, घोड़वा *ghŏṛ'wá*, or घोड़ौवा *ghŏṛauwá*, and so throughout.

[2] The genitival affixes remain unchanged before all genders and cases. Sometimes the genitive affix केरी *kerí* is borrowed from Mágadhí, and should be used only before feminine nouns, but this distinction is very little adhered to.

Plural.

Nom.	घोड़वनि *ghŏṛ'wani*,	'horses.'
Acc.	घोड़वनि कऽ *ghŏṛ'wani ka*, &c.,	'horses.'
Instr.	घोड़वनि सऽ *ghŏṛ'wani sa*, &c.,	'by horses.'
Dat.	घोड़वनि कऽ *ghŏṛ'wani ka*, &c.,	'to horses.'
	घोड़वनि ला *ghŏṛ'wani lá*, &c.,	'for horses.'
Abl.	घोड़वनि सऽ *ghŏṛ'wani sa*, &c.,	'from horses.'
Gen.	घोड़वनि कऽ *ghŏṛ'wani ka*, &c.,	'of horses.'
Loc.	घोड़वनि मेँ *ghŏṛ'wani mẽ*, &c.,	'in horses.'
Voc.	ए घोड़वनि *e ghŏṛ'wani*, &c.,	'O horses.'

This plural is not used in Jamuí, the periphrastic plural (§ 12) being used instead.

---

* See General Introduction, § 12.

† See General Introduction, §§ 12, 38, and ff.

§ 5. (b) Masculine Nouns ending in Silent Consonants.

Example of the declension of a masculine noun ending in a silent consonant:—

घर *ghar*, 'a house.'

Short form, { Weak, घर *ghar*. Strong, घरा *ghará*. } Long form,* घरऽवा *ghar'wá*. Redundant form,* घरौवा *gharauwá*

Singular and Plural.

Nom.	घर[1] *ghar*,	'a house.'
Acc.	घर कठ *ghar ka*, *&c.*,	'a house.'
Instr.	घरेँ *gharẽ*, घर सठ *ghar sa*, *&c.*,	'by a house.'
Dat.	घर ला *ghar lá*, *&c.*,	'for a house.'
Abl.	घर सठ *ghar sa*, *&c.*,	'from a house.'
Gen.	घर कठ *ghar ka*, *&c.*,	'of a house.'
Loc.	घरे *ghare*, घर मेँ *ghar mẽ*,	'in a house.'
Voc.	ए घर *e ghar !*	'O house!'

[1] Or घरऽवा *ghar'wá*, घरौवा *gharauwá*, and so throughout.

§ 6. It is not necessary to decline further any nouns in full, as the above examples suffice. All nouns ending in vowels are declined like घोड़ा *ghoṛá*, and all those ending in silent consonants like घर *ghar*. The final syllables of all long and redundant forms may optionally be nasalised by the addition of *anunásik :* thus घोड़ऽवा *ghŏṛ'wá* or घोड़ऽवाँ *ghŏṛ'wấ ;* घरौवा *gharauwá* or घरौवाँ *gharauwấ ;* मलिया *maliyá* or मलियाँ *maliyấ*.

Note, however, that—

(1) Occasionally in the case of masculine nouns ending in a silent consonant we find an instrumental in एँ *ẽ* and a locative in ए *e :* thus हम बलेँ ले जाएब *ham balẽ le jáĕb*, 'I shall take away by force,' where बलेँ *balẽ* is the instrumental of बल *bal*, 'force;' घाटे *gháṭe*, 'at a landing stage,' locative of घाट *gháṭ*, 'a landing stage:' so also घरे घरे *ghare ghare*, 'in every house,' 'from house to house.'

---

* See General Introduction, §§ 12, 38, and ff.

(2) Certain verbal nouns ending in ल *l* have an oblique form in ला *lá:* thus देखल *dekhal*, abl. देखला से *děkh'lá se*, 'from seeing;' also verbal nouns in the form of the root have an oblique form in अ *a* or ए *ě:* thus देख *dekh*, dat. देखत के *dekha ke* or देखे के *dekhě ke*, 'for seeing.' Full particulars concerning these nouns will be found in § 111.

An example of each of the more common forms of nouns follows:—

§ 7. (c) Masculine Tatsamas* in आ *á*.

राजा *rájá*, 'a king.'

Short form, राजा *rájá*. Long form,* रजऽवा *raj'wá*. Redundant form,* रजौवा *rajauwá*

Nom. plur. रजऽवनि *raj'wani*.

§ 8. (d) Masculine Nouns in ई *í*.

माली *málí*, 'a gardener.'

Short form, माली *málí*. Long form,* मलिया *maliyá*. Redundant form,* मलियवा *maliyawá* or मलीवा *malíwá*.

Nom. plur. मालियनि *maliyani*.

§ 9. (e) Masculine Nouns in ऊ *ú*.

लाऊ *láú*, 'a barber.'†

Short form, लाऊ *láú*. Long form,‡ लउआ *laüá* or लौआ *lauá* Redundant form,‡ लउअवा *laüawá* or लौअवा *lauawá*.

Nom. plur. लौअनि *lauani*.

§ 10. (f) Feminine Nouns in ई *í* and इ *i*.

पोथी *pothí*, 'a book.'

Short form, पोथी *pothí*. Long form,‡ पोथिया *pŏthiyá*. Redundant form,‡ पोथियवा *pŏthiyawá* or पोथीवा *pothíwá*.

Nom. plur. पोथियनि *pothiyani*.

---

* See General Introduction, §§ 12, 38, and ff., 34 and 36.

† Kellogg in his Hindí Grammar incorrectly gives आँसू *ású* as an example of a feminine noun in ऊ *ú:* it is masculine. आँसू *ású* is not used in Bihárí, लोर *lor* being the word for 'a tear.'

‡ See General Introduction, §§ 12, 38, and ff., 34 and 36.

CHAPTER II.

ADJECTIVES.

§ 14. Gender.

See General Introduction, § 42 and ff.

§ 15. Numeral Adjectives.

The cardinals are nearly the same as those in High Hindí. The following are the ones that present points of difference :—

1 = एक *ěk* or एगो *ego.*
2 = दू *dú* or दुइ *duí.*
9 = नउ *na* or नौँ *nõ.*
11 = एगारह *ěgára.*
23 = तैस *tais.*
29 = उन्तिस *untis.*
31 = एक॰तिस *ěk'tis.*
32 = बत्तिस *battis.*
33 = तेँतिस *tẽtis.*
34 = चौँतिस *chãũtis.*
35 = पैँतिस *pãĩtis.*
36 = छत्तिस *chhattis.*
37 = सैँतिस *sãĩtis.*
38 = अड़॰तिस *aṛ'tis.*
39 = उन॰चालिस *un'chális.*

40 = चालिस *chális.*
41 = एक॰तालिस *ěk'tális.*
42 = ब्यालिस *byális.*
43 = तेतालिस *tetális.*
44 = चौआलिस *chaŭális.*
45 = पैतालिस *paĩtális.*
46 = छियालिस *chhiyális.*
47 = सैतालिस *saĩtális.*
48 = अड़॰तालिस *aṛ'tális.*
57 = सँताओन *sãtáõn.*
58 = अँठाओन *ãṭháõn.*
63 = तिरेसठ *tiresaṭh.*
66 = छियर॰सठ *chhiyar'saṭh.*
100 = सै *sai.*

§ 16. Ordinals.

The ordinals up to 'sixth' are as follows :—

1st = पहिल *pahil* or पहिल॰का *pahil'ká ; obl.* पहिला *pahilá.**
2nd = दोसर *dosar* or दूसर *dúsar ; obl.* दोस॰रा *dŏs'rá* or दुस॰रा *dus'rá.**
3rd = तेसर *tesar* or तीसर *tísar ; obl.* तेस॰रा *tĕs'rá* or तिस॰रा *tis'rá.**

---

* The first three ordinals follow pronominal genitives in the formation of oblique forms. See *post*, § 34.

4th = चारिम *chárim* (not used in Jamuí) or चौठ *chauṭh* or चौठा *chauṭhá*.

5th = पँचन्वाँ *pãch'wã* or पँचन्मा *pãch'má*.

6th = छठन्वाँ *chhaṭh'wã* or छठन्मा *chhaṭh'má*.

The ordinals above 'sixth' are all formed by adding वाँ *wã* or मा *má* to the cardinals: as दसन्वाँ *das'wã* or दसन्मा *das'má*, 'tenth;' पचसन्वाँ *pachas'wã* or पचसन्मा *pachas'má*, 'fiftieth.'

§ 17. Fractional Numbers.

These are—

$\frac{1}{4}$ = पौ *pau* or पौआ *pauá*.

$\frac{1}{3}$ = तेखन्री *tĕkh'ri* or तेहाइ *tĕháï*.

$\frac{1}{2}$ = आधा *ádhá*, आध *ádh*, or अध *adh*.

$\frac{3}{4}$ = पौन *paun* or तीन पा *tín pá*.

$-\frac{1}{4}$ = पौने *paune*.

$1\frac{1}{4}$ or $+\frac{1}{4}$ = सावा *sáwá*.

$1\frac{1}{2}$ = डेढ़ *ḍeṛh*.

$2\frac{1}{2}$ = अढ़ाइ *aṛháï*.

$+\frac{1}{2}$ = साढ़े *sáṛhe*.

§ 18. Multiplicatives.

Multiplicatives, such as the English 'twice' and 'thrice,' are not found in this dialect. The Bihárí idiom is illustrated in such phrases as दू सते चौदह *dú sate chaudah*, 'two seven's, fourteen;' छ ती अठारह *chha tí aṭhárah*, 'six three's, eighteen,' which correspond to the English idioms 'seven times two' and 'three times six.' Numbers thus used are called multiplicatives, and differ in some respects from the cardinals. The following are the multiplicative numbers up to 10, including fractions:—

× 1, का *ká*.

× $1\frac{1}{4}$, सवा *sawá*.

× $1\frac{1}{2}$, डेओढ़ा *ḍĕoṛhá*.

× 2, दोबरा *dobará*.

× $2\frac{1}{2}$, अढ़ैया *aṛhaiyá*.

× 3, तौ *tí* or तेबरा *tebará*.
× 3½, ऊण्ठा *hunṭhá*.
× 4, चौका *chauká* or चौबरा *chaubará*.
× 4½, ढौँचा *ḍhõcha* or धौँचा *dhaũchá*.
× 5, पचे *pache* or पाँचब्बरा *pãch'bará*.
× 5½, पऊँचा *pahuṅchá*.
× 6, छके *chhake*.
× 7, सते *sate* or सातब्बरा *sát'bará*.
× 8, अट्ठे *áṭṭhe* or आठब्बरा *áṭh'bará*.
× 9, नमा *namá* or नौबरा *naubará*.
× 10, दाहीँ *dáhí* or दसब्बरा *das'bará*.

§ 19. Definite Cardinals.

These are as follows:—

एगो *ego*, 'the one.'

दूओ *dúo*, दुन्नो *dunno*, 'the two,' 'both;'

तीनो *tíno*, 'the three;'

चारो *cháro*, 'the four;' and so on,

adding ओ *o* to the numerals after omitting a final short vowel. Example: पाँचो भाइ जौरे छथी *pãchõ bhái jaure chhathí*, 'the five brothers are an undivided family.'

§ 20. Indefinite Cardinals.

The termination ओँ *õ* or अन *an* added to the numbers 'one hundred,' 'one thousand,' and so on, always denotes an indefinite number of these aggregates. In this idiom सैकर *saikar* is always substituted for सै *sai*, 'one hundred.' Examples are सैकरोँ पेड़ *saĭk'rõ peṛ*, 'hundreds of trees;' हजारन *hajáran*, 'thousands;' लाखोँ *lákhõ*, 'tens of thousands;' हजारोँ अदिमी मरल्ला *hajárõ adimí mar'lá*, 'thousands of men died.'

§ 21. Collective Numerals.

These—viz. जोड़ा *joṛá*, 'a pair,' गण्डा *gaṇḍá*, 'a four'—are the same as in High Hindí.

CHAPTER III.

PRONOUNS.

§ 22. The following tables show the declensional forms of the principal pronouns and pronominal forms.

The declension of pronouns presents some important points of difference from that of nouns, which must be carefully noticed.

While nouns frequently remain unchanged before post-positions, pronouns, with few exceptions, change to some other form, called the *oblique* or *inflected base.*

The accusative singular of pronouns is, with one or two exceptions, never the same as the nominative. In circumstances corresponding to those in which the accusative of a noun takes the nominative form, the accusative of a pronoun usually takes the oblique form without any post-position.

The genitive forms of pronouns ending in र *r* and न *n* are also to be noticed. They have all oblique forms ending in रा *rá* or ना *ná*, for which see § 34.

Pronouns have the same form, whether referring to masculine or feminine nouns. With the exception of the pronouns of the second person, they all want the vocative case.

§ 23. Pronouns of the First Person and of the Second Person Non-Honorific.

These pronouns have each two forms—a shorter and a longer. The shorter form in the singular is rarely used except in poetry.

हम *ham*, 'I.'

Singular.

	Shorter form.	*Longer form.*
Nom.	*Wanting.*	हम *ham*, हमऽ *hama*, हमेँ *hamẽ*, or हम्मेँ *hammẽ*.
Acc.	मोरा[1] *morá* or मोरा के *morá ke*.	हमरा[1] *ham'rá* or हमरा के *ham'rá ke*.
Instr.	मोरा से *morá se*.	हमरा से *ham'rá se*.
Dat.	मोरा ला *morá lá*.	हमरा ला *ham'rá lá*.
Abl.	मोरा से *morá se*.	हमरा से *ham'rá se*.
Gen.	मोर *mor*.	हम्मर *hammar*.
Loc.	मोरा में *morá mẽ*.	हमरा में *ham'rá mẽ*.
Voc.	*Wanting.*	*Wanting.*

[1] मोरो *moro* and हमरो *ham'ro* may be used for मोरा *morá* and हमरा *ham'rá* in an emphatic sense: thus हमरो दऽ *ham'ro da*, 'give to me also.' In poetry a shorter oblique form, मोहि *mŏhi*, instead of मोरा *morá*, is sometimes found.

Plural.

	Shorter form.	*Longer form.*
Nom.	हमनी *ham'ní*.	हमरा आर के *ham'rá ár ke*.[1]
Acc.	हमनी (के) *ham'ní (ke)*.	हमरा आर (के) *ham'rá ár (ke)*.
Instr.	हमनी से *ham'ní se*.	हमरा आर से *ham'rá ár se*.
Dat.	हमनी ला *ham'ní lá*.	हमरा आर ला *ham'rá ár lá*.
Abl.	हमनी से *ham'ní se*.	हमरा आर से *ham'rá ár se*.
Gen.	हमनी के *ham'ní kĕ*.	हमरा आर के *ham'rá ár kĕ*.
Loc.	हमनी में *ham'ní mẽ*.	हमरा आर में *ham'rá ár mẽ*.
Voc.	*Wanting.*	*Wanting.*

[1] Or हम सभ *ham sabh* (this only in the nominative), हमनी सभ *ham'ní sabh*, हमें आर के *hamẽ ár ke*, or हमनी आर के *ham'ní ár ke*, and so throughout.

तोँ *tõ*, 'thou.'

Singular.

	Shorter form.	*Longer form.*
Nom.	*Wanting.*	तोँ *tõ* or तोँहँ *tõhẽ.*
Acc.	तोरा[1] *torá* or तोरा के *torá ke.*	तोहरा[1] *tŏh'rá* or तोहरा के *tŏh'rá ke.*
Instr.	तोरा से *torá se.*	तोहरा से *tŏh'rá se.*
Dat.	तोरा ला *torá lá.*	तोहरा ला *tŏh'rá lá*
Abl.	तोरा से *torá se.*	तोहरा से *tŏh'rá se.*
Gen.	तोर *tor.*	तोहर *tohar.*
Loc.	तोरा मेँ *torá mẽ.*	तोहरा मेँ *tŏh'rá mẽ.*
Voc.	*Wanting.*	हो तोँ *ho tõ* or (when addressing a female) हे तोँ *he tõ.*

[1] तोरो *toro* and तोहरो *tŏh'ro* may be used for तोरा *torá* and तोहरा *tŏh'rá* in an emphatic sense: thus तोहरो देखैछी *tŏh'ro dekhaichhí*, 'I see you also.' In poetry, a shorter oblique form, तोहि *tŏhi* instead of तोरा *torá*, is sometimes found.

Plural.

	Shorter form.	*Longer form.*
Nom.	तोहनी *tŏh'ní.*	तोरा आर के *torá ár ke.*[1]
Acc.	तोहनी (के) *tŏh'ní (ke).*	तोरा आर (के) *torá ár (ke).*
Instr.	तोहनी से *tŏh'ní se.*	तोरा आर से *torá ár se.*
Dat.	तोहनी ला *tŏh'ní lá.*	तोरा आर ला *torá ár lá.*
Abl.	तोहनी से *tŏh'ní se.*	तोरा आर से *torá ár se.*
Gen.	तोहनी के *tŏh'ní kĕ.*	तोरा आर के *torá ár kĕ.*
Loc.	तोहनी मेँ *tŏh'ní mẽ.*	तोरा आर मेँ *torá ár mẽ.*
Voc.	*Wanting.*	हे तोरा आर *he torá ár.*

[1] Or तोँ सभ *tõ sabh* (this only in the nominative), तोहनी सभ *tŏh'ní sabh*, तोँहँ आर के *tõhẽ ár ke*, तोहनी आर के *tŏh'ní ár ke*, तोहरा आर के *tŏh'rá ár ke*, and so throughout.

§ 24. Pronoun of the Second Person Honorific and Reflexive Pronoun.

अपन्ने *ap'nĕ*, 'your honor.'

This pronoun is declined regularly like a substantive: thus—अपन्ने के *ap'nĕ ke*, अपन्ने से *ap'nĕ se*, &c.

The nominative plural is अपन्ने *ap'nĕ log*; or सभ *sabh* may be used instead of लोग *log*.

अपन्ने *ap'nĕ*, 'self.'

This presents some irregularities, and is therefore declined in full.

	Singular.	*Plural.*
Nom.	अपन्ने *ap'nĕ*.	अपन्ने सभ *ap'nĕ sabh*.
Acc.	अपन्ना (के) *ap'ná (ke)*.	अपन्ना सभ (के) *ap'ná sabh (ke)*.
Instr.	अपन्ना से *ap'ná se*.	अपन्ना सभ से *ap'na sabh se*.
Dat.	अपन्ना ला *ap'ná lá*.	अपन्ना सभ ला *ap'ná sabh lá*.
Abl.	अपन्ना से *ap'ná se*.	अपन्ना सभ से *ap'ná sabh se*.
Gen.	अप्पन *appan* or आपन *ápan*.	आपुस के or केर *ápus kĕ* or *ker*.
Loc.	अपन्ना में *ap'ná mẽ*.	आपुस में *ápus mẽ*.

§ 25. Demonstrative Pronouns.

These are (1) the proximate demonstrative ई *í*, 'this,' and (2) the remote demonstrative ऊ *ú*, 'that.'

Like the personal pronouns, they have each two forms, a shorter and a longer.

ई í, 'this.'

Singular.

	Shorter form.	*Longer form.*
Nom.	ई *í.*	*Wanting.*
Acc.	एहि (के) *ĕhi* (*ke*).	एकरा (के) *ĕk'rá* (*ke*).
Instr.	एहि से *ĕhi se.*	एकरा से *ĕk'rá se.*
Dat.	एहि ला *ĕhi lá.*	एकरा ला *ĕk'rá lá.*
Abl.	एहि से *ĕhi se.*	एकरा से *ĕk'rá se.*
Gen.	एहि के *ĕhi kĕ.*	एकर *ekar*, or एकरा के, केर *ĕk'rá kĕ, ker.*
Loc.	एहि मेँ, *ĕhi mẽ.*	एकरा मेँ *ĕk'rá mẽ.*

Plural.

	Shorter form.	*Longer form.*
Nom.	इन्ही *inhí*, हिन्ही *hinhí*, हिनी *hiní*, इन्ह *inh*, or इन *in.*	इनका आर के *in'ká ár ke.*[2]
Acc.	इन्ह[1] (के) *inh* (*ke*).	इनका आर (के) *in'ká ár* (*ke*).
Instr.	इन्ह से *inh se.*	इनका आर से *in'ká ár se.*
Dat.	इन्ह ला *inh lá.*	इनका आर ला *in'ká ár lá.*
Abl.	इन्ह से *inh se.*	इनका आर से *in'ká ár se.*
Gen.	इन्ह के, केर *inh kĕ, ker.*	इनका आर के *in'ká ár kĕ.*
Loc.	इन्ह मेँ *inh mẽ.*	इनका आर मेँ, *in'ká ár mẽ.*

[1] Or हिन्ह *hinh*, इन *in*, or हिन *hin*, and so throughout.

[2] Or इनकनी *in'kaní*, इन्हकनी *inh'kaní*, हिनकनी *hin'kaní*, हिन्हकनी *hinh'kaní*, or इनका *in'ká*, इन्हका *inh'ká*, हिनका *hin'ká*, हिन्हका *hinh'ká*, or इनकरा *in'kará*, इन्हकर *inh'kará*, हिनकरा *hin'kará*, हिन्हकरा *hinh'kará*, and so throughout.

NOTE.—The plural of this pronoun is used in a singular honorific sense. To form the non-honorific plural, the word सभ *sabh* is added to any of the above forms: thus, nominative plural ई सभ *í sabh*, एकरा सभ *ĕk'rá sabh*, इन्ह सभ *inh sabh*, हिन्हकरा सभ *hinh'kará sabh*, and so on.

ऊ *ú*, 'that.'

The close analogy between the declension of this pronoun and that of ई *í*, 'this,' will be manifest from the following paradigm:—

Singular.

	Shorter form.	*Longer form.*
Nom.	ऊ *ú.*	*Wanting.*
Acc.	ओहि (के) *ŏhi* (*ke*).	ओकरा (के) *ŏk'rá* (*ke*).
Instr.	ओहि से *ŏhi se.*	ओकरा से *ŏk'rá se.*
Dat.	ओहि ला *ŏhi lá.*	ओकरा ला *ŏk'rá lá.*
Abl.	ओहि से *ŏhi se.*	ओकरा से *ŏk'rá se.*
Gen.	ओहि के *ŏhi kĕ.*	ओकर *okar*, or ओकरा के, केर *ŏk'rá kĕ, ker.*
Loc.	ओहि में *ŏhi mẽ.*	ओकरा में *ŏk'rá mẽ.*

Plural.

	Shorter form.	*Longer form.*
Nom.	उन्ही *unhí*, हुन्ही *hunhí*, हुनी *huní*, उन्ह *unh*, or उन *un.*	उनका आर के *unká ár ke.*[2]
Acc.	उन्ह[1] (के) *unh* (*ke*).	उनका आर (के) *un'ká ár* (*ke*).
Instr.	उन्ह से *unh se.*	उनका आर से *un'ká ár se.*
Dat.	उन्ह ला *unh lá.*	उनका आर ला *un'ká ár lá.*
Abl.	उन्ह से *unh se.*	उनका आर से *un'ká ár se.*
Gen.	उन्ह के, केर *unh kĕ, ker.*	उनका आर के *un'ká ár kĕ.*
Loc.	उन्ह में *unh mĕ.*	उनका आर में *un'ká ár mĕ.*

[1] Or हुन्ह *hunh*, उन *un*, or हुन *hun*, and so throughout.

[2] Or उनकनी *un'kaní*, उन्हकनी *unh'kaní*, हुनकनी *hun'kaní*, हुन्हकनी *hunh'kaní*, or उनका *un'ká*, उन्हका *unh'ká*, हुनका *hun'ká*, हुन्हका *hunh'ká*, or उनकरा *un'kará*, उन्हकरा *unh'kara*, हुनकरा *hun'kará*, हुन्हकरा *hunh'kará*, and so throughout.

NOTE.—The plural of this pronoun is used in a singular honorific sense. To form the non-honorific plural, the word सभ *sabh* is added to any of the above forms: thus, nominative plural ऊ सभ *ú sabh*, ओकरा सभ *ŏk'rá sabh*, उन्ह सभ *unh sabh*, हुन्हकरा सभ *hunh'kará sabh*, and so on.

NOTE.—In the above two demonstrative pronouns the shorter form may be used either adjectivally or substantivally, but the longer form can only used as a substantive, and never as an adjective.

§ 26. Correlative Pronouns.

These are (1) the relative pronoun जे *je*, 'who;' (2) the correlative pronoun से *se*, 'that;' and (3) the interrogative pronoun के *ke*, 'who?'

The close analogy between their forms should be noted. Like the personal and demonstrative pronouns, they have each a shorter and a longer form.

It is not necessary to give their declension in full, as it is on exactly the same lines as that of the demonstrative pronouns. I shall therefore give only the nominative, genitive, and general oblique forms for each number.

Relative.

जे *je*, 'who.'

Singular.

	Shorter form.	*Longer form.*
Nom.	जे *je.*	*Wanting.*
Gen.	जेहि के *jĕhi kĕ.*	जेकर *jekar.*
Obl.	जेहि *jĕhi.*	जेकरा *jĕk'rá.*

Plural.

Nom.	जिन्ही *jinhi.*	जिनका आर के *jin'ká ár ke.*
Gen.	जिन्ह के *jinh kĕ.*	जिनका आर के *jin'ká ár kĕ.*
Obl.	जिन्ह *jinh.*	जिनका आर *ji'nká ár.*

Correlative.

से *se*, 'that.'

Singular.

	Shorter form.	*Longer form.*
Nom.	से *se.*	*Wanting.*
Gen.	तेहि के *tĕhi kĕ.*	तेकर *tekar.*
Obl.	तेहि *tĕhi.*	तेकरा *tĕk'rá.*

Plural.

Nom.	तिन्ही *tinhí.*	तिनन्का आर के *tin'ká ár ke.*
Gen.	तिन्ह के *tinh kĕ.*	तिनन्का आर के *tin'ká ár kĕ.*
Obl.	तिन्ह *tinh.*	तिनन्का आर *tin'ká ár.*

Interrogative.

के *ke*, 'who?'

Singular.

	Shorter form.	*Longer form.*
Nom.	के *ke* or कौन *kaun.*	*Wanting.*
Gen.	केहि के *kĕhi kĕ.*	केकर *kekar.*
Obl.	केहि *kĕhi.*	केकन्रा *kĕk'rá.*

Plural.

Nom.	किन्ही *kinhi.*	किनन्का आर के *kin'ká ár ke.*
Gen.	किन्ह के *kinh kĕ.*	किनन्का आर के *kin'ká ár kĕ.*
Obl.	किन्ह *kinh.*	किनन्का आर *kin'ká ár.*

Other optional forms as in the demonstrative pronouns.

NOTE.—In the above correlative pronouns the shorter form may be used either adjectivally or substantivally, but the longer form can only be used as a substantive, and never as an adjective. As in the case of the demonstrative pronouns, the non-honorific plural is formed by adding सभ *sabh*.

§ 27. Interrogative Pronoun.

SUBSTANTIVAL.

की *kí*, 'what?'

This pronoun is really a neuter form of के *ke*, and can only refer to inanimate things. Its plural is the same as that of के *ke*.

Singular.

Nom. की *kí* or का *ká.*

Obl. की *kí,* का *ká,* किथि *kithi,* or काहे *káhĕ,* कहि *kahi,* किये *kiye.*

Declined regularly like a substantive. Its dative, किथि ला *kithi lá* or किथि लाय *kithi láy,* 'for what?' is used as an adverb, meaning 'why?'

§ 28. Indefinite Pronoun.

केऊ *kĕú,* 'anyone,' 'some one.'

This is declined throughout the singular only.

Singular.

Nom. केऊ *kĕú,* कोइ *koï,* or कोय *koy.*

Obl. कोइ *koï,* केकऽरो *kĕk'rŏ,* or किथियो *kithiyŏ.*

Declined regularly like a substantive, except the genitive, which is केकऽरो *kĕk'rŏ.*

§ 29. किछु *kichhu,* 'anything,' 'something.'

Nom. किछु *kichhu,* कुछ *kuchh,* or कुच्छु *kuchchhu.*
Obl. कथू *kathú,* किछु *kichhu,* कुछ *kuchh,* or कथियो *kathiyŏ.*

Declined regularly like a substantive in the singular. The plural is wanting.

§ 30. The indefinite pronoun सभ *sabh,* सब *sab,* or सभो *sabhi,* 'all,' 'every one,' is declined regularly like a substantive. When plurality is to be emphasised, it has an oblique plural form सभन *sabhan*: thus, सभ के *sabh kĕ* 'of all,' *taken as a whole*; but सभन के *sabhan kĕ,* 'of all,' *taken severally.*

§ 31. The indefinite pronouns जेकेऊ *jekĕú,* 'whoever,' and जेकिछु *jekichhu,* 'whatever,' are compounds, and are declined regularly like their component parts: thus, acc. sing. जेह केकऽरो के *jěh kěk'rŏ ke*, जेह किछु के *jěh kichhu ke*; instr. जेह केकऽरो से *jěh kěk'rŏ se*, &c.

The indefinite pronominal adjective कऽ *ka*, कैक *kaik*, or कतेक *katěk*, signifies 'several.' It is also used as an interrogative, meaning 'how many?'

§ 32. Derivative Pronominal Forms.

The following table gives the more usual pronominal adjectives and adverbs in a succinct form.

		PRONOUN.	Manner.	
			Pron. Adj.	Pron. Adv.
Demonstrative ...	Proximate ...	ई *i*, 'this' ...	ऐसन *aisan*, एहन *ĕhan*, एना *ĕná*, इना *iná*, 'of this kind.'	एहिना *ĕhiná*, 'thus.'
	Remote ...	ऊ *ú*, 'that' ...	वैसन *waisan*, ओहन *ŏhan*, ओना *ŏná*, 'of that kind.'	ओहिना, *ŏhiná* 'in that way.'
Relative		जे *je*, 'who' ...	जैसन *jaisan*, जेहन *jĕhan*, जिना *jiná*, 'of what kind.'	जहिना *jahiná*, 'in what way.'
Correlative		से *se*, 'that' ...	तैसन *taisan*, तेहन *tĕhan*, तिना *tiná*, 'of that kind.'	तहिना *tahiná*, 'in that way.'
Interrogative		के *ke*, 'who?' ...	कैसन *kaisan*, केहन *kĕhan*, किना *kiná*, 'of what kind?'	कहिना *kahiná*, 'in what way?'

Pron. adj. of Quantity.	Pron. adv. of Time.	Pron. adv. of Place.	Pron. adv. of Direction.
एतऽना *ĕt'ná*, 'this much.'	एहिया *ĕhiyá*, 'now.'	हिँयाँ *hĩyā́*, 'here.'	इन्द० *inda*, इनैँ *inẽ*, 'hither.'
ओतऽना *ŏt'ná*, 'that much.'	ओहिया *ŏhiyá*, 'then.'	हुँआँ *hũā́*, 'there.'	उन्द० *unda*, उनैँ *unẽ* 'thither.'
जेतऽना *jĕt'ná*, 'how much.'	जहिया *jahiyá*, 'when.'	जहाँ *jahā́*, 'where.'	जिन्द० *jinda*, जनैँ *janẽ*, 'whither.'
तेतऽना *tĕt'ná*, 'so much.'	तहिया *tahiyá*, 'then.'	तहाँ *tahā́*, 'there.'	तिन्द० *tinda*, तनैँ *tanẽ*, 'thither.'
केतऽना *kĕt'ná*, 'how much?'	कहिया *kahiyá*, 'when?'	कहाँ *kahā́*, 'where?'	किन्द० *kinda*, कनैँ *kanẽ* 'whither?'

§ 33. Adjectival Pronouns.

The following sentences are designed to show the use of the various pronouns, both adjectivally and substantivally. Before doing so it is best to note here that colloquially the oblique forms एह *ĕh*, ओह *ŏh*, जेह *jĕh*, तेह *tĕh*, and केह *kĕh*, are frequently written and pronounced ई *í*, ऊ *ú*, जे *je*, ते *te*, and के *ke* respectively.

Note that while जे *je* and से *se* are used either as adjectives or substantives in both the nominative and oblique cases, के *ke* cannot be used as an adjective at all. When used as an adjective, के *ke* always becomes कौन *kaun* or कोन *kon*.

(1) जे ऐलै छल, से गेलै, *je ailai chhal, se gelai:* 'he who had come, went.

(2) जे अदिमी ऐलै छेलै, से अदिमी गेलै, *je adimí ailai chhĕlai, se adimí gelai:* 'the man who had come, went.'

(3) जेकर खेत, तेकर धान, *jekar khet, tekar dhán:* 'he who owns the field, owns the paddy.'

(4) जे अदिमी के खेत, से अदिमी के धान *je adimí kĕ khet, se adimí kĕ dhán:* 'the man who owns the field, owns the paddy.'

(5) के छिलै *ke chhilai?* 'who was it?'

(6) ऊ कोन अदिमी छिकै *ú kon adimí chhikai?* 'what man is he?'

(7) केकर घोड़ा छिकै *kekar ghoṛá chhikai?* 'whose is the horse?'

(8) कोन अदिमी के घोड़ा छिकै *kon adimí kĕ ghoṛá chhikai?* 'to what person does the horse belong?'

(9) की छिकै *kí chhikai?* 'what is it?'

(10) की गाछ छिकै *kí gáchh chhikai?* 'what tree is it?'

(11) किथि मेँ पानि नानऽलऽ छऽ *kithi mẽ páni nán'la chha?* 'in what have you brought the water?'

(12) कोन लोटा मेँ पानि नानऽलऽ छऽ *kon loṭá mẽ páni nán'la chha?* 'in what *loṭa* have you brought the water?'

(13) कोय नहीँ ऐलै *koy nahí ailai,* 'no one came.'

(14) कोय लरिका नहीं ऐलै *koy lariká nahí ailai*, 'no boy came.'

(15) ऊ गाँव में केकरो किछु नहीं छै *ú gãw mẽ kĕk'rŏ kichhu nahí chhai*, 'in that village no one has anything.'

(16) ऊ गाँव के कोइ बनियाँ से किछु नै मिलतै *ú gãw kĕ koï baniyã se kichhu nai mil'tai*, 'in that village nothing will be got from any shopkeeper.'

(17) ऊ दवाय कऽ किथियो में धरे* होतै *ú dawáy ka kithiyŏ mẽ dharĕ* * *hotai*, 'it will be (necessary) to put that medicine into something.'

(18) कऽ अदिमी ऐलहैन्ह *ka adimí ăil'hainh*, 'several men came,' or 'how many men came?'

§ 34. The Pronominal Oblique Genitive.

The following are examples of pronominal genitives which end in र *r* or न *n*, and which have an oblique form ending in रा *rá* or ना *ná*. These oblique forms occur for all pronominal genitives ending in र *r*, and are used with nouns in any form except that of the nominative singular or plural:—

Direct Genitive.	Meaning.	Oblique form.
मोर *mor*.	'My.'	मोरा *morá*.
हम्मर *hammar*.	'My.'	हमरा *ham'rá*.
तोर *tor*.	'Thy.'	तोरा *torá*.
तोहर *tohar*.	'Thy.'	तोहरा *tŏh'rá*.
अप्पन *appan*.	'Own.'	अपना *ap'ná*.
एकर *ekar*.	'Of this.'	एकरा *ĕk'rá*.
ओकर *okar*.	'Of that,' 'his.'	ओकरा *ŏk'rá*.
जेकर *jekar*.	'Whose.'	जेकरा *jĕk'rá*.
तेकर *tekar*.	'His.'	तेकरा *tĕk'rá*.
केकर *kekar*.	'Whose?'	केकरा *kĕk'rá*.

* Dative of the verbal noun.

The following examples will show the use of the genitive in—(*a*) its direct form, (*b*) its oblique form :—

a.—GENITIVES AGREEING WITH NOUNS IN THE NOMINATIVE FORM, *i.e.* DIRECT GENITIVES.

ओकर तिरिया कैसन सुन्दर छै *okar tiriyá kaisan sundar chhai*, 'how beautiful his wife is !'

केकर बेटा छै *kekar beṭá chhai ?* 'whose son is he ?'

हम्मर धन्धा बिगरत्तै *hammar dhandhá bigar'tai*, 'my profession will be ruined.'

ओकर कानल सुन के *okar kánal sun kĕ*, 'on hearing her lamentations.'

ओकर इकरार लिखउ *okar ik'rár likha*, 'write a bond to that effect' (*lit.* of that).

अप्पन धन उड़ाय, भिखारी होय गेल *appan dhan uṛáy, bhikhárí hoy gel*, 'having wasted all his substance, he became poor.'

b.—GENITIVES AGREEING WITH NOUNS NOT IN THE NOMINATIVE FORM, *i.e.* OBLIQUE GENITIVES.

ओकरा चढ़े के घोड़ा *ŏk'rá chaṛhĕ kĕ ghoṛá*, 'his riding-horse' (*lit.* the horse of his riding).

ऊ ओकरा फुलवारी में ऐलै *ú ŏk'rá phul'wárí mẽ ailai*, 'he came into *his* (some one else's) garden.'

हमरा सिरकी में *ham'rá sir'kí mẽ*, 'in my hovel.'

तोहरा घर में *tŏh'rá ghar mẽ*, 'in your house.'

तोहरा हथवा से *tŏh'rá hath'wá se*, 'from thy hand.'

हमरा दरवाजा से ओकर दरवाजा बाँस भर दूरि छै *ham'rá dar'wájá se okar dar'wájá bā̃s bhar dúri chhai*, 'his doorway is a rod distance from mine.'

गिरहस्त अपना जी में कहलकै *gir'hast ap'ná jí mẽ kahal'kai*, 'the husbandman said in his heart.'

Sometimes, by the vulgar, the direct form is used instead of the oblique, but the oblique form is never used instead of the direct. It should be observed, moreover, that in South Munger these rules are by no means universally followed. There the direct form is the rule, and the oblique the exception.

DIVISION II.

CONJUGATION.

CHAPTER IV.

INTRODUCTORY.

§ 35. It must be noted with respect to the following paradigms that colloquially the plural is commonly used in the place of the singular: thus तोँ छ *tõ chha*, 'thou art,' is commonly used instead of तोँ छैँ *tõ chhẽ*, which is the more correct form.

NOTE also that there is great laxity colloquially in regard to gende. The forms given for the feminine are only those which are specially confined to that gender; but instead of these, the masculine forms are often used colloquially. In the following paradigms when the masculine and feminine forms coincide, the latter are not given. As a matter of fact feminine forms are rarely used except in the west of the district referred to in this grammar.

As already observed (§ 1), the language spoken in South Munger is in the main Maithilí. In the western portions, however, of the Jamuí subdivision of Munger, and in Báṛh, many Mágadhí forms are used, and such will be noted in the proper place.

§ 36. With regard to the spelling of the various tense-forms, it must be noted that ऐ *ai* and औ *au* are frequently written अइ *aï* and अउ *aü* respectively: thus such forms as देखै *dekhai* and देखौन्ह *dekhaunh* are often written देखइ *děkhaï* and देखउन्ह *děkhaünh*. It has not been thought necessary to put both these varieties of spelling into the paradigms: hence only देखै *dekhai*, देखौन्ह *dekhaunh*, &c., will be found therein. With regard to this and to the shortening of ante-penultimate vowels, see General Introduction, §§ 34—37.

Every plural form ending in न्ह *nh* can also be spelt as ending in न *n*: thus गिरल्हैन्ह *gir'lainh* or गिरल्हैन *gir'lain*. Only the fuller form in न्ह *nh* will be given in the paradigms.

When a stem terminates in an unaspirated letter, and is followed by a termination beginning with ह *h*, the final letter of the stem and the initial ह *h* of the termination generally coalesce into the cognate aspirate of the final letter of the stem. Thus देखबन्हो *dĕkhab'ho* becomes देखन्भो *dĕkh'bho*, and छिकन्हैँ *chhik'hẽ*, छिखैँ *chhikhẽ*.

§ 37. Conjugational System.

The conjugation of the verb √ देख *dekh*, 'see,' being given in full, it is not necessary to give here the details of conjugation at length.

§ 38. There are three moods—the Indicative, Conjunctive, and Imperative. These may again be divided into *simple tenses*—formed from the root direct, and *periphrastic tenses*—formed with the aid of auxiliary verbs added to the present or past participle, or to the conjugated preterite indicative.

§ 39. The *simple tenses* are as follows:—

INDICATIVE.	CONJUNCTIVE.	IMPERATIVE.
Preterite.	Present.	Present.
Future.	Preterite.	

Of these, the present imperative is always the same as the present conjunctive.

§ 40. The *periphrastic tenses* are as follows:—

a) From the present participle, direct form—

Indicative—

Definite present	with auxiliary	present.
Imperfect	„	preterite.
Durative future	„	future.

Conjunctive—

Future	with auxiliary	present	conjunctive.
Durative present	„	preterite	„

b) From the past participle: direct form in the neuter verb, oblique form in the active verb—

Indicative—

Perfect (form II)	with auxiliary	present.
Pluperfect (form II)	„	past.
Future exact (form II)	„	future.

Conjunctive—

Future exact (form II)	with auxiliary	present	conjunctive.
Preterite (form II)	„	preterite	„

c) From the preterite indicative—

Indicative—

Perfect (form I)	with auxiliary	present.
Pluperfect (form I)	„	preterite.
Future exact (form I)	„	future.

Conjunctive—

Future exact (form I)	with auxiliary	present	conjunctive.
Preterite (form I)	„	preterite	„

Concerning the use of the auxiliary in tenses formed from the past participle, see General Introduction, p. 13, cl. (4).

§ 41. The Simple Tenses.

The personal terminations are nearly the same for all these tenses. They are added to a tense-stem, the formation of which will be described afterwards. They are exactly the same for the present conjunctive, the preterite indicative, and the preterite conjunctive.

The terminations of these three tenses are given in the following table. It will be observed that there are many optional forms of terminations for each person. They are all used with nearly equal frequency. They should be carefully committed to memory.

It must be noted that the termination अह *ah* or अ *a* of the 2nd plural masculine is pronounced with a peculiar drawl, something like the English word 'awe.' Thus, देखऽ *dekh*'awe.'

Table showing the Personal Terminations of the Present Conjunctive, the Preterite Indicative, and the Preterite Conjunctive.

Person.	SINGULAR.		PLURAL.	
	Masculine.	Feminine.	Masculine.	Feminine.
1st	ऊँ *ú*, ओँ *õ*.		ई *í*, इऐ *iai*, इऐन्ह *iainh*, इऔ *iau*, इऔन्ह *iaunh*.	
2nd	आ *á*, ए *e*, एँ *ẽ*, ऐ *ai*, ऐँ *aĩ*, न्हीँ *'hí*.	ई *í*.	अ *a*, न्हू *'hú*, न्हो *'ho*, न्हौ *'hau*.	
3rd	ए *e*, ऐ *ai*, औ *au*, अ *a*.		ऐन्ह *ainh*, औन्ह *aunh*, अथ *ath*, न्थी *'thí*.	न्थीँ *'thí*, न्थीन्हि *'thínhi*.
			न्हीँ *'hí*, न्हिन्ह *'hinh*.	ई *í*.

The first person is often used honorifically in the sense of the second person: thus आबोँ *ábõ*, 'come.'

§ 42. These terminations are added to various tense-stems, and it is by these tense-stems that the tenses are distinguished. The formation of each tense-stem will be given separately under the heading of each tense, and the conjugation of each tense will now be described in the order in which they will subsequently be given in the conjugation of the model verb √देख *dekh*, 'see.'

§ 43. The Preterite Indicative.

The stem of this tense is formed by adding अल *al* or इल *il* to the root. To this the terminations in § 41 are added. Thus √ देख *dekh*, 'see,' preterite stem देखल *dekhal* or देखिल *dekhil*, to which the terminations are added: thus देख्लूँ *dĕkh'lú* or देखिलूँ *dĕkhilú*, 'I saw.' This tense has in the case of transitive verbs the following terminations instead of those given in § 41:— अक *ak*, ’कै *'kai*, or ’कौ *'kau* for the third person singular, and ’का *'ká*, ’कैन्ह *'kainh*, ’कौन्ह *'kaunh*, ’कथ *'kath*, or ’कथी *'kathí* for the third person plural masculine, and ’की *kí*, ’कथीं *'kathī*, ’कथीन्हि *'kathīnhi* for the third person plural feminine. In the case of neuter verbs—

(1) in the third singular masculine either no termination is added to the stem at all, or else the following are the terminations:— ऐ *ai*, औ *au*, or अ *a*;

(2) in the third plural masculine, in addition to the termination in § 41, the terminations ’हैन्ह *'hainh*, ’हौन्ह *'haunh*, or आ *á*.

In addition to the above, the following terminations may be used in the past tense of all verbs, whether transitive or neuter:—first sing., अँ *ã*; second do., ’है *'haí*, ’हैँ *'hãĩ*; first plural इहौन्ह *ihaunh*; third do., ’खीं *'khī*, ’खिन्ह *'khinh*.

Examples.

देख्लक *dĕkh'lak*, देखल्कै *dĕkhal'kai*, 'he saw.' देखल्का *dĕkhal'ká*, देखल्खिन्ह *dĕkhal'khinh*,* 'they saw' (masc.), and देखल्की *dekhal'kí*, 'they saw' (fem.). Similarly for the other forms.

§ 44. The Future Indicative.

This tense has two stems—one for the first and second persons, and one for the third person. The first stem is formed by adding अब *ab* to the root; the second is the root itself.

The following are the terminations of this tense. All should be added to the root direct.

---

* This is really a contraction of देख्लक हिन्ह *dĕkh'lak hinh*.

After certain vowels, *e.g.* आ *á*, the stem termination may be एब *eb* instead of अब *ab*.

Terminations of the Future.

Person.	Singular.		Plural.	
	Masculine.	Feminine.	Masculine.	Feminine.
1st	॰बै *'bai*, ॰बौ *'bau*.		अब *ab*, ॰बैन्ह *'bainh*, ॰बौन्ह *'baunh*.	
2nd	॰बा *'bá*, ॰बे *'be*, ॰बैँ *'bẽ*, ॰बै *'bai*, ॰बैँ *'bãĩ*. ॰भीँ *'bhí*.*	॰बी *'bi*	॰बठ *'ba*. ॰भू *'bhú**, ॰भो *'bho*.* ॰भौ *'bhau*.*	
3rd	अत, ॰तै, ॰तौ, ॰तठ. *at*, *'tai*, *'tau*, *'ta*.		॰तैन्ह *'tainh*, ॰तौन्ह *'taunh*, ॰ता *'tá*, ॰तहीँ *'tahí*, ॰तहिन्ह *'tahinh*, ॰तथ *'tath*, ॰तथी *'tathí*. अत॰खीँ *at'khí*,† अत॰खिन्ह *at'khinh*.†	॰ती *'tí*, ॰तथीँ *tath*, ॰तथीन्ह *'tathính*.

* These are contractions for ॰ब हीँ *'b hí*, ॰ब हू *'b hú*, &c.

† Contractions for अत॰क हीँ *at'k hí*, अत॰क हिन्ह *at'k hinh*.

§ 45. The Present Conjunctive and Imperative.

In this tense the terminations are added to the root itself: thus देखूँ *dekhũ*, 'let me see.' As already stated, the terminations are those given in § 41. Besides these, this tense may in the first person masculine singular take औँ *aũ*, and in the second person masculine singular take अँ *ã*. It also optionally takes no termination whatever in the latter person.

In the plural, it may in the first person masculine also take the termination इहुन्ह *ihunh*, and in the third person the terminations ॰हुन्ह *'hunh*, ॰हेँ *'hẽ*.

§ 46. The Preterite Conjunctive.

In this tense अत *at*, इत *it*, ऐत *ait*, or अति *ati* is added to the root to form the stem. The personal terminations in § 41 are then added: thus देख॰तूँ *dĕkh'tũ* or देख॰तिऊँ *dĕkh'tiũ*, '(if) I had seen.'

In the third person singular it may drop the usual terminations and end in ऐत *ait*, added simply to the root. In the first person singular masculine it optionally takes the termination अँ *ã*, in the first person plural masculine इहौन्ह *ihaunh*, and in the third person plural masculine ॰हैन्ह *'hainh*, ॰हौन्ह *'haunh*, or आ *á*.

§ 46a. The Use of the Various Verbal Terminations.

It will be noticed that each person has many terminations, but they do not all mean exactly the same thing. At the same time it must be noted that this multiplicity of verbal forms is partly due to local and personal circumstances—an inhabitant of one place using one set of forms, and an inhabitant of another, another. This is due to the want of a literature, which would fix each verbal form in its proper and exact shade of meaning. The following instructions will help to explain approximately the more customary uses of the forms.

In the first place it must be noted that in the Maithilí dialect generally number is continually disregarded, verbs in the singular form being used with plural subjects, and *vice versâ*. Thus, take देख॰लक *dĕkh'lak*, which is properly third singular preterite. The following examples show that it can be used both in a singular and in a plural sense:—

(Singular) ऊ हम॰रा नदी भीर देख॰लक *ú ham'rá nadí bhír dĕkh'lak*, 'he saw me beside the river.'

(Plural) ऊ सभ हम॰रा नदी किछार देख॰लक *ú sabh ham'ra nadí kichhár dĕkh'lak*, 'they saw me on the bank of the river.'

So also देखलꣳकथ *dèkhal'kath* (properly 3rd plural) may be used as a singular: viz. ऊ देखलꣳकथ *ú dĕkhal'kath*, 'he saw,' as well as ऊ सभ देखलꣳकथ *ú sabh dĕkhal'kath*, 'they saw.' It may be asked, then, why these terminations have been divided into singular and plural. The answer is twofold,—first, that though no longer used in their proper sense, the terminations were originally singular and plural as written, and in songs (which always conserve an older form of the language) they are so used to the present day. Secondly, at the present day there is this important difference in their use,—singular terminations (especially in the second and third persons) are always used non-honorifically, and plural terminations honorifically, as regards the subject; thus, ऊ देखꣳलक *ú dĕkh'lak* (singular) means 'he (that humble person) saw,' but ऊ देखलꣳकथ *ú dĕkhal'kath* (plural) 'he (that respectable person) saw.' In the first person, however, this distinction has been lost, and singular and plural are used indiscriminately.

There is another way of looking at a verbal form, and that is the relation it bears to the object. There is nothing like this in any European language; so it requires more careful exemplification in the present case. For the purposes of the present explanation a sentence may be divided into subject, verb, and object. The object may be direct or remote. Thus, in 'the king gave a village to the bráhman,' 'the king' is the subject, 'gave' is the verb, 'a village' is the direct object, and 'the bráhman' is the remote object. So in 'the child fell on the ground,' for the purposes of the present explanation 'the ground' may be considered as the remote object. In European grammar the form of a verb depends on the subject, *i.e.*, we say that it agrees with its subject in number and person, but the object (direct or remote) has no effect at all on the form of the verb. In Bihárí, on the contrary, the selection of the verbal form to be used largely depends upon the object. Thus, while in Europe we must say that the verb agrees with its subject in number and person, in Bihár we must say that it agrees with its subject, and also with its object, in honour and person.

The following are approximately the rules on this point:—

(*a*) The terminations ending in औ *au* are used when the object (direct or remote) is in the second person and is considered inferior to the speaker. If, however, the termination is pronounced with a drawl. something like *a-o*, the object is mentioned with some, but not great, respect,

Exception.—If the verb itself is in the second person, the object may be in the first or third person.

(*b*) The terminations ending in औन्ह *aunh* are used when the object (direct or remote) is in the second person and is spoken of with respect.

(*c*) The terminations ending in न्हीँ *'hí* and ऐ *ai* are used when the object (direct or remote) is in the first or third person and is considered inferior to the subject.

(*d*) The terminations ending in ऐन्ह *ainh* are used generally when the object (direct or remote) is mentioned with great respect. In this case the object may be in the first, second, or third person.

The following examples will make the above clear :—

हम्मेँ तोर बैरी छेलिऔ *hammĕ tor bairí chhĕliau*, '(you fool), I was your enemy.'

हम तोहर पोथी बिहान देख॰बौ *ham tohar pothí bihán dĕkh'bau*, 'I will see your book (my humble friend) to-morrow.'

(Here the direct object, 'your book,' being inferior and in the second person, a termination ending in औ *au* is used.)

जब तोँ हम॰रा छोड़ि देब॰, तब कह॰बौ *jab tŏ ham'rá chhoṛi deba, tab kah'bau* 'when you (my humble friend) let me go, I will tell you.'

जे तोँ हम॰रा मारि डाल॰तिअ, त॰ मोती तोरा हाथ लग॰तिऔ *je tŏ ham'rá mári ḍál'tia, ta moti torá háth lag'tiau*, 'if you had killed me, the pearl would have come (my humble friend) into your hand.'

तोह॰रा गाड़ी मेँ की माल छौ *tŏh'rá gáṛí mĕ kí mál chhau ?* '(My humble friend), what goods are in your cart ?'

एखनि जाहौ, आज साँझ के तोहर पाती देख॰बौ *ĕkh'ní jáhau, áj sẵjh ke tohar pátí dĕkh'bau* (pronounced *dĕkh'ba-o*), 'go now, Sir ; I will see your letter this evening.'

देखल॰नौ कुकुर नै परा सक॰लै *dĕkhal'nau kukur nai pará sak'lai ?* 'Did you see the dog (inferior), how it could not run away ?' (Here, although the object is in the third person, still a termination ending in औ *au* is used, because the subject is in the second person.)

हम्मेँ तोर भला मानऽबौन्ह, आरो सदई गुन गैबौन्ह *hammẽ tor bhalá mán'baunh, árŏ sadaí gun gaĭbaunh*, 'I will be grateful to you, sir, and will always sing your praises.' (Here the object is in the second person, and is mentioned with respect.)

तोहऽरा कन कऽ मोट चलैछौन्ह *tŏh'rá kan ka moṭ chalaichhaunh ?* 'how many well-buckets are at work in your (farm), (my respected friend) ?'

तोँ ओकऽरा चाकर के देखलऽहीँ है *tŏ ŏk'rá chákar ke dĕkhal'hí hai ?* 'Have you (my humble friend) seen his servant ?' (Here both subject and object are non-honorific.)

देखलऽहौ मुरऽता नूनू के कैसन चाट खीँच के मारलऽकै *dĕkhal'hau Mur'tá núnú ke kaisan cháṭ khích kĕ máral'kai ?* 'Did you see how Mur'tá gave a severe slap to the child ?' (Here the object, 'the child,' is inferior.)

हम अपऽने के देखऽबैन्ह *ham ap'nĕ ke dĕkh'bainh*, 'I will see your honour.' (Here the object is mentioned with great respect.)

अपऽने हमऽरा नूनू के देखऽलोँ छै *ap'nĕ ham'rá núnú ke dĕkh'lŏ chhai*, 'has your honour seen my child ?' (Here the first person of the verb is used honorifically instead of the second person, and no special reference being made to the person of and respect due to the object, the form देखऽलिऐ *dĕkh'liai* is not used.)

रे छौँड़ा, हम्मर बही देखऽलेँ छै ? *re chhaŭṛá, hammar bahí dĕkh'lẽ chhai ?* 'Ho ! you boy, there, have you seen my book ?' (Here the subject is non-honorific, and there is no reference to the object.)

मजिष्टर साहेब हमऽरा देखलऽकथ *Majisṭar Sáhĕb ham'rá dĕkhal'kath*, 'His Honor the Magistrate saw me.' (Here the subject is honorific, and no reference is made to the honour of the object.)

हो काका, देखऽलऽ मोहन के बौह केना डाकऽलक *ho káká, dĕkh'la Mohan kĕ bauh kená ḍák'lak ?* 'Hallo, uncle, did you see how Mohan's wife called me ?' (Here no special reference is made to the honour of the object.)

CHAPTER V.

AUXILIARY VERBS.

§ 47. There are two classes of auxiliary verbs—the *defective* and the *complete.*

§ 48. There is, properly speaking, only one *defective auxiliary verb* in use in this dialect,—that derived from the √ अछ *achh.* In the western portion of Jamúí, however, and in Báṛh, another verb is used, derived from the √ अह *ah.*

(*a*) The first of these is used only in the present and preterite tenses, and always in this dialect loses its initial vowel. It has in the present tense two forms,—a weak (*e.g.* छी *chhí*, 'I am') and a strong (*e.g.* छिकाँ *chhikõ* 'I am'). In the preterite tense it is used only in the weak form (*e.g.* छलाँ *chhalõ*, 'I was'). I shall call it the *first defective auxiliary verb.*

(*b*) The second of these, derived from the √ अह *ah*, belongs properly to the Mágadhí dialect. In the dialect under consideration it is used only in the present and preterite tenses. It always in this dialect loses its initial vowel. In the present tense it has two forms,—a weak (*e.g.* ही *hí*, 'I am'), and a strong (*e.g.* हिकाँ *hikõ*, 'I am'). In the preterite tense it is used only in the weak form (*e.g.* हलाँ *halõ*, 'I was'). I shall call it the *second defective auxiliary verb*.

§ 49. The complete auxiliary verb is formed from the √ हो *ho*, 'become,' which is conjugated through all moods and tenses. Its preterite is irregular, and is never used as an auxiliary, but only as a verb substantive, meaning 'I became.'

§ 50. First Defective Auxiliary Verb.

√ अछ *achh*, 'be.'

Present : '*I am*,' *&c.*

WEAK FORM.

Person.	SINGULAR.		PLURAL.	
	Masculine.	Feminine.	Masculine.	Feminine.
1st	*Not used.*		छी, छिऐ, छिऐन्ह, *chhí*, *chhiai*, *chhiainh*, छिऔ, छिऔन्ह, छिउन्ह, *chhiau*, *chhiaunh*, *chhihunh*.	
2nd	छा *chhá*, छे *chhe*, छें *chhẽ*, छै *chhai*, छैं *chhãi*, छहीं *chhahí*, छँ *chhã*.	छी *chhí*.	छ० *chhȧ*, छहू *chhahú*, छहो *chhaho*, छहौ *chhahau*.	
3rd	छे *chhe*, छै *chhai*, छौ *chhau*. छ० *chha*.		छैन्ह *chhainh*, छौन्ह *chhaunh*, छथ *chhath*, छथी *chhathí*, छहीं *chhahí*, छहिन्ह *chhahinh*, छहुन्ह *chhahunh*, छहें *chhahẽ*.	छथीं *chhathí*, छथीन्हि *chhathínhi*.

STRONG FORM.

Person.	SINGULAR. Masculine.	SINGULAR. Feminine.	PLURAL. Masculine.	PLURAL. Feminine.
1st	छिकूँ, छिकों, *chhikū̃, chhikõ,* छिकौं *chhikaũ.*		छिकी, छिकिऐ, *chhikí, chhikiai,* छिकिऐन्ह, छिकिऔ, *chhikiainh. chhikiau,* छिकिऔन्ह, छिकिहुन्ह, *chhikiaunh, chhikihunh.*	
2nd	छिका, छिके, छिकें, *chhiká, chhike, chhikẽ,* छिकै, छिकैं *chhikai, chhikaĩ.*	छिकी *chhikí.*	छिक०, छिखू, छिखो, *chhika, chhikhú**, *chhikho.**	
	छिखीं *chhikhí.**		छिखौ, *chhikhau.**	
3rd	छिके, छिकै, *chhike, chhikai,* छिकौ *chhikau.*		छिकैन्ह, छिकौन्ह, *chhikainh, chhikaunh,* छिकथ, छिकऽथी, *chhikath, chhik'thí,*	छिकऽथीं, छिकऽथीन्हि, *chhik'thí, chhik'thinhi.*
	छिक० *chhika.*		छिखीं, छिखिन्ह, *chhikhí,** *chhikhinh,** छिखुन्ह, छिखें, *chhikhunh,** *chhikhẽ.**	छिकी *chhikí.*

* For छिकऽहीं *chhik'hí*, &c., see § 36, last paragraph.

Preterite : '*I was,*' *&c.*

Person.	SINGULAR.		PLURAL.	
	Masculine.	Feminine.	Masculine.	Feminine.
1st	छलूँ, छलों, छलँ, *chhalũ*,* *chhalõ*, *chhalã*.		छली, छलिऐ, छलिऐन्ह, *chhalí*, *chhaliai*, *chhaliainh*, छलिऔ, छलिऔन्ह *chhaliau*, *chhaliaunh*, छलिहौन्ह, *chhalihaunh*.	
2nd	छला, छले, छलेँ, *chhalá*, *chhale*, *chhalẽ*, छलै, छलैँ, *chhalai*, *chhalaĩ*, छलऽहीं, छलऽहै, *chhal'hĩ*, *chhal'hai*, छलऽहैँ, *chhal'haĩ*.	छली *chhalí*.	छलऽ, छलऽहू, छलऽहो, *chhala*, *chhal'hú*, *chhal'ho*. छलऽहौ *chhal'hau*.	
3rd	छल *chhal*. छलै, छलौ, छलऽ *chhalai*, *chhalàu*, *chhala*.		छलैन्ह, छलौन्ह, *chhalainh*, *chhalaunh*, छलथ, छलऽथी, *chhalath*, *chhal'thí*, छलऽहीं *chhal'hĩ*, छलऽहिन्ह, *chhal'hinh*. छलऽखीं, छलऽखिन्ह, *chhal'khĩ*, *chhal'khinh*, छलऽहैन्ह, छलऽहौन्ह, *chhal'hainh*, *chhal'haunh*, छला *chhalá*.	छलऽथीं, *chhal'thĩ*, छलऽथीन्हि, *chhal'thínhi*. छली *chhalí*.

* Or छिलूँ *chhilũ* or छेलूँ *chhelũ*, and so throughout.

§ 51. Second Defective Auxiliary Verb.

√ अह *ah*, 'be.'

Present, '*I am*,' *&c.*

WEAK FORM.

Person.	SINGULAR.		PLURAL.	
	Masculine.	Feminine.	Masculine.	Feminine.
1st	*Not used.*		ही *hī*.	
2nd	हैँ *hẽ*.	ही *hī*.	हऽ *ha*.	
3rd	है *hai*.		हैन्ह *hainh*.	हथीं *hathī*.

Optional forms as in the present of √ अछ *achh*.

STRONG FORM.

Person.	SINGULAR.		PLURAL.	
	Masculine.	Feminine.	Masculine.	Feminine.
1st	हिकूँ *hikū*.		हिकी *hikī*.	
2nd	हिकैँ *hikẽ*.	हिकी *hikī*.	हिकऽ *hika*.	
3rd	हिकै *hikai*.		हिकैन्ह *hikainh*.	हिकन्थीं *hik'thī*.

Optional forms as in छिकूँ *chhikū*.

§ 52. Preterite : '*I was,*' *&c.*

Person.	Singular.		Plural.	
	Masculine.	Feminine.	Masculine.	Feminine.
1st	हलूँ *halũ.*		हली *halí.*	
2nd	हलैँ *halẽ.*	हली *halí.*	हलऽ *hola.*	
3rd	हल *hal.*		हलैन्ह *halainh.*	हलन्थीं *hal'thí.*

Optional forms as in छलूँ *chhalũ.*

§ 53. The Complete Auxiliary Verb.

√ हो *ho, 'be,' 'become.'*

INDICATIVE MOOD.

(*a*)—Preterite : '*I became,*' *&c.*

NOTE.—This tense is never used as an auxiliary, छलूँ *chhalũ* or रही *rahí* (see above) being used instead.

Person.	Singular.		Plural.	
	Masculine.	Feminine.	Masculine.	Feminine.
1st	होलूँ *holũ.*		होली *holí.*	
2nd	होलैँ *holẽ.*	होली *holí.*	होलऽ *hola.*	
3rd	होल *hol.*		होलैन्ह *holainh.*	होलन्थीं *hŏl'thí.*

Optional forms as in छलूँ *chhalũ.*

In Báṛh and Western Jamuí the following form is used:—

Person.	Singular.		Plural.	
	Masculine.	Feminine.	Masculine.	Feminine.
1st	भेलूँ *bhelú.*		भेली *bhelí.*	
2nd	भेलें *bhelẽ.*	भेली *bhelí.*	भेलह *bhela.*	
3rd	भेल *bhel.*		भेलैन्ह *bhelainh.*	भेल॰थीं *bhĕl'thí.*

Optional forms as in छलूँ *chhalú.*

§ 54. (*b*)—Future : '*I shall be,*' *&c.*

Person.	Singular.		Plural.	
	Masculine.	Feminine.	Masculine.	Feminine.
1st	होबै, होबौ. *hobai, hobau.*		होब, होबैन्ह, होबौन्ह. *hob, hobainh, hobaunh.*	
2nd	होबा, होबे, होबें, *hobá, hobe, hobẽ,* होबै, होबैं, होभीं. *hobai, hobai, hŏbhí.*	होबी *hobi.*	होबह, होभू, होभो, होभौ. *hoba, hŏbhú, hŏbho, hŏbhau.*	
3rd	होत, होअत, होतै, *hot, hoat, hotai,* होतौ, होतह. *hotau, hota.*		होतैन्ह, होतौन्ह, होता, *hotainh, hotaunh, hotá,* होतहीं, होतहिन्ह, होतथ, *hŏtahí, hŏtahinh, hotath,* होतथी, होत॰खीं, होत॰खिन्ह. *hŏtathi, hŏt'khí, hŏt'khinh.*	होती *hoti.* होतथीं, होत॰थीन्हि. *hŏtathí, hŏtathinhi.*

CONJUNCTIVE MOOD.

§ 55. (*c*)—Present: '*(If) I be,*' *&c.*

Person.	SINGULAR.		PLURAL.	
	Masculine.	Feminine.	Masculine.	Feminine.
st	होऊँ *hoū́*, होओँ *hoõ*, होअऊँ *hoaū̃*.		होइ, होइऐ, होइऐन्ह, *hoi*, *hoïai*, *hoïainh*, होइऔ, होइऔन्ह, *hoïau*, *hoïaunh*, होइउन्ह, *hoïhunh*.	
d	होआ, होए, होएँ, होऐ, *hoá*, *hoe*, *hoẽ*, *hoai*, होऐँ, *hoaĩ*. होहीँ *hohí*, होअँ, *hoã*. हो *ho*.	होइ *hoi*.	होअ *hoa*. होहू *hohú*, होहो *hoho*. होहौ *hohau*.	
	होए *hoë*. होऐ *hoai*, होऔ *hoau*. होअ *hoa*.		होऐन्ह, होऔन्ह, *hoainh*, *hoaunh*, होअथ or होथ, होथी, *hoath* or *hoth*, *hothí*. होहीँ, होहिन्ह, *hohí*, *hohinh*. होउन्ह, होहेँ, *hohunh*, *hohẽ*.	होइ *hoi*, होथीँ, होथीन्हि, *hothí*, *hothínhi*.

§ 56. (*d*)—Preterite: '*(If) I had been,*' *&c.*

Person.	Singular.		Plural.	
	Masculine.	Feminine.	Masculine.	Feminine.
st	होतूँ *hotū́**, होतोँ *hotõ*, होतँ *hotã*.		होती *hotí*. होतिऐ, होतिऐन्ह, होतिऔ, *hŏtiaï, hŏtiainh, hŏtiau*, होतिऔन्ह *hŏtiaunh*, होतिहौन्ह *hŏtihaunh*.	
nd	होता, होते, होतेँ, होतै, *hotá, hote, hotẽ, hotai*, होतैँ, होथीँ, *hotaĩ, hŏthī*.	होती *hoti*.	होतह *hota*. होथु *hŏthu*, होथो *hŏtho*. होथौ, *hŏthau*.	
d	होऐत *hoait* or होत *hot*, होते *hote*. होतै, होतौ, होतऽ, *hotai, hotau, hota*.		होतथ, होतःथी, होतैन्ह, *hotath, hot'thi, hotainh*, होतौन्ह, होथीँ, होथिन्ह, *hotaunh, hŏthī, hŏthinh*, होथैन्ह *hŏthaïnh*. होथौन्ह *hŏthaunh*. होता *hotá*.	होती *hoti*. होतःथीँ, होतःथीन्हि, *hŏt'thī, hŏt'thīnhi*.

* Or होअतूँ *hoatū́*, and so throughout.

§ 57. Imperative Mood.

Present: '*Let me see,*' *&c.*

The same as the present conjunctive.

Precative Forms.

Non-honorific—

होइहऽ *hoïha*, होइअ *hoïa*.

Honorific—

होई *hoí*, होइएँ *hoïẽ*, 'be good enough to be.'

The periphrastic tenses are quite regular, and need not be given.

§ 58. Present Participle, '*being.*'

Singular and Plural.

होइत *hŏait.*

Past Participle, '*been.*'

होल *hol;* or in West Jamuí and Báṛh, भेल *bhel.*

Conjunctive Participle, '*having been.*'

भै के *bhai kĕ.*

Infinitive, '*to be.*'

होअल *hoal.*

CHAPTER VI.

THE REGULAR ACTIVE VERB.

§ 59. There is only one conjugation of active verbs, if we except a few irregular verbs to be noted further on. The conjugation of neuter verbs differs from that of active verbs only in certain of the past tenses, and these will be treated of in a future page. Verbs whose roots end in vowels also exhibit slight variations, which will be explained at the proper place. For the sake of uniformity the tenses are given in the same order, and under the same names, as those in Dr. Hoernle's grammar.

Reference is again made to General Introduction, §§ 34 to 36, with regard to the changes of the root-vowel.

§ 60. √देख *dekh*, 'see.'

PRESENT PARTICIPLE: देखैत *dekhait.*

PAST PARTICIPLE: देखल *dekhal.*

Simple Tenses.

INDICATIVE MOOD.

§ 61. (*a*)—Preterite: '*I saw,*' *&c.*

Person.	SINGULAR.		PLURAL.	
	Masculine.	Feminine.	Masculine.	Feminine.
1st	देख॰लूँ *dĕkh'lú̃**, देख॰लों [*dĕkh'lõ.* देख॰लाँ *dĕkh'lã.*		देख॰ली *dĕkh'lí.* देख॰लिऐ *dĕkh'liai,* देख॰लिऐन्ह *dĕkh'liainh,* देख॰लिऔ *dĕkh'liau,* देख॰लिऔन्ह *dĕkh'liaunh,* देख॰लिहौन्ह, *dĕkh'lihaunh.*	
2nd	देख॰ला, देख॰ले, देख॰लें, *dĕkh'lá, dĕkh'le, dĕkh'lẽ.* देख॰लै, देख॰लैं, *dĕkh'lai, dĕkh'lãi,* देखल॰हीं, देखल॰है, *dĕkhal'hí, dĕkhal'hai.* देखल॰हैं *dĕkhal'hãi.*	देख॰ली *dĕkh'lí.*	देख॰लह, *dĕkh'la.* देखल॰हू, देखल॰हो *dekhal'hú, dĕkhal'ho.* देखल॰हौ, *dĕkhal'hau.*	
3rd	देख॰लक *dĕkh'lak.* देखल॰कै, देखल॰कौ, *dĕkhal'kai, dĕkhal'kau.*		देखल॰का, देख॰कैन्ह, *dĕkhal'ká, dĕkhal'kainh,* देखल॰कौन्ह, *dĕkhal'kaunh.* देखल॰कथ, देखल॰कथी, *dĕkhal'kath, dĕkhal'kathi.* देखल॰खीं *dĕkhal'khí.* देखल॰खिन्ह *dĕkhal'khinh.*	देखल॰की *dĕkhal'kí.* देखल॰कथीं *dĕkhal'kathí.* देख॰लक॰थीन्हि, *dĕkh'lak'thínhi.*

* O देखिलूँ *dĕkhilú̃*, and so throughout.

§ 62. (*b*)—Future: '*I shall see,*' &c.

Person.	Singular. Masculine.	Singular. Feminine.	Plural. Masculine.	Plural. Feminine.
1st	देख॰बै, देख॰बौ, *dĕkh'bai, dĕkh'bau.*		देखब, देख॰बैन्ह, *dekhab, dĕkh'bainh,* देख॰बौन्ह, *dĕkh'baunh.*	
2nd	देख॰बा, देख॰बे, *dĕkh'bá, dĕkh'be,* देख॰बेँ *dĕkh'bẽ.* देख॰बै *dĕkh'bai,* देख॰बैँ [*dĕkh'bãĩ.* देख॰भीँ *dĕkh'bhĩ.*	देख॰बी, *dĕkh'bi.*	देख॰बऽ, देख॰भू, *dĕkh'ba, dĕkh'bhú,* देख॰भो, *dĕkh'bho.* देख॰भौ, *dĕkh'bhau.*	
3rd	देखत *dekhat.* देख॰तै, *dĕkh'tai.* देख॰तौ, देख॰तऽ, *dĕkh'tau, dĕkh'ta.*		देख॰तैन्ह *dĕkh'tainh.* देख॰तौन्ह *dĕkh'taunh.* देख॰ता *dĕkh'tá.* देख॰तहीँ *dĕkh'tahĩ,* देख॰तहिन्ह *dekh'tahinh,* देख॰तथ *dĕkh'tath,* देख॰तथी *dĕkh'tathi,* देख॰तखीँ *dĕkhat'khĩ,* देखत॰खिन्ह *dĕkhat'khinh.*	देख॰ती *dĕkh'ti.* देखत॰थीँ *dĕkhat'thĩ,* देखत॰थीन्हि *dĕkhat'-* [*thinhi.*

CONJUNCTIVE (CONDITIONAL) MOOD.

§ 63. (c)—Present: '*(If) I see;*' rarely '*I see,*' or '*I shall see,*' *&c.*

Person.	Singular.		Plural.	
	Masculine.	Feminine.	Masculine.	Feminine.
1st	देखूँ *dekhú.* देखोँ, देखौँ, *dekhõ, dekhaũ.*		देखी, देखिऐ, *dekhí, dĕkhiai,* देखिऐन्ह, देखिऔ, *dĕkhiainh, dĕkhiau,* देखिऔन्ह, देखिहुन्ह, *dĕkhiaunh, dĕkhihunh.*	
2nd	देखा, देखे, देखेँ, *dekhá, dekhe, dekhẽ,* देखै *dekhai,* देखैँ *dekhaĩ.* देखहीँ, देखँ, देख, *dekh'hí, dĕkhã, dekh.*	देखी *dekhí.*	देखऽ, देखहू, *dekha, dĕkh'hú,* देखहो, देखहौ, *dĕkh'ho, dĕkh'hau.*	
3rd	देखे, देखै, देखौ, *dekhe, dekhai, dekhau.* देखऽ *dekha.*		देखैन्ह, देखौन्ह, *dekhainh, dekhaunh,* देखथ, देखथी, *dekhath, dĕkh'thí.* देखहीँ देखहिन्ह, *dĕkh'hí, dĕkh'hinh.* देखहुन्ह, देखहेँ, *dĕkh'hunh, dĕkh'hẽ.*	देखथीँ, देखथीन्हि, *dĕkh'thí, dĕkh'thínhi.* देखी *dekhí.*

§ 64. (*d*)—Preterite : ‘(*If*) *I had seen,*’ *&c.*

Person.	Singular.		Plural.	
	Masculine.	Feminine.	Masculine.	Feminine.
1st	देखऽतूँ, देखऽतों, *dĕkh’tū́,* dĕkh’tŏ,* देखऽतँ *dĕkh’tā̃.*		देखऽती *dĕkh’tī.* देखऽतिऐ, देखऽतिऐन्ह, *dĕkh’tiai, dĕkh’tiainh.* देखऽतिऔ, देखऽतिऔन्ह, *dĕkh’tiau, dĕkh’tiaunh,* देखऽतिहौन्ह *dĕkh’tihaunh.*	
2nd	देखऽता, देखऽते, *dĕkh’tá, dekh’te,* देखऽतेँ *dekh’tẽ.* देखऽतै, देखऽतैँ, *dĕkh’tai dekh’taĩ.* देखऽथीँ *dĕkh’thī̃.*	देखऽती *dĕkh’tī.*	देखऽतह *dĕkh’ta.* देखऽथू, देखऽथो. *dĕkh’thū́, dĕkh’tho.* देखऽथौ *dĕkh’thau.*	
3rd	देखैत *dekhait.* देखऽते, देखऽतै, *dĕkh’te, dĕkh’tai,* देखऽतौ, देखऽतह. *dĕkh’tau, dĕkh’ta.*		देखऽतैन्ह, देखऽतौन्ह, *dĕkh’tainh, dĕkh’taunh.* देखऽतथ, देखऽतथी, *dĕkh’tath, dĕkh’tathī,* देखतऽथिन्ह *dĕkhat’thinh.* देखऽथीँ देखऽथिन्ह, *dĕkh’thī̃, dekh’thinh,* देखऽता, देखऽथैन्ह, *dĕkh’tá, dĕkh thainh,* देखऽथौन्ह *dĕkh’thaunh.*	देखऽतथीँ *dĕkh’tathī̃.* देखऽतथीन्हि, *dĕkh’tathīnhi.* देखऽती *dĕkh’tī.*

* Or देखितूँ *dĕkhitū́*, or देखऽतिऊँ *dĕkh’tiū́*, or देखैतूँ *dĕkhaitū́*, and so throughout.

Note.—The word छल *chhal* (or in Western Jamuí and Báṛh, हल *hal*) may optionally be added to any of the above forms: thus देखऽतूँ छल *dĕkh’tū́ chhal.*

IMPERATIVE MOOD.

§ 65. (*e*)—Present.—Same as Present Conjunctive.

Precative Forms.

Non-honorific—

2nd person: देखिहठ *dĕkhiha*, देखिअ *dĕkhia*.

Honorific—

2nd person: देखी *dekhi*, देखिऐ *dĕkhiĕ*.

(B)-Periphrastic Tenses.

INDICATIVE MOOD.

§ 66. In the following paradigms the optional forms and dialectic forms of the auxiliary verbs will not all be given, as taking up too much valuable space. For similar reasons feminine forms are generally omitted. When not given, they only differ from the masculine in assuming the feminine form of the auxiliary verb. Thus the second singular definite present is—masculine देखैछँ *dekhaichhẽ* and feminine देखैछी *dekhaichhí*.

§ 67. (*g*)—Definite Present: '*I am seeing,*' &c.

Person.	Singular.	Plural.
1st	*Not used.*	देखैछी *dekhaichhí*.
2nd	देखैछँ *dekhaichhẽ*.	देखैछठ *dekhaichha*.
3rd	देखैछै *dekhaichhai*.	देखैछैन्ह *dekhaichhainh*.

§ 68. To form the feminine, use feminine forms of the auxiliary verb. Thus second singular देखैछी *dekhaichhí*.

Any optional form of the present of the defective auxiliary verb may be used; also the strong form of the defective auxiliary verb. Thus, first plural देखैछिऐ *dekhaichhiai* or देखैछिकी *dekhaichhikí*. The word देखै *dekhai* is only the present participle देखैत *dekhait* with the final त *t* dropped. In Báṛh and Western Jamuí ही *hí*, &c., may be substituted for छी *chhí*, &c. Thus, first plural, देखैही *dekhaihí*. देखे *dekhĕ* or देखऽ *dekha* is often substituted for देखै *dekhai*. Thus, first plural, देखेही *dekhĕhí* or देखऽही *dekhahí*.

§ 69. (*i*)—Imperfect: '*I was seeing.*'

Person.	Singular.	Plural.
1st	देखैछलौं *dekhaichhalõ.*	देखैछली *dekhaichhalí.*
2nd	देखैछलें *dekhaichhalẽ.*	देखैछलऽ *dekhaichhala.*
3rd	देखैछल *dekhaichhal.*	देखैछला *dekhaichhalá.*

To form the feminine, use feminine forms of the auxiliary verb, as in the definite present.

Any optional form of the preterite of the defective auxiliary verb may be used. In Báṛh and Western Jamuí हलौं *halõ* is substituted for छलौं *chhalõ*. Thus, first singular देखैहलौं *dekhaihalõ*. देखे *dekhĕ* is often written for देखै *dekhai*. Thus, first singular देखेहलौं *dekhĕhalõ*.

§ 70. (*j*)—Durative Future: '*I shall be seeing,*' *&c.*

Person.	Singular.	Plural.
1st	देखैहोबै *dekhaihobai.*	देखैहोब *dekhaihob.*
2nd	देखैहोबैं *dekhaihobẽ.*	देखैहोबऽ *dekhaihoba.*
3rd	देखैहोत *dekhaihot.*	देखैहोता *dekhaihotá.*

To form the feminine, use feminine forms of the auxiliary verb, as in the definite present.

Any optional form of the future of the complete auxiliary verb may be used throughout.

§ 71. (*k*)—Perfect: '*I have seen,*' *&c.*

This tense has two forms of conjugation, used with equal frequency.

FORM I.

Person.	Singular.	Plural.
1st	देखलौं छै *děkh'lõ chhai.*	देखली छै *děkh'lí chhai.*
2nd	देखलें छै *děkh'lẽ chhai.*	देखलऽ छै *děkh'la chhai.*
3rd	देखलक छै *děkh'lak chhai.*	देखलका छै *děkhal'ká chhai.*

To form the feminine, use feminine forms of the preterite: thus, second singular feminine देखली छै *děkh'li chhai.*

Any optional form of the preterite may be used, and any optional form of the third singular of the present tense of the auxiliary verb. In Báṛh and Western Jamuí, है *hai* is substituted for छै *chhai* throughout.

FORM II.

Person.	Singular.	Plural.
1st	*Not used.*	देखलें छी *dĕkh'lẽ chhi.*
2nd	देखलें* छें *dĕkh'lẽ chhẽ.*	देखलें छ *dĕkh'lẽ chha.*
3rd	देखलें छै *dĕkh'lẽ chhai.*	देखलें छैन्ह *dĕkh'lẽ chhainh.*

* Or देखल *dĕkh'la*, and so throughout.

To form the feminine, use feminine forms of the auxiliary verb: thus, second singular feminine देखलें छी *dĕkh'lẽ chhi*, and so on, as in the definite present. In Báṛh and Western Jamuí ही *hi*, &c., is substituted for छी *chhi*, &c.

As in the definite present, any optional form of the present of the defective auxiliary verb may be used, and also the strong form of the defective auxiliary verb: thus, first plural देखलें छिऐ *dĕkh'lẽ chhiai*, देखलें छिकी *dĕkh'lẽ chhiki*, and so on.

§ 72. (*l*)—Pluperfect: '*I had seen,*' &c.

This also, like the perfect, has two forms of conjugation.

FORM I.

Person.	Singular	Plural.
1st	देखलों छल *dĕkh'lõ chhal.*	देखली छल *dĕkh'li chhal.*
2nd	देखलें छल *dĕkh'lẽ chhal.*	देखलह छल *dĕkh'la chhal.*
3rd	देखलक छल *dĕkh'lak chhal.*	देखलका छल *dĕkhal'kạ́ chhal.*

To form the feminine, use feminine forms of the preterite: thus, second singular feminine देखली छल *dĕkh'li chhal.*

Any of the other forms of the preterite may be used throughout.

In Báṛh and Western Jamuí हल *hal* is substituted for छल *chhal.*

FORM II.

Person.	Singular.	Plural.
1st	देख॰लेँ* छलोँ *dĕkh'lẽ chhalŏ̃.*	देख॰लेँ छली *dĕkh'lẽ chhalí.*
2nd	देख॰लेँ छलेँ *dĕkh'lẽ chhalẽ.*	देख॰लेँ छलऽ *dĕkh'lẽ chhala.*
3rd	देख॰लेँ छल *dĕkh'lẽ chhal.*	देख॰लेँ छला *dĕkh'lẽ chhalá.*

* Or देख॰लऽ *dĕkh'la,* and so throughout.

To form the feminine, use feminine forms of the auxiliary, as in the imperfect.

Any optional form of the preterite of the defective auxiliary verb may be used. In Báṛh and Western Jamuí हलोँ *halŏ̃,* &c., is substituted for छलोँ *chhalŏ̃,* &c.

§ 73. (*m*)—**Future Exact**: '*I shall have seen,*' '*I may have seen,*' *&c.*

This tense also has two forms of conjugation.

FORM I.

Person.	Singular.	Plural.
1st	देख॰लोँ होत *dĕkh'lŏ̃ hot.*	देख॰ली होत *dĕkh'lí hot.*
2nd	देख॰लेँ होत *dĕkh'lẽ hot.*	देख॰लऽ होत *dĕkh'la hot.*
3rd	देख॰लक होत *dĕkh'lak hot.*	देखल॰का होत *dĕkhal'ká hot.*

To form the feminine, use feminine forms of the preterite: thus, second singular feminine देख॰ली होत *dĕkh'lí hot.*

FORM II.

Person.	Singular.	Plural.
1st	देखन्लें * होबै *dĕkh'lĕ hobai.*	देखःलें होब *dĕkh'lĕ hob.*
2nd	देखन्लें होबें *dĕkh'lĕ hobĕ.*	देखःलें होबऽ *dĕkh'lĕ hoba.*
3rd	देखन्लें होत *dĕkh'lĕ hot.*	देखःलें होता *dĕkh'lĕ hotá.*

* Or देखन्लऽ *dĕkh'la*, and so throughout.

To form the feminine, use feminine forms of the auxiliary verb, as in the definite present.

Any other form of the future of the complete auxiliary verb may be used instead throughout.

CONJUNCTIVE (CONDITIONAL) MOOD.

§ 74. (*n*)—Future Conditional : '(*If*) *I be seeing*,' *&c.*

Person.	Singular.	Plural.
1st	देखैहोऊँ *dekhaihoû.*	देखैहोई *dekhaihoi.*
2nd	देखैहोएँ *dekhaihoĕ.*	देखैहोअ *dekhaihoa.*
3rd	देखैहोऐ *dekhaihoai.*	देखैहोऐन्ह *dekhaihoainh.*

To form the feminine, use feminine forms of the auxiliary verb.

Any other form of the present conjunctive of the complete auxiliary verb may be used instead throughout.

§ 75. (*o*)—Durative Present Conditional: '(*If*) *I were seeing*,' *&c.*

Person.	Singular.	Plural.
1st	देखैहोतौं *dekhaihotŏ.*	देखैहोती *dekhaihotí.*
2nd	देखैहोतैं *dekhaihotĕ.*	देखैहोतह *dekhaihota.*
3rd	देखैहोइत *dekhaihoait.*	देखैहोता *dekhaihotá.*

To form the feminine, use feminine forms of the auxiliary verb.

Any other form of the preterite conditional of the complete auxiliary verb may be used instead throughout.

§ 76. (*p*)—Future Exact Conditional: '(*If*) *I have seen*,' *&c.*

This tense also has two forms of conjugation.

Form I.

Person.	Singular.	Plural.
1st	देखलौं होइ *dĕkh'lŏ hoai.*	देखली होइ *dĕkh'lí hoai.*
2nd	देखलैं होइ *dĕkh'le hoai.*	देखलऽ होइ *dĕkh'la hoai.*
3rd	देखलक होइ *dĕkh'lak hoai.*	देखलका होइ *dĕkhal'ká hoai.*

To form the feminine, use feminine forms of the preterite: thus, second singular feminine देखली होइ *dĕkh'lí hoai.*

FORM II.

Person.	Singular.	Plural.
1st	देखऽलैं* होऊँ *dĕkh'lẽ hoū̃.*	देखऽलैं होई *dĕkh'lẽ hoī.*
2nd	देखऽलैं होएँ *dĕkh'lẽ hoẽ.*	देखऽलैं होअ *dĕkh'lẽ hoa.*
3rd	देखऽलैं होए *dĕkh'lẽ hoai.*	देखऽलैं होएन्ह *dĕkh'lẽ hoainh.*

* Or देखऽलऽ *dĕkh'la,* and so throughout.

To form the feminine, use feminine forms of the auxiliary verb.

Any other form of the present conjunctive of the complete auxiliary verb may be used instead throughout.

§ 77. (*q*)—Preterite Conditional: '(*If*) *I had seen,' &c.*

This tense also has two forms of conjugation.

FORM I.

Person.	Singular.	Plural.
1st	देखऽलौं होएत *dĕkh'lõ hoait.*	देखऽली होएत *dĕkh'li hoait.*
2nd	देखऽलैं होएत *dĕkh'lẽ hoait.*	देखऽलऽ होएत *dĕkh'la hoait.*
3rd	देखऽलक होएत *dĕkh'lak hoait.*	देखलऽका होएत *dĕkhal'ká hoait.*

To form the feminine, use feminine forms of the preterite: thus, second singular feminine देखऽली होएत *dĕkh'li hŏait.*

FORM II.

Person.	Singular.	Plural.
1st	देखलें* होतों *dĕkh'lĕ hotŏ.*	देखलें होती *dĕkh'lĕ hoti.*
2nd	देखलें होतें *dĕkh'lĕ hotĕ.*	देखलें होतह *dĕkh'lĕ hota.*
3rd	देखलें होइत *dĕkh'lĕ hoait.*	देखलें होता *dĕkh'lĕ hotá.*

* Or देखलह *dĕkh'la,* and so throughout.

To form the feminine, use feminine forms of the auxiliary verb.

Any other form of the preterite conditional of the complete auxiliary verb may be used instead throughout.

§ 78. Participles.

ADJECTIVAL.

Present, 'seeing' . . . देखैत *dekhait; obl.* देखते *dĕkh'te* or देखतह *dĕkh'ta.*

Past, 'seen' . . . . . a) देखल *dekhal; fem.* देखलि *dekhali; obl.* देखलें *dĕkh'lĕ* or देखलह *dĕkh'la.*
b) देखल भेल *dekhal bhel.*

CONJUNCTIVE.

'Having seen' . . . . देख* कें *dekh kĕ,* देख कह *dekh ka,* देखि कें *dekhi kĕ,* देखि कह *dekhi ka.*

§ 79. Infinitives or Verbal Nouns, *'to see,' 'the act of seeing.'*

Nominative.	Oblique.
देख *dekh,** देखि *dekhi.*	देखें *dekhĕ* or देखह *dekha.*
देखल *dekhal.*	देखला *dĕkh'lá.*

§ 80. Noun of Agency, *'one who sees.'*

देखनिहार *dĕkh'nihár,* देखेवाला *dĕkhĕwálá,* or देखवैया *dĕkh'waiyá.*

* This form of the verbal noun is always the same as the root. So also in the conjunctive participle.

CHAPTER VII.

THE REGULAR NEUTER VERB.

§ 81. This verb differs from the active verb only in the formation of certain of its past tenses. The three more usual past tenses are here given; the conjugation of the rest of the verb can be learnt from the conjugation of the √ देख *dekh*.

NOTE that throughout the periphrastic tenses of the neuter verb, in which the past participle occurs, the past participle takes the form गिरल *giral* or गिरऽलऽ *gir'la*, and not the form गिरऽलेँ *gir'lẽ*, which might be expected: thus हम गिरल होब *ham giral hob*, 'I shall have fallen,' and not हम गिरऽलेँ होब *ham gir'lẽ hob*.

§ 82. √ गिर *gir*, 'fall.'

PAST PARTICIPLE: गिरल *giral*; fem. गिरलि *girali*.

•

INDICATIVE MOOD.

§ 83. (*a*) Preterite: '*I fell,*' *&c.*

Person.	SINGULAR.		PLURAL.	
	Masculine.	Feminine.	Masculine.	Feminine.
1st	गिर॰लूँ, गिर॰लोँ, *gir'lú,* gir'lõ,* गिरलँ *gir'lã.*		गिर॰ली *gir'lí.* गिर॰लिऐ, गिर॰लिऐन्ह, *gir'liai, gir'liainh,* गिर॰लिऔ, गिर॰लिऔन्ह, *gir'liau, gir'liaunh,* गिर॰लिहौन्ह *gir'lihaunh.*	
2nd	गिर॰ला *gir'lá,* गिर॰ले, गिर॰लेँ, *gir'le, gir'lẽ,* गिर॰लै, गिर॰लैँ, *gir'lai, gir'laĩ,* गिरल॰हीँ, गिरल॰है, *giral'hí, giral'hai,* गिरल॰हैँ, *giral'haĩ.*	गिर॰ली *gir'lí.*	गिर॰लऽ *gir'la.* गिरल॰हू, गिरल॰हो, *giral'hú, giral'ho,* गिरल॰हौ *giral'hau.*	
3rd	गिरल *giral,* गिर॰लै *gir'lai,* गिर॰लौ, गिर॰लऽ, *gir'lau, gir'la.*		गिर॰लैन्ह, गिर॰लौन्ह, *gir'lainh, gir'launh,* गिर॰लथ *gir'lath,* गिरल॰थी, *giral'thí,* गिरल॰हीँ *giral'hí,* गिरल॰हिन्ह, *giral'hinh,* गिरल॰खीँ, गिरल॰खिन्ह, *giral'khí, giral'khinh,* गिरल॰हैन्ह, गिर॰हौन्ह, *giral'hainh, giral'-* [*haunh,* गिर॰ *gir'lá.*	गिरल॰थीँ, *giral'thí,* गिरल॰थीन्हि, *giral'thinhi.* गिर॰ली *gir'lí.*

* Or गिरिलूँ *girilú*, and so throughout.

§ 84. (*k*)—Perfect: '*I have fallen,*' *&c.*

FORM I.

Person.	Singular.	Plural.
1st	गिरलौं छै *gir'lŏ chhai.*	गिरली छै *gir'li chhai.*
2nd	गिरलैं छै *gir'lĕ chhai.*	गिरलऽ छै *gir'la chhai.*
3rd	गिरल छै *giral chhai.*	गिरला छै *gir'lá chhai.*

To form the feminine, use feminine forms of the preterite: thus, second singular feminine गिरली छै *gir'lí chhai.*

Any of the other forms of the preterite may be used throughout. In Baṛh and Western Jamuí है *hai* is used instead of छै *chhai.*

FORM II.

This form means, '*I am fallen,*' rather than '*I have fallen.*'

Person.	Singular.	Plural.
1st	*Not used.*	गिरल* छी *giral chhí.*
2nd	गिरल छैं *giral chhĕ.*	गिरल छऽ *giral chha.*
3rd	गिरल छै *giral chhai.*	गिरल छैन्ह *giral chhainh.*

* Or गिरलऽ *gir'la,* and so throughout.

To form the feminine, use feminine forms of the past participle and of auxiliary: thus, first plural feminine गिरलि छी *girali chhí*, and so on.

Any optional form of the present of the defective auxiliary verb may be used, and the strong form of the defective auxiliary verb: thus, गिरल छिऐ *giral chhiai*, गिरल छिकी *giral chhiki*, *&c.* In Báṛh and Western Jamuí ही *hí*, &c., is used instead of छी *chhí*, &c.

§ 85. (*l*)—Pluperfect: '*I had fallen,*' &c.

FORM I.

Person.	Singular.	Plural.
1st	गिरलौं छल *gir'lõ chhal.*	गिरली छल *gir'li chhal.*
2nd	गिरलैं छल *gir'lẽ chhal.*	गिरलह छल *gir'la chhal.*
3rd	गिरल छल *giral chhal.*	गिरला छल *gir'lá chhal.*

To form the feminine, use feminine forms of the preterite: thus, second singular feminine गिरली छल *gir'li chhal.*

Any of the other forms of the preterite may be used throughout. In Báṛh and Western Jamuí हल *hal* is used instead of छल *chhal.*

FORM II.

This form means '*I was fallen,*' rather than '*I had fallen.*'

Person.	Singular.	Plural.
1st	गिरल* छलौं *giral chhalõ.*	गिरल छली *giral chhalí.*
2nd	गिरल छलैं *giral chhalẽ.*	गिरल छलह *giral chhala.*
3rd	गिरल छल *giral chhal.*	गिरल छला *giral chhalá.*

* Or गिरलह *gir'la*, and so throughout.

To form the feminine, use feminine forms of the past participle and auxiliary: thus, first plural feminine गिरलि छलौं *girali chhalõ*, and so on.

Any optional form of the preterite of the second auxiliary verb may be used. In Báṛh and Western Jamuí the form हलौं *halõ* is used instead of छलौं *chhalõ.*

CHAPTER VIII.

VOCALIC ROOTS.

§ 86. Many verbs have roots ending in vowels, and the junction of the root with the termination frequently causes some slight apparent irregularity.

For this reason the following examples are given of the conjugation of verbs having roots ending in vowels. They are here conjugated in the masculine gender, and through the four radical and participial tenses. From these the periphrastic tenses can easily be formed. It has not been thought necessary to give the conjugation in full for each person.

With regard to the shortening of the root-vowel, see General Introduction, § 36.

§ 87. Example of a verb whose root ends in आ *á*:—

The conjugation of these verbs should be carefully studied, as a large class of active and causal verbs follows it.

In the preterite indicative these verbs insert a junction vowel between the root and the ल *l* of the termination: thus ख* + ए + लौँ *kha* + *ĕ* + *lõ*, or खैलौँ *khailõ*, 'I ate,' and प* + ए + लौँ *pa* + *ĕ* + *lõ*, or पैलौँ *pailõ*, 'I got,' where ए *ĕ* is the junction vowel. As will be subsequently seen the same peculiarity exists in other tenses besides the preterite.

All verbs which take ए *ĕ* in the preterite indicative insert ए *e* or य *y* in the future, in the past participle, and in that form of the 3rd singular preterite which is the same as the past participle.

---

* With regard to the shortening of the root-vowel and contraction of concurrent vowels, see General Introduction, §§ 34, 36.

§ 88. The first verbal noun, or root, of these verbs sometimes ends in आब *áb* or आव *áw* and sometimes in आ *á*, according to the following rule:—

1) All active (including causal) roots end in आब *áb*: thus पाब *páb* or पाव *páw*, 'obtain;' obl. पाबे *pábĕ* or पाबऽ *pába*.

Exception.—The √ खा *khá*, 'eat,' although active, ends in आ *á*.

2) All neuter roots end in आ: thus अघा *aghá*, 'satiate;' obl. अघाए *agháĕ*.

Exceptions.—The √ गाब *gáb*, 'sing,' and the √ आब *áb*, 'come,' though neuter, end in आब *áb*.

Verbs whose roots end in आब *áb* may optionally insert a ब *b* or व *w* in the present conjunctive and in the present participle, but not those whose roots end in आ *á*.

Note also that all verbs whose roots end in आब *áb* may drop the ब *b* and be conjugated like simple verbs in आ *á*.

§ 89. √पा *pá*, 'get.'

INFINITIVE (1ST FORM): पाब *páb* or पाव *páw*; obl. पाबे *pábĕ*, पाबऽ *pábu*, or पाए *páĕ* or पा *pá*.*

„ (2ND FORM): पाएल *páĕl*; obl. पैला *pailá*. (See General Introduction, § 37.)

PRES. PART. पाबैत *pábait* or पाइत *páit*.†

---

* But from √ खा *khá*; *Dir.* only खा *khá*. *Obl.* only खाए *kháĕ* or खा *khá*.

† But from √खा *khá*, only खाइत *kháït* or खात *khát*.

INDICATIVE MOOD.

Person.	PRETERITE. (See remarks above.)		FUTURE.	
	Singular.	Plural.	Singular.	Plural.
1st	पैलों *pailõ.*	पैली *paili.*	पैबै *paibai.*	पाएब *páĕb.*
2nd	पैलँ *pailẽ.*	पैलऽ *paila.*	पैबँ *paibẽ.*	पैबऽ *paiba.*
3rd	पैलक *pailak.*	पैलन्का *paĭl'ká.*	पैत *paitai.*	पैता *paitá.*

CONDITIONAL MOOD.

Person.	PRESENT.		PRETERITE.	
	Singular.	Plural.	Singular.	Plural.
1st	पाऊँ *páũ** or [पाबों *pábõ.*	पाई *pái* or [पाबी *pábi.*	पैतों *paitõ.*	पैती *paiti.*
2nd	पाएँ *páẽ* or पाबँ [*pábẽ.*	पाहू *páhú* or [पाबऽ *pába.*	पैतँ *paitẽ.*	पैतऽ *paita.*
3rd	पाऐ *páai* or पाबै [*pábai.*	पाऐन्ह *páainh* or पाबैन्ह *pábainh.*	पाबैत *pábait* or पाइत [*páït.*†	पैता *paitá.*

* From √ खा *khá*, and other roots ending in आ *á*, the forms are only—
Sing.—(1) खाऊँ *kháũ*, (2) खाएँ *khaẽ*, (3) खाऐ *kháai*;

Plur.—(1) खाई *khái*, (2) खाहू *kháhú*, (3) खाऐन्ह *kháainh*, and not खाबों *khábõ*, &c.

† But from √ खा *khá*, only खाइत *kháït*, and not खाबैत *khábait*.

§ 90. Example of a verb whose root ends in ई í:—

√पी pí, 'drink.'

INFINITIVE (2ND FORM): पीअल *píal*; obl. पीला *pilá*, 'to drink.'
PRES. PART. पीऐत *piait*.

INDICATIVE MOOD.

Person.	Preterite.		Future.	
	Singular.	Plural.	Singular.	Plural.
1st	पीलौं *pilõ*.*	पीली *píli*.	पीबै *píbai*.†	पीअब *piab*.
2nd	पीलैं *pilẽ*.	पीलऽ *pila*.	पीबैं *píbẽ*.	पीबऽ *piba*.
3rd	पिलन्कै *pil'kai*.	पिलन्का *pil'ká*	पीतै *pitai*.	पीता *pitá*.

* Or पीअलौं *píalõ*, and so throughout.
† Or पीअबै *píabai*, and so throughout.

CONDITIONAL MOOD.

Person.	Present.		Preterite.	
	Singular.	Plural.	Singular.	Plural.
1st	पीऊँ *píū*.	पीइ *píi*.	पीतौं *pitõ*.*	पीती *píti*.
2nd	पीएँ *píẽ*.	पीअ *pia*.	पीतैं *pitẽ*.	पीतऽ *pita*.
3rd	पीऐ *piai*.	पीऐन्ह *piainh*.	पीऐत *piait*.	पीता *pitá*.

* Or पीऐतौं *piaitõ*, and so throughout.

§ 91. **Example of a verb whose root ends in ऊ *ú*:—**

√चू *chú*, 'drip.'

INFINITIVE (2ND FORM): **चूअल** *chúal*, 'to drip.'

PRES. PART. **चूऐत** *chúait.*

INDICATIVE MOOD.

Person.	PRETERITE.		FUTURE.	
	Singular.	Plural.	Singular.	Plural.
1st	चूलौँ* *chúlõ.*	चूली *chúli.*	चूबै *chúbai.*	चूअब *chúab.*
2nd	चूलेँ *chúlẽ.*	चूलह *chúla.*	चूबेँ *chúbẽ.*	चूबह *chúba.*
3rd	चूअल *chúal.*	चूला *chúlá.*	चूतै *chútai.*	चूता *chútá.*

* Or चूअलौँ *chúalõ*, and so throughout, except in third singular.

CONDITIONAL MOOD.

Person.	PRESENT.		PRETERITE.	
	Singular.	Plural.	Singular.	Plural.
1st	चूऊँ *chúú.*	चूई *chúí.*	चूतौँ* *chútõ.*	चूती *chúti.*
2nd	चूएँ *chúẽ.*	चूअ *chúa.*	चूतेँ *chútẽ.*	चूतह *chúta.*
3rd	चूऐ *chúai.*	चूऐन्ह *chúainh*	चूऐत *chúait.*	चूता *chútá.*

* Or चूअतौँ *chúatõ*, and so on throughout.

§ 92. Example of a verb whose root ends in ओ *o*:—

√ रो *ro*, 'weep.'

INFINITIVE (2ND FORM): रोअल *roal*, 'to weep.'
PRES. PART. रोइत *roït* or रोऐत *roait*.

INDICATIVE MOOD.

Person.	PRETERITE.		FUTURE.	
	Singular.	Plural.	Singular.	Plural.
1st	रोअलों *roälõ*.*	रोअली *roäli*.	रोअबै *roäbai*.†	रोअब *roäb*.
2nd	रोअलें *roälẽ*.	रोअलठ *roäla*.	रोअबें *roäbẽ*.	रोअबठ *roäba*.
3rd	रोअल *roäl*.	रोअला *roälá*.	रोतै *rotai*.	रोअता *roätá*.

* Or रोलों *rolõ*, and so throughout.
† रोबै *robai*, and so throughout the first and second persons.

CONDITIONAL MOOD.

Person.	PRESENT.		PRETERITE.	
	Singular.	Plural.	Singular.	Plural.
1st	रोऊँ *roũ*.	रोई *roí*.	रोअतों *roatõ*.*	रोअती *roati*.
2nd	रोएँ *roẽ*.	रोअ *roa*.	रोअतें *roatẽ*.	रोअतठ *roata*.
3rd	रोऐ *roai*.	रोऐन्ह *roainh*.	रोइत *roit* or [रोऐत *roait*.	रोअता *roatá*.

* Or रोतों *rotõ*, and so throughout.

For further examples of verbs of this class, see conjugation of √ हो *ho*, § 53 & ff. This root √ रो *ro* is not much used in Southern Maithilí, the √ कान *kán* or काँद *kãd* being preferred. It is, however, given as an example for the sake of uniformity with the other grammars of this series.

CHAPTER IX.

IRREGULAR VERBS.

§ 93. The verbs √ कर *kar*, 'do;' √ धर *dhar*, 'seize' or 'place;' √ जा *já*, 'go;' and √ हो *ho*, 'become,' are irregular in their preterite tense indicative. The conjugation of √ कर *kar* and √ जा *já* is therefore given in that tense only. √ धर *dhar* is conjugated exactly like √ कर *kar*, and is therefore not given. Besides the irregular forms, √ कर *kar* and √ धर *dhar* have also each a regular form of the preterite indicative. The √ मर *mar*, 'die,' which is irregular in most Bihárí dialects, is regular in the one under notice.

The conjugation of √ हो *ho* has been already given in § 53 and ff., and is not given here.

The verbs √ दे *de*, 'give,' and √ ले *le*, 'take,' are more or less irregular throughout all the tenses. The verb √ दे *de* is therefore given conjugated throughout the four radical and participial tenses. The verb √ ले *le* is conjugated precisely like the verb √ दे *de*.

§ 94. √कर *kar*, 'do.'

INFINITIVE (2ND FORM) : करल *karal* or कैल *kail*.

PRES. PART. करैत *karait*.

PAST PART. करल *karal* or कैल *kail*.

√धर *dhar*, 'seize,' 'place.'

INFINITIVE (2ND FORM) : धरल *dharal* or धैल *dhail*.

PRES. PART. धरैत *dharait*.

PAST PART. धरल *dharal* or धैल *dhail*.

INDICATIVE MOOD.

Person.	Irregular Preterite.		Regular Preterite.	
	Singular.	Plural.	Singular.	Plural.
1st	कैलौँ *kailõ.*	कैली *kailí.*	करऽलौँ *kar'lõ.*	करऽली *kar'lí.*
2nd	कैलेँ *kailẽ.*	कैलह *kaila.*	करऽलेँ *kar'lẽ.*	करऽलह *kar'la.*
3rd	कैलक *kailak.*	कैलऽका *kail'ká.*	करलऽकै *karal'kai* or (irregularly) करऽकै *kar'kai.*	करलऽका *karal'ká* or (irregularly) करऽकैन्ह *kar'kainh.*

The irregular form is used chiefly in Báṛh, and the regular one in South Munger.

Similarly is conjugated √ धर *dhar* (धैलौँ *dhailõ*, धरऽलौँ *dhar'lõ*, &c.).

§ 95. The √ मर *mar*, 'die,' is conjugated regularly.

§ 96. √जा *já*, 'go.'

This root is conjugated like √ खा *khá* in all tenses but the preterite indicative, which is therefore here given. (See § 87 and ff.) With it is given the same tense of √ आब *áb*, 'come,' for the sake of comparison.

	√ आब	√ जा
VERBAL NOUN (2ND FORM) :	आएल *áĕl.*	जाएल *jáĕl* or गेल *gel.*
PRES. PART.	आबैत *ábait.*	जाइत *jáït.*
PAST PART.	आएल *áĕl.*	गेल *gel.*

Person.	√ आ *á*, PRETERITE INDICATIVE.		√ जा *já*, PRETERITE INDICATIVE.	
	Singular.	Plural.	Singular.	Plural.
1st	ऐलौँ *ailŏ*.	ऐली *ailí*.	गेलौँ *gelŏ*.	गेली *gelí*.
2nd	ऐलँ *ailĕ*.	ऐलऽ *aila*.	गेलँ *gelĕ*.	गेलऽ *gela*.
3rd	आएल *áĕl*.	ऐला *ailá*.	गेल *gel*.	गेला *gelá*.

The second plural imperative of √जा *já* is irregularly जो *jo*.

§ 97. √दे *de*, 'give.'

VERBAL NOUN { 1ST FORM : दऽ *da*, दे *de*, or दै *dai*; obl. देवऽ *dewa*.
2ND FORM : देल *del*, 'to give.' }

PRES. PART. देत *dait*.

PAST PART. देल *del*.

INDICATIVE MOOD.

Person.	PRETERITE.		FUTURE.	
	Singular.	Plural.	Singular.	Plural.
1st	देलौँ *delŏ*.	देली *delí*.	देबै *debai*.	देब *deb*.
2nd	देलँ *delĕ*.	देलऽ *dela*.	देबँ *debĕ*.	देबऽ *deba*.
3rd	देलन्कै *dĕl'kai*.	देलन्का *dĕl'ká*.	देतै *detai*.	देता *detá*.

CONDITIONAL MOOD.

Person.	Present.		Preterite.	
	Singular.	Plural.	Singular.	Plural.
1st	दौँ *daũ*, देऊँ *deũ*, or दीओँ *díõ*.	दी *dí*.	देतोँ *detõ*.	देती *deti*.
2nd	दे *de*, देँ *dẽ*, दै *dai*, दैँ *daĩ*, or देही [*dehí*.	दऽ *da*, दहो *daho* or देहू *dehú*.	देतेँ *detẽ*.	देतऽ *deta*.
3rd	दै *dai*, दीऐ *díai*.	देथ *deth* or दैन्ह *dainh*.	दैत *dait*.	देता *detá*.

PRECATIVE: दीहऽ *díha*, दीही *dihí*.

Similarly is conjugated the √ले *le*, 'take,' the letter ल *la* being substituted for the letter द *da* throughout.

CHAPTER X.

THE PASSIVE VERB.

§ 98. The passive verb is formed by conjugating the verbal noun ending in अल *al* with the verb √ जा *já*, 'go:' thus देखल जाएल *dekhal jáĕl*, 'to be seen.' This verbal noun is not altered for gender, number, person, or tense, only the verb जाएल *jáĕl* being conjugated. Thus—

Indicative Preterite Masculine: *'I was seen,' &c.*

Person.	Singular.	Plural.
1st	देखल गेलौँ *dekhal gelŏ.*	देखल गेली *dekhal gelí.*
2nd	देखल गेलेँ *dekhal gelĕ.*	देखल गेलह *dekhal gela.*
3rd	देखल गेल *dekhal gel.*	देखल गेला *dekhal gelá.*

§ 99. This verbal noun in अल *al* must be carefully distinguished from the past participle having the same termination. The former even in irregular verbs is sometimes quite regular, so that we have verbal nouns such as जाएल *jáĕl*, besides past participles like गेल *gel*. At the same time it must be remembered that the verbal noun can also take the form of the past participle as well as its proper form: so that we may have गेल *gel* as a verbal noun as well as जाएल *jáĕl*. An example of an irregular passive verb is जाएल जाइछै *jáĕl jäichhai* (impersonal), 'it is gone'—*itum est*; but, used in the sense of the potential, 'it can go.' When neuter verbs are used in the passive voice, they are always used in an impersonal potential sense: thus, हमन्रा से चलल नइँ जाइछै *ham'rá se chalal naí jäichhai*, 'by me it cannot be gone,' *i.e.* 'I cannot go.'

§ 100. Another common form of the passive is made by adding to the direct form of the first variety of the verbal noun (which is the same in form as the root) the verb परल *paral*, 'to fall;' the whole then forms an intensive compound. (See § 114.)

An example of this form is—

> कुच्छु उठल नहीँ देख परैछै *kuchchhu uṭhal nahi dekh paraichhai*, 'it is not seen to be at all increased in size.'

§ 101. The Potential Passive Voice.

This voice is formed in the same manner as the causal verb (see § 103). It has a potential force, intimating not so much that a thing *is* done as that it *can be* done. Examples of its use are—

> कुच्छु कुच्छु जनाबैछै, *kuchchu kuchchhu janábaichhai*, 'a little can be known, *i.e.*, is evident.'

> ई तऽ कोय नया ढङ्ग के आदिमी देखाइछै *i ta koy nayá ḍhang kẽ adimí dèkháïchhai*, 'this (fellow) appears to be a man of strange habit.'

§ 102. The Periphrastic Passive Voice.

A very common kind of passive voice is formed by placing the verb √ आब *áb* after the first or shortest form of a verbal noun in the locative case: thus देखे मेँ आएल *dekhĕ mẽ áĕl*, 'the coming into seeing,' *i.e.* 'to be seen.' The person by whom the action is done is put in the oblique genitive form of the noun or pronoun when there is one: thus तोरा आर हमऽरा देखे मेँ ऐलऽ *torá ár ham'rá dekhĕ mẽ aila*, 'you came into my seeing,' 'you were seen by me.' The following example shows a verb in this voice conjugated in the preterite indicative masculine:—

Singular.	Plural.
1. देखे मेँ एलोँ *dekhĕ mẽ ailõ.*	1. देखे मेँ ऐली *dekhĕ mẽ ailí.*
2. देखे मेँ ऐलेँ *dekhĕ mẽ ailẽ.*	2. देखे मेँ ऐलऽ *dekhĕ mẽ aila.*
3. देखे मेँ आएल *dekhĕ mẽ áĕl.*	3. देखे मेँ ऐला *dekhĕ mẽ ailá.*

EXAMPLE.—हमऽरा आर तोरा देखे मेँ ऐलियै *ham'rá ár torá dekhĕ mẽ aïliai*, 'we were seen by you.'

CHAPTER XI.

CAUSAL VERBS.

§ 103. A causal verb is formed by adding आ *á* to the root of the simple verb, and a double causal by adding वा *wá*. The stems thus formed are conjugated exactly like verbs whose roots end in आ *á* (see § 87)—that is, like the √ पा *pá*, taking आब *áb* or आव *áw* in the first verbal noun, the present conjunctive, and present participle. (See § 88.)

Simple Verb.	Causal.	Double Causal.
√ उठ *uṭh*, ‘rise.’	उठा *uṭhá*, ‘raise.’	उठ॰वा *uṭh’wa*, ‘cause to raise.’
√ कह *kah*, ‘say.’	कहा *kahá*, ‘cause to speak.’	कह॰वा *kah’wá*, ‘cause to cause to speak.’
√ छिप *chhip*, ‘be hidden.’	छिपा *chhipá*, ‘hide.’	छिप॰वा *chhip’wá*, ‘cause to hide.’
√ नुक *nuk*, ‘be hidden.’	नुका *nuká*, ‘hide.’	नक॰वा *nuk’wá*, ‘cause to hide.’
√ पक *pak*, ‘be cooked.’	पका *paká*, ‘cook.’	पक॰वा *pak’wá*, ‘cause to cook.’
√ मिल *mil*, ‘meet.’	मिला *milá*, ‘mix.’	मिल॰वा *mil’wá*, ‘cause to mix.’
√ सुन *sun*, ‘hear.’	सुना *suná*, ‘tell.’	सुन॰वा *sun’wá*, ‘cause to tell.’

§ 104. If the simple root contains a long vowel it is shortened, viz. आ *á* to अ *a*, ई *í* to इ *i*, ऊ *ú* to उ *u*, ए *e* to ऍ *ĕ*, ओ *o* to ओ *ŏ*, ऐ *ai* to ऐ *aĭ*, and औ *au* to औ *aŭ*.

Similarly, if a root ends in a double consonant, it is made single : thus—

Simple Verb.	Causal.	Double Causal.
जाग *jág*, 'be awake.'	जगा *jagá*, 'awaken.'	जगवा *jag'wá*, 'cause to awake.'
पाक *pák*, 'be cooked.'	पका *paká*, 'cook.'	पकवा *pak'wá*, 'cause to cook.'
जीत *jít*, 'conquer.'	जिता *jitá*, 'cause to conquer.'	जितवा *jit'wá*, 'cause to cause to conquer.'
सीख *síkh*, 'learn.'	सिखा *sikhá*, 'teach.'	सिखवा *sikh'wá*, 'cause to teach.'
पी *pí*, 'drink.'	पिआ *piá*, 'cause to drink.'	पिअवा *piawá*, 'cause to cause to drink.'
भीग *bhíg*, 'wet.'	भिगा *bhigá*, 'moisten.'	भिगवा, *bhig'wá* 'cause to moisten.'
घूम *ghúm*, 'be turned.'	घुमा *ghumá*, 'turn.'	घुमवा *ghum'wá*, 'cause to turn.'
बूड़ *búṛ*, 'sink.'	बुड़ा *buṛá*, 'immerse.'	बुड़वा *buṛ'wá*, 'cause to immerse.'
सूत *sút*, 'sleep.'	सुता *sutá*, 'put to sleep.'	सुतवा *sut'wá*, 'cause to put to sleep.'
देख *dekh*, 'see.'	देखा *dĕkhá*, 'show.'	देखवा *dĕkh'wá*, 'cause to show.'
बैस *bais*, 'sit.'	बैसा *baĭsá*, 'seat.'	बैसवा *baĭs'wá*, 'cause to sit.'
दौर *daur*, 'run.'	दौरा *daŭrá*, 'cause to run.'	दौरवा *daŭr'wá*, 'cause to cause to run.
नुक्क *nukk*, 'be hidden.'	नुका *nuká*, 'hide.'	नुकवा *nuk'wá*, 'cause to hide.

Note in connection with the above:—

Simple Verb.	Causal.
√ कह *kah*, 'speak'	कहला *kah'lá*, also regular.
√ खा *khá*, 'eat'	खिआ *khiá*.
√ पी *pí*, 'drink'	पिला *pilá*, also regular.

§ 105. Some primitive neuter verbs, having a monosyllabic root enclosing a short vowel, form the first causal by simply lengthening that vowel. The double causal is formed in the usual way, *e.g.*—

Simple Verb.		Causal.
√ कट *kaṭ*,	'be cut'	काट *káṭ*, 'cut.'
√ बन्ध *bandh*,	'be tied'	बाँध *bẫdh*, 'tie.'
√ लद *lad*,	'be loaded'	लाद *lád*, 'load.'
√ खिंच *khiṅch*,	'be dragged'	खीँच* *khîch*, 'drag.'

§ 106. Sometimes a cognate diphthong is substituted for the long vowel, *e.g.*—

खुल *khul*, 'be open.'	खोल *khol*, 'open.'
घुर *ghur*, 'melt.' (*Neut.*)	घोर *ghor*, 'melt.' (*Act.*)

§ 107. The verb √ निकल *nikal* or निकस *nikas*, 'come out,' makes its causal निकाल *nikál* or निकास *nikás*, 'take out,' on the analogy of the above. So also √ पसर *pasar*, 'be scattered,' makes पसार *pasár*, 'scatter,' 'extend;' √ ससर *sasar*, 'slip,' ससार *sasár*, 'cause to slip;' √ उपर *upar*, 'be rooted up,' उपार *upár*, 'root up;' and √ उखर *ukhar*, 'be rooted up,' उखार *ukhár* 'root up.'

---

* When the vowel is lengthened, *anuswár* becomes *anunásik*. (Compare General Introduction, § 28.)

§ 108. The following are irregular :—

Simple Verb.	Causal.	Double Causal.
अट *aṭ*, 'be stopped.'	आर *ár*, 'stop.'	अरा *ará*.
फट *pkaṭ* or फाट *pháṭ*, 'be torn.'	फार *phár*, 'tear,'	फरा *phará*.
छूट *chhúṭ*, 'be separated.'	छोर *chhor* or छार *chhár*, 'separate.'	छोरा *chhŏrá*.
जूट *júṭ*, 'be joined.'	जोर *jor*, 'join.'	जोरा *jŏrá*.
टूट *ṭúṭ*, 'be broken.'	तोर *tor*, 'break.'	तोरा *tŏrá*,
फूट *phúṭ*, 'be burst.'	फोर *phor*, 'burst.'	फोरा *phŏrá*.
बिक *bikk*, 'be sold.'	बेँच *bĕch* or बिका *biká*, 'sell.'	बेँचा *bĕchá*.
रह *rah*, 'remain.'	राख *rákh* or रक्ख *rakkh*, 'place.'	रखा *rakhá*.
मर *mar*, 'die.'	मार *már* or मुआ *muá*, 'cause to die.'	

CHAPTER XII.

COMPOUND VERBS.

§ 109. Compound verbs are either intensives, potentials, completives, frequentatives, desideratives, continuatives, staticals, inceptives, permissives, or acquisitives.

§ 110. Compound verbs may be classed as—(1) those formed with the verbal noun, and (2) those formed with the participles.

(1) Those formed with the verbal noun are—

a) Intensives.
b) Potentials.
c) Completives.
d) Frequentatives.
e) Desideratives.
f) Inceptives.
g) Permissives.
h) Acquisitives.

(2) Those formed with the participles—

a) Continuatives.
b) Staticals.

Class I.—Compounds formed with the Verbal Noun.*

§ 111. There are two varieties of the verbal noun—

a) In अ *a* (silent) or इ *i*, oblique form ए *ĕ* or अ *a*; as देख *dekh* or देखि *dekhi*, obl. देखे *dekhĕ* or देखऽ *dekha*.

b) In अल *al*, oblique form ल्ला *'lá*; as देखल *dekhal*, obl. देखल्ला *dĕkh'lá*.

The direct first form in अ *a* (silent) is always the same as the root.

Compound verbs are either formed with the direct form of the first or second variety of the verbal noun, or with the oblique form of the first variety.

---

* Much of the succeeding matter is based on Kellogg's Hindí Grammar.

§ 112. ***Intensives*** are formed with the direct form of the first variety; ***Frequentatives*** are always, and ***Desideratives*** are sometimes, formed with the direct form of the second variety; ***Potentials, Completives, Inceptives, Permissives,*** and ***Acquisitives,*** are always formed with the oblique form of the first variety.

§ 113. ***Intensive*** compounds intensify or otherwise modify the meaning of the verb whose root stands first in the compound. They are formed by adding to a verbal noun of the first variety in the direct form one of certain other verbs, which latter verb in conjunction with the verbal noun is then conjugated as usual. This second conjugated member does not, however, retain its separate character and significance, but only modifies, in accordance with the general idea which it embodies, the meaning of the unconjugated verbal noun to which it is annexed. Examples are—

फेँकल *phěkal*, 'to throw.'	फेँक (or फेँकि) देल *phěk* (or *phěki*) *del*, 'to throw away.'
तोरल *toral*, 'to break.'	तोर डालल *tor ḍálal*, 'to break in pieces.'
बनल *banal*, 'to be made.'	बन आएल *ban áěl* or बन जाएल *ban jáěl*, 'to be completed.'
खाएल *kháěl*, 'to eat.'	खा जाएल *khá jáěl*, 'to eat up.'
बोलल *bolal*, 'to speak.'	बोल उठल *bol uṭhal*, 'to speak suddenly.'
काटल *káṭal*, 'to cut.'	काट लेल *káṭ lel*, 'to cut for oneself.'
राखल *rákhal*, 'to place.'	राख लेल *rákh lel*, 'to lay by.'

§ 114. The auxiliary verbs usually employed to form intensives are—

देल *del*,	'to give,'	implying	*intensity.*
डालल *ḍálal*,	'to throw,'	"	*violence.*
आएल *áěl*,	'to come,'	"	*completion.*
जाएल *jáěl*,	'to go,'	"	*completion.*
परल *paral*,	'to fall,'	"	*chance.*
उठल *uṭhal*,	'to rise,'	"	*suddenness.*
लेल *lel*,	'to take,'	"	*reflexiveness.*

परल *paral* is also used in intensive compounds to form passives of transitive verbs. (See § 100.)

§ 115. *Potentials* are formed by adding to the oblique form of the first verbal noun of any verb the verb सकल *sakal*, 'to be able,' or the verb पारल *páral* 'be able,' which may then be conjugated throughout. Examples are—

बोलें पारल *bolĕ páral*, 'to be able to speak.'

ऊ दौरें पारैछै *ú daurĕ páraichhai*, or ऊ दौरऽ सकैछै *ú daura sakaichhai* 'he can run.'

हमें जाए सकब्बै (or पारब्बै) *hamĕ jáĕ sak'bai* (or *pár'bai*), 'I shall be able to go.'

§ 116. *Completives* are formed by adding to the same form of the verbal noun of a verb the verb चुकल *chukal*, 'to be finished,' which may then be conjugated throughout. This compound denotes the *completion* of the act denoted by the primary member of the compound. Examples are—

ऊ खाए चुकब्लै *ú kháĕ chuk'lai*, 'he has done eating.'

जब ऊ खाए चुकब्तै *jab ú kháĕ chuk'tai*, 'when he shall have eaten.'

ऊ तऽ जाए चुकब्लै है *ú ta jáĕ chuk'lai hai*, 'he is indeed already gone.'

§ 117. *Frequentatives* are formed by affixing to the direct form of the second variety of the verbal noun of any verb the verb करल *karal*, 'to do,' which may then be used in any tense. Examples are—

आएल करऽ *áĕl kara*, 'come often,' *lit.* 'do the act of coming.'

हमें सास्त्र पढ़ल करैछी *hamĕ sástr paṛhal karaichhí*, 'I am in the habit of reading the shástras.'

तोँ हम्मर बाता मानल करऽ *tŏ hammar bátá mánal kara*, 'always obey my words.'

तोँ कहिनऽ ऐसन करल करैछऽ *tŏ kahina aisan karal karaichha*, 'why do you always do so?'

ऊ जाएल करैछै *ú jáĕl karaichhai*, 'he often goes.'

§ 118. *Desideratives* are formed, like frequentatives, with the direct form of the verbal noun in अल *al*, substituting the verb चाहल *cháhal*, 'to wish,' for करल *karal* as the second or conjugated member. They denote primarily *desire* to do the action expressed of the principal member; secondarily, the *immediate futurity* of that action. An example is—

ऊ बोलल चाहैछै *ú bolal cháhaichhai*, 'he wishes to speak.'

Sometimes the principal verb is put in the oblique form of the first variety of the verbal noun with or without the dative postposition के *ke* or ला *lá*, लेल *lel*. Examples are—

ऊ बोलें लेल चाहैछै *ú bolĕ lel cháhaichhai*, 'he wishes to speak.'

घड़िया बाजे (or बाजे लेल) चाहैछलै *ghaṛiyá bájĕ* (or *bájĕ lel*) *cháhaichhalai*, 'the clock was about to strike.'

ऊ जाए लेल चाहैहै *ú jáĕ lel cháhaihai*, 'he wishes to go.'

ऊ मरे के (or ला) चाहैछै *ú marĕ ke* (or *lá*) *cháhaichhai*, 'he is about to die.'

The desiderative compound in the precative form is idiomatically used to express obligation or duty. Examples are—

ई पोथिया के पढ़ल चाही *i pŏthiyá ke paṛhal cháhí*, '(one) ought to read this book.' (*lit.* 'be good enough to wish to read').

तोरा उहाँ जाए के चाहिअ *torá uhã jáĕ ke cháhia*, 'it is right for you (*i.e.* you ought) to go there.'

§ 119. *Inceptives* are formed by using the inflected form of the first variety of the verbal noun in construction with the verb लागल *lágal*, 'to be joined,' 'to begin,' and denote the action of the verbal noun as *beginning*. Examples are—

कहे लग्लै *kahĕ lag'lai*, 'he began to say.'

मारे लागल *márĕ lágal*, 'he began to beat.'

बाघा खाए लग्लै *bághá kháĕ lag'lai*, 'the tiger began to eat.'

§ 120. *Permissives* are formed by combining the same form of the verbal noun with the verb देल *del*, 'to give,' and express *permission* to do the act denoted by the verbal noun. Examples are—

> हमऽरा जाए दऽ *ham'rá jáĕ da*, 'let me go.'
>
> हमऽरा बोलें दऽ *ham'rá bolĕ da*, 'be good enough to let me speak.'
>
> ऊ ओकऽरा खाए देलऽकै *ú ŏk'rá kháĕ dĕl'kai*, 'he allowed him to eat.'

§ 121. *Acquisitives* are the exact converse of the preceding, and are formed in the same way, substituting पाएल *páĕl*, 'to get,' for देल *del*. Examples are—

> तोरा आर के उहाँ जाए नऽ पैबऽ *torá ár ke uhī̃ jáĕ na paiba*, 'you will not obtain permission to go there.'
>
> हमें बैसे नऽ पैलूँ *hamẽ baisĕ na pailú̃*, 'I was not allowed to sit.'

Class II.—Compounds formed from the Participles.

§ 122. *Continuatives* are formed by combining the present or past participle of any verb with the verbs जाएल *jáĕl*, 'to go,' or रहल *rahal*, 'to remain.' The participle may be either in the direct or oblique form. It must be remembered that in the case of neuter verbs the oblique form of the past participle is the same as the direct: thus, गिरल *giral*, obl. गिरल *giral*; while in the case of active verbs it is formed by adding एँ *ẽ* or अ *a*: thus, देखल *dekhal*, obl. देखऽलें *dĕkh'lẽ* or देखऽलऽ *dĕkh'la*. The present participle always has its oblique form in तेँ *tẽ* or तऽ *ta*, both in active and neuter verbs: thus, देखैत *dekhait*, obl. देखऽतेँ *dĕkh'tẽ* or देखऽतऽ *dĕkh'ta*; गिरैत *girait*, obl. गिरऽतेँ *gir'tẽ* or गिरऽतऽ *gir'ta*.

The compound with जाएल *jáĕl* expresses *steady progression*, and with रहल *rahal* the *continuance* of a complete action. Examples :—

> ऊ लिखऽलेँ जाइछै *ú likh'lẽ jáichhai*, 'he is going on writing.'
>
> ऊ छौँड़ियनि पढ़ऽतेँ जाइछलऽथी *ú chhaũṛiyani paṛh'tẽ jáichhal'thi*, 'those girls were going on reading.'
>
> पनिया बहल जाइछै *paniyá bahal jáichhai*, 'the water keeps flowing away.'

ऊ गाबैत रहैछै *ú gábait rahaichhai*, 'she continues singing.'

लद्दी के धारा बहैत (or बंहन्तेँ) रहैछै *ladí kĕ dhárá bahait* (or *bah'tẽ*) *rahaichhai*, 'the stream of the river keeps flowing on.'

तोहेँ किथि ला हसन्तऽ रहैछहो *tohẽ kithi lá has'ta rahaichhaho*, 'why do you keep laughing?'

Closely connected with the above is a common combination in which the past participle in its direct form, and changing in gender according to the subject, takes the first place and a verb of motion the second place. Examples are—

एक बाघ परल फिरैछै *ĕk bágh paral phiraichhai*, 'a tiger is prowling about.'

नौँड़ी चललि जाइछलै *nãũṛí chalali jáichhalai*, 'the girl was going along.'

§ 123. *Staticals* denote motion in a state of doing anything. They are formed by combining a verb of motion with a present or past participle, direct or oblique. Examples are—

ऊ कानल (or कानन्तेँ) आबैछै *ú kánal* (or *kán'tẽ*) *ábaichhai*, 'he comes weeping.'

एगो मौगी गाबैत (or गैलेँ) आबैछलै *ego maugí gábait* (or *gailẽ*) *ábaichhalai*, 'a woman was coming singing.'

Note with regard to Baṛh.

In the Báṛh subdivision, and in the western portion of South Munger, some of the above rules do not apply. In Báṛh *Potentials* and *Completives* are formed from the direct, and not from the oblique form of the first verbal noun, and *Continuatives* and *Progressives* always from the direct form of the present participle. Examples are—

Potentials.—ऊ दौर सकैछथ *ú daur sakaihath*, 'he can run.'

हम जा सकब *ham já sakab*, 'I shall be able to go.'

जऽ ऊ सभ आ सकथ *ja ú sabh á sakath*, 'if they be able to come.'

हम नइँ जा सकेही *ham naí já sakĕ hí*, 'we cannot go.'

मिलि सक॰तै *mili sak'tai*, 'it will be able to be found.'

Completives.—ऊ खा चुकल *ú khá chukal* 'he has done eating.'

ऊ तो जा चुक॰लै है *ú to já chuk'lai hai*, 'he is indeed gone.'

जब ऊ खा चुक॰ता *jab ú khá chuk'ta*, 'when he will have done eating.'

Continuatives.—ऊ लिखैत जाहै *ú likhait jáhai*, 'he is going on writing.'

ऊ सभ लड़िकी पढ़ैत जाइहथ *ú sabh laṛikí paṛhait jäïhath*, 'those girls are going on reading.'

पानी बहैत जाहै *páni bahait jáhai*, 'the water keeps flowing on.'

ऊ गाबैत रहऽ है *ú gábait raha hai*, 'she continues singing.'

तोँ काहे हसैत रहऽ हो *tõ káhĕ hasait raha ho?* 'why do you keep laughing?'

नदी के धार बहैत रहऽ है *nadi kĕ dhár bahait raha hai*, 'the stream of the river keeps flowing on.'

Staticals.—ऊ कानैत आबैहै *ú káṇait ábaihai*, 'he comes crying.'

एक स्त्री गाबैत आबऽ हल *ĕk strí gábait ábá hal*, 'a woman was coming singing.'

DIVISION III.

INDECLINABLES.

§ 124. See General Introduction.

APPENDIX.

THE following selections are in the dialect of the northern part of South Munger. Note that in the formation of potential verbs they have a tendency to the forms in vogue in Báṛh. The conversation and fables were translated for me by Anant Lál, Guru of Basdeopúr, in that district. An English translation of them, and of the conversation, will be found in the General Introduction. If the corresponding forms of √अह *ah* are substituted for those of √अछ *achh* throughout, they will be in the dialect of Báṛh and Jamuí. This remark, indeed, applies to all the examples through this Grammar.

SELECTIONS IN THE SOUTH MAITHIL-MÁGADHI DIALECT.

CONVERSATION BETWEEN TWO VILLAGERS.

१ प्रश्न। कहऽ भाइ, कहाँ से आवैछऽ।

उत्तर। परःसिया गाँम से आवैछी॥

२ प्र.। ऊँआँ से कहिया चलल छेलऽ।

उ.। भिन्निएँ चलल छेलँ।

३ प्र.। किथि लाय ऊँआँ गेल छेलऽ॥

उ.। ऊँआँ हम्मर खेत छऽ, तेकऽरा देखऽ गेल छेलँ॥

४ प्र.। ओकऽरा मेँ की बुनऽलऽ छऽ।

उ.। खाली राहर बूनल गेल छै॥

५ प्र.। कहऽ भाइ, अबऽरी के फसिल के कैसन रङ्ग छै।

उ.। ई फसिल के हाल की पुछैछऽ, पानी के नहीँ पड़ऽला सऽ बड़ी खराबी होलै॥

६ प्र.। आज काल तोहर भाइ कऽ देखै नै छिऊन्ह*।

उ.। हम्मर भाइ आज काल किल्ला मेँ नौकर छ, इन्हऽ बऊत कम आवैछै।

---

* For नँ देखैछिइन्ह, the auxiliary being separated from the principal verb.

७ प्र. । तोहर बड़-की गाय के कैसन हाल छउन्ह ।

उ. । ऊ आज काल गभ-नायल छै ; मगर चारा नहीं मिल-ला सऽ टूटि गेल छै ॥

८ प्र. । कऽ महीना सऽ गभ-नायल छै ।

उ. । होलै तऽ आठ महीना, मगर पेट ओकर कुछु उठल नहीं देख पड़ैछै ॥

९ प्र. । कोराबैछै कि एख-नी नै ।

उ. । हाँ कुछु कुछु जनाबैछै ॥

१० प्र । ई कौन बियान छिकै, आरो केत-ना दूध दैछै ।

उ. । अठ-मा बियान छिकै. दू अढ़ाय सेर दूध एक बेरा में दैछै ॥

११ प. । हम-रा एक बक-री लेवऽ के छऽ, तोह-रा गाँम में मिल-तै ।

उ. । हम-रा गाँम में बक-री सब तऽ बहुत छै. मगर दामे तऽ कड़ा छै ॥

१२ प्र. । तोहर बक-री की भेल-हौन्ह ।

उ. । हम्में चरऽ खातिर ओक-रा गामे में छोड़-लउ छिऐ ॥

१३ प्र. । कुछ दूध दैछै ।

उ. । छौँरी के पीए जुकुर होइछै ॥

१४ प्र. । अब-री केतारी बुन-लऽ छऽ की नै ।

उ. । केतारी तऽ बुनलऽ छिऐ, मगर ओक-रा में कुछु फैदा नै छै ॥

१५ प्र. । तोह-रा कन सऽ मार मोँट मँगै-नी में मिलि सक-तै ।

उ. । कहिने नऽ ; पटाओन होय देलऽ, तऽ ले लिहऽ ॥

१६ प्र. । तोह-रा कन कऽ मोट चलैछौन्ह ।

उ. । तीन मोट तऽ लाध-लऽ छिऐ ।

१७ प्र. । तोहर आम के बगीचा कुछु फरैछौन्ह की नै ।

उ. । अब-री बेर तऽ बद-री सऽ गाछ सब में लाही लगि गेलै । नै तऽ बहुत होऐछिलै ॥

१८ प्र. । थोड़ा सन आम हम-रो* औंवार खातिर दीहऽ ।

उ. । अहिया तोहर मन चाहौन्ह आय कऽ तोड़-वाय लऽ ॥

१९ प्र. । तोहर लड़िका कुछु पढ़ैछौन्ह की नै ।

उ. । हाँ गुरू कन जाइछै, ओ ना मा सी तऽ सब पढ़ि गेलै । अब थोड़ा पढ़ैछै ॥

---

* Emphatic for हम-रा, 'to me also.'

२० प्र.। इसकूल में कथिने नठ भेजैछहो

उ.। कुच्छु सीखि ले, तठ भेजि देबै॥

२१ प्र.। हमूँ* अपन्ना लड़िका कठ इस्कूल में भेजठ लाय चाहैछिऐ।

उ.। अच्छा; हमऽरो लड़िका के साथ ओऽकरो† भेजि दहो॥

FÁBLES.

॥ १ बात ॥

मुर्गा आरो मोती के दाना।

एक मुर्गा गोबर के ढेरी कठ गोड़ सठ उकटि रहल छिलै। ओकऽरा मेँ सठबड़ऽका ठो मोती निकलि ऐलै। मुर्गा बोलऽलै, वाह कैसन रङ्ग रूप आरो चमक दमक छै, जौहऽरी एकऽरा पैतिऐ, तठ फूलि कठ नै समैतिऐ। पर हमऽरा पेट के लागिन एकऽरा सठ नै मिँझतै। हाय, एक चाउर के दाना हम्मर हाथ लगतिऐ, तठ से मोती सठ बढ़ि कठ छिलै॥ सचे छिकै।

जे अप्पन काम नै आबै से चूल्हा भाड़ मेँ जाय॥

॥ २ बात ॥

कँगऽला के पूछल आरो फकीर के उतारा देल।

एक कँगऽला के ठियाँ कोय फकीर ऐलऽ छिलै, तेकऽरा सठ पुछलऽकै कि, हमैँ ता भुक्खल मरौँ, आरो हम्मर परोसिया गद्दी तकिया पर लोटैछै, रात दिन चैन करैछै। ओकऽरा मे कौन गुन छै, जे भगऽमान ओकऽरा निहाल करलऽकै, आरो हमऽरा कँगऽला करलऽकै। ई सुनि कठ फकीर उतारा देलऽकै कि, बाबा तोँ ई नै सुनलठ छठ की,

रामऽजी झरोखा पर बैठल सबै के हिसाब लैछै।
आरो जैसन जेकर काम तेकऽरा तैसन दैछै॥

---

* Emphatic for हमैँ, 'I also.'

† Emphatic for ओकऽरा, 'him also.'

॥ ३ बात ॥

देस बिदेस घुमऽ के फेदा।

कोय भला अद॰मी एक गोसाँय सऽ कहलन्है। महऽराज देस देस आरो गाँम गाँम घुम॰ला सऽ की फेदा छिकै, एक जगह रहि कऽ गोसैँया मैँ लौ कहिने ने लगावैछऽ, आरो कोय मध मैँ बैठि कऽ भग॰मान के गुन कहिनऽ ने गावैछऽ। जोगी कहलन्है कि, बाबा ई सब सच्चे छै, पर तों ई कहानी ने सुनलऽ छऽ कि, बहल पानी निर॰मल होइछै आे बाँधल मैला होइछै, तै से साधू अद॰मी बुलन्तैँ फ़ल, कि कोय दाग ने लगै।

॥ ४ बात ॥

एक दिन जाड़ा के दिन मैँ कोय बड़ः अद॰मी के घर मैँ आगिन लगन्लै। सब चीज जरि कऽ बानी होइ गेलै। ज बाहर खड़ा हाथ मलि रहल छिलै, कि एक गरीब परोसिया जाड़ा के मार॰लऽ थर थर काँपन्तऽ घर सऽ निकलि ऐलै, आरो हाथ सेंदऽ लगन्लै। तब ज धन॰बाला बोलन्लै कि, बाह बाह। केकन्रो घर जरै, आरो कोय तापै॥

॥ ५ बात ॥

बाँधल लकन्ड़ी आरो छुटल लकन्ड़ी।

एक गिरन्हस्त के लड़िका आपुस कैँ बहुत लड़ाय झगन्ड़ा करैछिलै। बहुत समन्झौलन्है पर कोय कुच्छु ने मानलन्है। तऽ गिरन्हस्त अपन्ना जी मैँ कहलन्है, जे इनन्का कुच्छु करि कऽ, देखाय दौँ, तऽ चाहे ई कुच्छु बुझि जाय। एक दिन ज अप्पन बेटा कऽ बोलैलन्है, आरो कहलन्है कि, थोड़ा ऐसन लकन्ड़ी हम्मर आगू ले आन। ज लकन्ड़ी कऽ ज गिरन्हस्त एक रस्सी सऽ बाँधलन्है, फनू एक एक गो सऽ कहलन्है कि, रस्सी ने खोलऽ आरो लकन्ड़ी कऽ तोड़ि डालऽ। सबै थकि गेलै, पर कुच्छु ने भेलै। फनू गिरन्हस्त खोलि कऽ एक एक लकन्ड़ी देलन्है, तऽ ज ओकन्रा तुरन्ते तोड़ि देलन्है। तब ओकर बाप कहलन्है कि, बेटा जे तोँ बाँधल लकन्ड़ी के ऐसन आपुस मैँ मिलन्लऽ रहऽ, तऽ सब बैरी के दाँत खट्टा करन्थऽ, आरो अब अरक फरक हो गेलऽ, तऽ बुझऽ कि बिगड़ि गेलऽ॥

॥ जे बिखरन्लऽ, से बिगन्ड़ल ॥

॥ ६ बात ॥

॥ ऊड़ाड़ सब आरो भेँड़ी सब के साथ ॥

एक दिन ऊड़ाड़ सब भेँड़ी सब सऽ कहाय भेजलन्कै कि, आबँ, हम्मँ आरो तोँ आपुस मेँ मेल करि लौँ, किथि लाय आपुस मेँ लड़ौँ, आरो एक दोसन्रा के लहू के पिआसल रहौँ। पाजी कुत्ता सब समुझे लड़ाय के जड़ छिकै। एहिना सदई भूँकि भूँकि कऽ हमन्रा भड़कावैछे, आरो हमन्रा तोरा सऽ लड़ावैछऽ। इनन्का हमन्रा पास भेजि दऽ, फनू की झगन्ड़ा छिकै। हमन्रा तोरा मेँ सदई पियार आरो मिलाप रहितऽ, तऽ तोहर बाल टेढ़ा नै होतौन्ह। गँमार भेँड़ी ई नटन्खट ऊड़ाड़ के बात मानि लेलन्कै, आरो कुत्ता कऽ ऊड़ाड़ के पास भेजि देलन्कै। पहिले तऽ ऊड़ाड़ कुत्ता कऽ खा गेलै, फनू भेँड़ी के पाछे गोड़ हाथ तोड़ कऽ पड़न्लै, थोड़िये दिन मेँ सब भेँड़ी कऽ खा गेलै। सच्चे छिकै, कि बैरी सदई धोखा देहै। ऊ बड़ी गँमार छिकै, जे बैरी कऽ सच्चा समन्झे ॥

॥ ७ बात ॥

॥ बाघ ऊड़ाड़ आरो कँदुआ ॥

एक दिन बाघ ऊड़ाड़ आरो कँदुआ आपुस मेँ ई ठहन्रैलन्कै कि, सब कोय मिलि कऽ सिकार मारौँ, फनू आपुस मेँ बाँटी लौँ। ई बात* ठहन्राइ कऽ जङ्गल मेँ कूद फाँद करऽ लगन्लै, आरो जब एक बड़न्का ठो हरिन मारि लेलन्कै, तऽ बाघ बोलन्लै, आबऽ एकन्रा बाँटौँ। आरो तुरन्ते ओकर तीन टुकन्ड़ा करि देलन्कै, आरो गरजि कऽ बोलन्लै कि, पहिला टुकन्ड़ा तऽ हम्मँ लेबै कहिनऽ कि हम्मँ जङ्गल के राजा छिकूँ, आरो दोसन्रो हमी* लेबै कहिनऽ कि हम्मँ एकन्रा मारऽ मेँ बहुत दौड़न्लौँ, आरो तेसर टुकन्ड़ा ई धरल छै, देखिये तऽ केकर मूँह पड़ैछै, हम्मर आगू सऽ उठाय कऽ ले जाइछऽ। ई सुनि कऽ कँदुआ आरो ऊड़ाड़ पुच्छी दबाय कऽ भागि गेलै, आरो बाघ हरिन कऽ एकेले खा गेलै। ई कहानी सच्चे छिकै कि।

॥ जेकर लाठी तेकर भैँस ॥

---

* Emphatic for हम, 'I indeed.'

॥ ८ बात ॥

॥ माँटी आरो पित्तर के घैला के बात॰चीत ॥

एक दिन कहूँ लड़ी चढ़॰लै, तऽ एक पित्तर के घैला आरो एक माँटी के घैला भाँसि चल॰लै। पित्तर के घैला माँटी के घैला सऽ कहल॰कै हम॰रे साथे आबऽ, तऽ हम्में तोरा बचाय लेबौं। माँटी के घैला बोल॰लै,ऽ ई तोँ बहुत अच्छा बात कहिलऽ, हम्में तोर भला मान॰बौन्ह, आरो सदई गुन गैबौन्ह। मगर सच्चे पूछऽ, तऽ हम॰रा ई डर छै, कि कहूँ पानी के लहर के धक्का सऽ तोरा पास नै जाय रहौं। कहिने जे तोरा सऽ दूर रहलौं, तऽ एहिना डोलल झूलल कहूँ किनारा पर जाय लग॰बै। पर जो तोरा सऽ भेँट होएऽ आरो कहूँ धोखा सऽ ठोकर लगि गेलऽ, तऽ हम॰रो पेट फटि जैतै। सच्चे छिकै, कि।

॥ बड़ा सऽ आस रक्खी पर पास नै जाई ॥

॥ ९ बात ॥

एक मुन्सी बजार में बैठल चिट्ठी लिक्खि रहल छिलै। एक बिदेसी ऐलै, आरो बोल॰लै कि, मुन्सी जी, की लिक्खै छऽ। मुन्सी उतारा देल॰कै कि, भाय चिट्ठी लिक्खै छी। ऊ कहल॰कै कि हम॰रो * सलाम लिक्खि दीअ। मुन्सी जी कहल॰कै, नै जी, अर॰जी लिक्खै छी। ऊ कहल॰कै, तऽ हम॰रो सही करि दीअ। मुन्सी अकुताय कऽ बोल॰लै कि, तमस्सुक लिक्खै छी। ऊ बोल॰लै हम॰रो गुआही लिक्खि दीअ। मुन्सी सोचल॰कै कि, ई तऽ कोय नया ढङ्ग के अदिमी देखाइ छै। पुछल॰कै कि, तोहर नाम की छिकौन्ह। ऊ हँस कऽ बोल॰लै, हम्मर नाम छिकऽ।

॥ मानऽ चाहे नऽ मानऽ हम्में तोर पहुना छिकौं ॥

॥ १० बात ॥

एक बड़ा अदिमी के घर रात कें बेरा आगि लग॰लै। ऊ तऽ अप्पन बाल बच्चा समेत निकलि कऽ भग॰लै आरो नौकर कऽ हुकुम देल॰कै कि, चीज बस्त निकालऽ। एत॰ने में आगिन बहुत उठि गेलै, समुच्चा घर लहरि के लह लह होय गेलै। नौकर

* Emphatic for हम्मर, 'my also.'

बोलन्हे हम्मेँ की की निकालौँ। तब ऊ बड़ऽ अदिमी ठण्ढा साँस लेऽन्कै आरो कहलन्कै कि बाबा।

॥ आगि लगन्लऽ मेँ झोँपन्ड़ी सऽ जे निकन्ले से ही लाभ ॥

॥ ११ बात ॥

॥ गमारी गोआरिन ॥

एक गमारी गोआरिन माथा पर दही के हँड़िया रक्खलऽ चललि जाइछेले। जैतऽ जैतऽ ओकन्रा जी मेँ ई बात ऐले कि, ई दही कऽ बेचन्बे, आरो पैसा सऽ आम मोल लेबै। कुछु आम हमन्रा पास छै। सभे मिलाय कऽ तीन से से कुछु बढ़ि जैतै। एकन्रा मेँ कुछु सड़ि जैतै, पर अढ़ाय से तऽ बचि रहन्तै; आरो ओकन्रा मेँ सऽ जे बचि निकलन्तै ओकर अच्छा दाम लगन्तै। तऽ दिवाली मेँ एक हरिअर सारी लेबै। हाँ हाँ हरिअर सारी हमन्रा मूँह पर अच्छा लगन्तै। अबन्तो हम्मेँ तऽ हरिअरे सारी लेबै, आरो ओकन्रा पीन्हि कऽ मेला जैबै, आरो खूब ऐँठि कऽ अप्पन गहिना हुक्का के सोभा आरो मूँह के चमक देखैबै। आरो एकके चाल मेँ से से झुकाव देखैबै। ई सोच बिचार मेँ ऊ गमारी गोआरिन चमकि कऽ झूकि कऽ चलन्ले। तऽ दही के हँड़िया माथा सऽ गिरि कऽ, चूर होय गेले, आरो सबे बनल बनाएल घर बिगड़ि गेले॥

॥ १२ बात ॥

॥ चील्ह आरो कौआ ॥

एक चील्ह के ठोर मेँ एक घोँघा छेलै। केतन्नोँ भुँइयाँ मेँ पटन्कलन्कै, मगर घोँघा ने टूटन्ले। तऽ एक कौआ ई राह बतैलन्कै कि, ई घोँघा कऽ ठोर मेँ ले कऽ बहुत उच्चा उड़ि जो, आरो उहाँ से गिराय दे, तऽ घोँघा टूटि जैतै। चील्ह कहलन्कै कि, ई बात बहुत अच्छा छिकै, आरो घोँघा कऽ ले कऽ उड़न्ले, आरो बहुत उच्चा मेँ जाय कऽ छोड़ि देलन्कै। जेखननियेँ घोँघा भूँईं मेँ गिरन्ले टुकन्ड़ा टुकन्ड़ा होय गेलै, आरो कौआ ओकर गुद्दा खाय गेलै। थोड़ा देरी मेँ चील्ह हेँठ उतरन्लै, तऽ छिलन्का के छोड़ कऽ कुछु न पलन्कै॥

॥ १३ बात ॥

खट्टा अंगुर।

एक लोमन्ड़ी कोय बगीचा मेँ जाय निकललन्है; देखलन्है, कि अँगूर के ऐसन गुच्छा पक्कल पक्कल टट्टी मेँ लटकि रहल छै, कि जेकन्रा से रस चूऐछै, आरो कोय अगोरन्वाहा नै छै। ई देखि क० ओकर मूँह मेँ पानी भरि अएलै। बहुत उछललन्है कुदलन्है मगर अँगूर के गुच्छा लग नै पहुँच सकलन्है। जब कौनोँ तरह से दाँव नै लगलन्है, त० एना बकैत बढ़लन्है उहाँ से चललन्है कि।

॥ खट्टा अँगूर के छैतै ॥

॥ १४ बात ॥

॥ रसायन्नी ॥

एक रसायन्नी कोय अदिमी से कहलन्है कि, जोँ तोँ कुच्छु चाँदी हमन्रा आगू ले आनऽ, त० हम्मेँ एक ऐसन जड़ी डालौँ, कि तुरन्ते ऊ चाँदी के सोना हो जाय। ऊ सोझा अदिमी ओकर दरुन्पट्टी मेँ आय गेलै, आरो कहूँ से, दुख सुख सहि क०, दू सै रुपैया के चाँदी ऊ रसायन्नी क० लानि देलन्है। रसायन्नी ओही रात क० बिछौना लऽ क० कहूँ चलि देलन्है। अब ऊ बेचारा बीपत के मारल ऊ नटन्खट रसायन्नी के खोजे लगलन्है। जङ्गल जङ्गल खोज-लन्है, मगर ऊ रसायन्नी के कहूँ पता नै लगलन्है। ओकन्रा एना घबराएल देखि क०, एक अदिमी कहलन्है कि, तोरा से भूल होयलौन्ह, कि ऊ नटन्खट फकीर के फन्दा मेँ फँसि गेल०। अब सोच आरो ओकर खोज मेँ दौड़ धूप करन्ला से कुच्छु नै होतौन्ह ई बात पर हम्मेँ एक बात तोरा सुनाबैछी, जेकन्रा सदई याद रक्खँ क० चाही॥

॥ १५ बात ॥

एक चिड़ैया कोय किसान के बगीचा मेँ जाय क० कच्चा पक्कल फल सब के सब काटि खाय करैछेलै। किसान सदई ओकर खोज मेँ रहैछेलै। एक दिन अँगूर के टट्टी पर जाल लगाय क० ओकन्रा पकड़ क० मारऽ चाहलन्है। चिड़ैया किसान से कहलन्है कि, जे तोँ हमन्रा छोड़ि दे, त० हम्मेँ ई भलाई के बदन्ला मेँ तोरा तीन ठो बात बताय देबौ, कि जेकन्रा मेँ

तोरा बड़ फैदा होतौ। किसान कहलन्कै कि तोँ पहन्हे बताय दे, तऽ हम्मेँ तोरा छोड़ि देबौ। चिड़ैया ओकन्रा तीन बात कहलन्कै। एक तऽ ई कि, बैरी जे अपन्ना बसऽ में आबऽ, तऽ छोड़ऽ के नै चाही। दोसर, जे बात मन में नै समाबऽ ओकन्रा नै मानऽ के चाही। तेसर, गेल चीज के खातिर सोचऽ कै नै चाही। आरो चौठा एक बात आरो छऽ, कि अब तोँ हमन्रा छोड़ि देबऽ तब कहन्बौ। किसान ई बात सुनि कऽ जेसन कहन्लऽ छेलै, तेसन्ने करन्कै, आरो ऊ चिड़ैया कऽ छोड़ि देलन्कै। तऽ चिड़ैया भीत पर बैठि कऽ कहलन्कै कि, हमन्रा पेट में मुर्गी के अण्डा सऽ ओ बड़न्को ठो एक मोती छेलऽ। जे तोँ हमन्रा नै छोड़न्तिअ आरो मारि डालन्तिअ. तऽ ऊ मोती तोरा हाथ लगन्तिऔ। किसान पछन्तावऽ लन्गलै, ऊ कहलन्कै, गमार, तोँ हम्मर तीनोँ बात एखन्निये भूलि गेलै। कहिनऽ कि, हम्मेँ तोर बैरी छेलिऔ, ओकन्नो पकड़ि पैलऽ छेलँ, तऽ छोड़न्लऽ कहिने। आरो मुर्गी के अण्डा के बराबर. तऽ हम्मेँ अपन्ने नै छी। कहिया मन में आय सकैछे, कि मुर्गी के अण्डा सऽ बढ़ि कऽ मोती हमन्रा पेट में होय। मगर तोँ ई बात पर भरोसा करन्ले, आरो अब जे हम्मेँ तोरा हाथ से निकलि गेलियौ, तऽ पछन्ताय कऽ की होतौ। एकन्रा सऽ ई फल निकन्लछै, कि पहन्ले सऽ सब काम कऽ सोचि बिचारि कऽ करऽ के चाही। आरो जे कोय काम बिगड़ि जाय, तऽ फनू पछतावऽ के नै चाही॥

॥ १९ बात ॥

कोय धनन्मान कऽ दु बेटा छेलै। जब ओकर बाप मरि गेलै. तब दुओ भाय ओकर सम्पत आपुस में बाँटि लेलन्कै। बड़न्का भाय अप्पन रुपैया पैसा खुब चैन आरो खेल तमासा में उड़ाबऽ लगन्लै, आरो छोटन्का भाय बड़ी जतन से बेपार करऽ लगन्लै। एक दिन बड़ा भाय छोटा भाय सऽ ओलहन्ना दे कऽ कहलन्कै कि, भाय किथि लाय दिन भर अनाज जोखल करै छऽ। हमन्रा साथे रहऽ। खा। पीअ। चैन करऽ। ढेर दिन के बाद, जब छोटन्का भाय लेन देन करि कऽ बहुत रुपैया जमा करि लेलन्कै; तब ओकर बड़न्का भाय जे राग रङ्ग आरो खेल तमासा में अप्पन सबे सम्पत उड़ाय कऽ भिखारी होय गेल छेलै, ओकन्रा दुआरी पर आय कऽ, कहऽ लगन्लै कि, भाय हम्मेँ तोरा पहन्ले ठट्ठा में उड़ैलिऔन्हल। जो हमूँ तोड़न्रे ऐसन तजारत करतिऔं, आरो अनाज तौलतिऔं तऽ आज पा भर अनाज इन्हऽ उन्हऽ सऽ माँगि कऽ नै खैतिऔं। सच्चे छिकै कि।

॥ आलस ऐसन कीड़ा छिकै, कि धन कऽ भूरा करि डालैछै॥

* Emphatic for हम्मेँ, 'I also.'

॥ १६ बात ॥

॥ लल॰ची कुत्ता ॥

कोय कुत्ता नद्दी के किनारा पर एक हाड़ पैल॰कै, आरो मूँह मेँ लेल॰कै। जौँ पर॰छाहीँ ओकर पानी मेँ देखल॰कै समझल॰कै कि, दोसर हाड़ छिकै। लालच के मारल मूँह खोलल॰कै, कि ओक॰रो* पानी सठ निकालौँ। ऊ हाड़ जे मूँह मेँ छेलै से हो गमैल॰कै। सच्चे छिकै कि।

मक्खी बैठ॰ले दूध पर, पङ्ख गेले लप॰टाय।
हाथ मलै आरो माथा धुनै। लालच बुरा बलाय॥

* Emphatic for ओक॰रा, 'it also.'

Reg. No. 5436J—510—3.7-86.

SEVEN

GRAMMARS

OF THE DIALECTS AND SUBDIALECTS OF THE

BIHARI LANGUAGE.

SPOKEN IN THE PROVINCE OF BIHÁR, IN THE EASTERN PORTION OF THE NORTH-WESTERN PROVINCES, AND IN THE NORTHERN PORTION OF THE CENTRAL PROVINCES.

PART VII.

SOUTH MAITHILÍ-BAN'GÁLÍ DIALECT

OF SOUTH BHAGAL'PÚR.

Compiled under orders of the Government of Bengal,

By GEORGE A. GRIERSON, B.C.S.,
JOINT-MAGISTRATE OF PATNA.

CALCUTTA:
PRINTED AT THE BENGAL SECRETARIAT PRESS.
1887.

CONTENTS.

CHAPTER VI.—THE REGULAR ACTIVE VERB.

CHAPTER VII.—THE REGULAR NEUTER VERB.

CHAPTER VIII.—VOCALIC ROOTS.

CHAPTER IX.—IRREGULAR VERBS.

CHAPTER X.—THE PASSIVE VERB.

CHAPTER XI.—CAUSAL VERBS.

CHAPTER XII.—COMPOUND VERBS.

DIVISION III.

INDECLINABLES.

APPENDIX.

SELECTIONS IN THE SOUTH MAITHILI-BAN'GÁLÍ DIALECT.

INTRODUCTION.

§ 1. The following grammar treats of the subdialect spoken in South Bhagal'púr. The basis of this subdialect is Maithilí, but it is largely affected by the Mágadhí dialect to its south-west, and to a less extent, and principally in verbal inflexions, by the Ban·gálí to its east. South Bhagal'púr is, in fact, one of the meeting grounds of Bihárí and Ban·gálí, and the dialect spoken there is essentially a border tongue.*

§ 2. The alphabet and rules for spelling will be found in the General Introduction to this series of grammars, and the remarks therein found are not repeated here.

* The author has to express his thanks to Bábú Wooma Churn Bose, Subdivisional Officer of Banká, and to Bábú Gour Chunder Roy, 8th Teacher in the Government School, Bhagal'púr for most valuable assistance rendered in the compilation of this part.

DIVISION I.

DECLENSION.

CHAPTER I.

NOUNS.

§ 3. For general remarks, see the General Introduction, § 38 and ff.

The following are the post-positions used in declining the noun in this dialect:—

		Power.
Nom.	*Wanting.*	
Acc.	*Wanting* or कै *kai* or *कैँ *kaĩ.*	
Instr.	सेँ *sẽ* or सैँ *saĩ.*	'By.'
Dat.	कै *kai* or *कैँ *kaĩ.*	'To.'
	लै *lai.*	'For.'
Abl.	सेँ *sẽ* or सैँ *saĩ.*	'From.'
Gen.	क *k*, *के *kĕ* ; केरा *kera*, केरी *keri.*	'Of.'
Loc.	मैँ *maĩ*, मेँ *mẽ.*	'In.'
Voc.	*Wanting.*	

All these post-positions will only be used in one example, that of घोड़ा *ghoṛá*, 'a horse;' but they can all be used with all nouns. Those forms which are preceded by an asterisk (*) are peculiar to the south of the district.

Except that for the genitive, they can be used with all pronouns. In the genitive singular many pronouns do not take these post-positions, but have other forms subject to special rules.

The plural is the same as the singular.

The following are examples of declension.

§ 4. (a) Masculine Tadbhavas in आ *á*.

Example of the declension of a *tadbhava** masculine noun in आ *á* :—

घोड़ा *ghoṛá*, 'a horse.'

Short form, { Weak, घोड़ *ghoṛ*. Strong, घोड़ा *ghoṛá*. } Long form,* घोड़वा *ghoṛ'wá*. Redundant form,† *not used*.

Singular.

Nom.	घोड़ा,[1] *ghoṛá*,	'a horse.'
Acc.	घोड़ा *ghoṛá* or घोड़ा कै *ghoṛá kai* or *कैँ *kaĩ*,	'a horse.'
Instr	घोड़ा सँ *ghoṛá sẽ* or सैँ *saĩ*,	'by a horse.'
Dat.	घोड़ा कै *ghoṛá kai* or *कैँ *kaĩ*,	'to a horse.'
	घोड़ा लै *ghoṛá lai*,	'for a horse.'
Abl.	घोड़ा सँ, *ghoṛá sẽ* or सैँ *saĩ*,	'from a horse.'
Gen.	घोड़ाक *ghoṛák*, *घोड़ा के *ghoṛá kĕ*, or केरा *kera*, केरी *keri*,[2]	'of a horse.'
Loc.	घोड़ा मैँ *ghoṛá maĩ*, or मँ *mẽ*,	'in a horse.'
Voc.	हे घोड़ा *he ghoṛá*,	'O horse !'

[1] Or घोड़ *ghoṛ*, or घोड़वा *ghŏṛ'wá*, and so throughout.

[2] घोड़ाक *ghoṛák* and घोड़ा के *ghoṛá kĕ* do not change for gender. घोड़ा केरा *ghoṛá kera* and घोड़ा केरी *ghoṛa kerí* can only be used in certain cases. केरा *kera* (like the Hindí का *ká* and के *ke*) can only be used before masculine nouns, and केरी *kerí* (like the Hindí की *kí*) only before feminine nouns.

Forms preceded by an asterisk (*) are peculiar to the south of the district.

Plural.

The plural is the same as the singular.

---

* See General Introduction. § 12.

† See General Introduction, § 12.

§ 5. (b) Masculine Nouns ending in Silent Consonants.

Example of the declension of a masculine noun ending in a silent consonant:—

घर *ghar*, 'a house.'

Short form, { Weak, घर *ghar*. / Strong, घरठ *ghara*. } Long form,* घरऽवा *ghar'wá*. / Redundant form,* *not used*.

Singular and Plural.

Nom.	घर[1] *ghar* or घरठ *ghara*,	'a house.'
Acc.	घर *ghar* or घरठ कै *ghara kai*, *&c.*,	'a house.'
Instr.	घरैँ *gharaĩ*, घरठ सैँ *ghara saĩ*, *&c.*,	'by a house.'
Dat.	घरठ लै *ghara lai*, *&c.*,	'for a house.'
Abl.	घरठ सैँ *ghara saĩ*, *&c.*,	'from a house.'
Gen.	घरक *gharak*, *&c.*,	'of a house.'
Loc.	घरे *ghare*, घरठ मैँ *ghara maĩ*,	'in a house.'
Voc.	हे घर *he ghar !*	'O house !'

[1] Or घरऽवा *ghar'wá*, and so throughout.

§ 6. It is not necessary to decline further any nouns in full, as the above examples suffice. All nouns ending in vowels are declined like घोड़ा *ghoṛá*, and all those ending in silent consonants like घर *ghar*. The final syllables of all long forms may optionally be nasalised by the addition of *anunásik*: thus घोड़वा *ghoṛ'wá* or घोड़वाँ *ghoṛ'wã*; मलिया *maliyá* or मलियाँ *maliyã*.

NOTE, however, that—

(1) All nouns ending in a silent consonant take अ *a* in the oblique form singular: as, nom. घर *ghar*, acc. घरठ कै *ghara kai*. Occasionally also in the case of these nouns we find an instrumental in ऐँ *aĩ* and a locative in ए *e*: thus हम्मै बलैँ लै जैबठ *hammai balaĩ le jaiba*, 'I shall take away by force,' where बलैँ *balaĩ* is the instrumental of बल *bal*, 'force;' भूखैँ मरै छी *bhúkhaĩ marai chhi*, 'I die of (by) hunger;' घाटे घाटे *gháṭe gháṭe*, 'at every landing place,' locative of घाट *gháṭ*, 'a landing place:' so also घरे घरे *ghare ghare*, 'in every house,' 'from house to house.'

---

* See General Introduction, §§ 12, 38, and ff.

Locatives in ए *e* are confined to phrases like the above. The instrumental sometimes inserts the letter ह *h*, *e.g.* बल्हैं *balhaĩ* instead of बलैं *balaĩ*.

(2) Certain verbal nouns ending in ल *l* have an oblique form in ला *lá*; thus देखल *dekhal*, obl. देखला सँ *dĕkh'lá saĩ*, 'from seeing:' also verbal nouns in the form of the root have a noblique form in ए *ĕ* or ऐ *aĩ*; thus देख *dekh*. dat. देखे लै *dekhĕ lai* or देखैं लै *dekhaĩ lai*, 'for seeing.' Full particulars concerning these nouns will be found in § 111.

An example of each of the more common forms of nouns follows :—

§ 7. (c) Masculine Tatsamas in आ *á*.

राजा *rájá*, 'a king.'

Short form, राजा *rájá*. Long form,* रजवा *raj'wá*. Redundant form,* *wanting*.

Gen. sing. राजाक *ráják*, *&c*.

§ 8. (d) Masculine Nouns in ई *í*.

माली *málí*, 'a gardener.'

Short form, माली *málí*. Long form* मलिया *maliyá*. Redundant form,* मलियवा *maliyawá* or मलीवा *malíwá*.

Gen. sing. मालीक *málík*, *&c*.

§ 9. (e) Masculine Nouns in ऊ *ú*.

नाऊ *náú* 'a barber.'†

Short form, नाऊ *náú*. Long form,‡ नउआ *naüá* or नौआ *nauá*. Redundant form,‡ नउअवा *naüawa* or नौअवा *nauawá*.

Gen. sing. नाऊक *náúk*, *&c*.

---

* See General Introduction, §§ 12, 38, and ff., 34 and 36.

† Kellogg in his Hindí Grammar incorrectly gives आँसू *ãsú* as an example of a feminine noun in ऊ *ú* : it is masculine. आँसू *ãsú* is not used in Bihárí, लोर *lor* being the word for 'a tear.'

‡ See General Introduction, §§ 12, 38, and ff., 34 and 36.

§ 10. (f) Feminine Nouns in ई í and इ i.

पोथी pothí, 'a book.'

Short form, पोथी pothí. Long form,* पोथिया pŏthiyá. Redundant form,* पोथियवा pŏthiyawá or पोथीवा pŏthíwá.
Gen. sing. पोथीक pothík, &c.

राति rati, 'a night.'

Short form, राति ráti. Long form,* रतिया ratiyá. Redundant form,* रतियवा* ratiyawá or रतीवा ratíwá.
Gen. sing. रातिक rátik, &c.

§ 11. (g) Feminine Nouns ending in a Silent Consonant.

बात bát, 'a word.'

Short form, बात bát. Long form,* बतिया batiyá. Redundant form,* (rare) बतियवा batiyawá or बतीवा batíwa.
Acc. sing. बातऽ कें báta kaĩ, &c.
Gen. sing. बातक bátak, &c.

§ 12. Periphrastic Plural.

With reference to the statement that the plural forms are the same as the singular, it must be noted that every noun can also form a periphrastic plural by the addition of the words आरःहिन ár'hin, सन्ही sanhí, सब sab, or सभै sabhai. Thus, nom. plur. घोड़ा आरःहिन ghoṛá ár'hin, घोड़ा सन्ही ghoṛá sanhí, &c.; acc. plur. घोड़ा आरःहिनकै ghoṛá ár'hin kai, घोड़ा सन्ही कै ghoṛá sanhí kai, and so on. In the case of rational beings the word लोग log, 'people,' may also be used: thus, माली लोग máli log, 'gardeners.'

---

* See General Introduction, §§ 12, 38, and ff., 34 and 36.

§ 13. Genitival Affixes.

The following examples have been specially designed to exhibit the use of the genitival affixes :—

1. ई राजा केरऽ मन्दिर छिकै.
Í rájá kera mandir chhikai.
'This is the king's temple.'

2. हमेँ कन्सऽ केरी दाई* छिकिऐ.
Hamẽ Kansa keri dái chhikiai.*
'I am the maid-servant of King Kans.'

3. मधुमाँछी केरऽ झुण्ड उड़ि गेलै.
Madhumàchhi kera jhuṇḍ uṛi gelai.
'A swarm of bees flew away.'

4. कप॰टी कै मार॰ला सैँ कुछु दोस नई.
Kap'ṭi kai már'lá sẽ kuchhu dos nai.
'There is no sin in slaying a deceiver.'

5. मथुरा केरी जनानी* सभै कान॰ली चल॰ली गेलै.
Mathurá keri janáni sabhai kán'lí chal'li gelai.*
'The women of Mathurá departed weeping.'

6. बहुत रङ्गऽ केरऽ बात* सुन॰लऽ गेलै.
Bahut ranga kera bát sun'la gelai.*
'Matters of many kinds were heard.'

7. अस्फटिकऽ केरऽ चार फाटक टूटि गेलै.
Asphaṭika kera chár pháṭak ṭúṭi gelai.
'Four gates of crystal broke.'

8. देसऽ देसऽ केरऽ राजा ऐलात.
Desa desa kera rájá ailát.
'Kings of all countries came.'

9. हौ सन्ही मालीक बेटा छिकै
Hau sanhi málik beṭá chhikai.
'They are the sons of the gardener.'

10. हम्मै राजा केरऽ गाँवऽ मेँ ऐलाँव
Hammai rájá kera gãwa mẽ ailãw.
'I came into the king's villages.'

11. पण्डित आर॰हिन केरऽ घरऽ मेँ बहुत पुस्तक छैन्ह
Paṇḍit ár'hin kera ghara mẽ bahut pustak chhainh.
'There are many books in *paṇḍits'* houses.'

---

* केरी *kerí* is always used before nouns which are not only feminine grammatically, but which are also words representing female living creatures, such as दाई *dáí*, 'a maid-servant,' नारी *nárí*, 'a woman.' Before nouns which are only grammatically feminine, such as बात *bát*, 'a matter,' 'a word,' केरऽ *kera* is used.

CHAPTER II.

ADJECTIVES

§ 14. Gender.

See General Introduction, § 42 and ff.

In this dialect there are some adjectival peculiarities which are not noted in the General Introduction. Adjectives in the strong form in आ *á* do not change for gender. Thus अच्छा *achchhá*, 'good'; fem. अच्छा *achchhá*, and not अच्छी *achchhi*. But adjectives in the weak form, and every participle used adjectivally, may have a strong form in अ *a*, forming its feminine in ई *i*: thus—

WEAK FORM.	STRONG FORM. Masculine.	STRONG FORM. Feminine.
काँच *kắch*, 'unripe.'	काँचऽ *kắcha.*	काँची *kắchi.*
बड़ *bar*, 'great.'	बड़ऽ *bara.*	बड़ी *bari.*
पाकल *pákal*, 'cooked,' 'ripe.'	पकल्लऽ *pak'la.*	पकल्ली *pak'li.*

Examples of the use of these strong forms are the following :—ऊ बिपत्तक के मारल्लऽ ऊ रसायन्नी केरऽ खोजऽ मेँ दौड़ धूप करे लगल्लै *ú bip'tak már'la ú rasáy'ni kera khoja mẽ daur dhúp karĕ lag'lai*, 'that man, smitten by adversity, began to run about in search of the alchemist.'

काँचऽ पकल्लऽ फल *kắcha pak'la phal*, 'fruit, ripe and unripe.'

बड़ी अच्छा बात *bari achchhá bát*, 'a very excellent sentiment.'

In Bhagal'púr the weak form of adjectives is rarely used, the strong form in अ *a* being preferred.

§ 15. Numeral Adjectives.

The cardinals are nearly the same as those in High Hindí. The following are the ones that present points of difference :—

1 = एक *ěk* or एके *eke.*
2 = दू *dú* or दुइ *duí.*
29 = उन्तिस *untis.*
31 = एकतिस *ěk'tis.*
32 = बत्तिस *battis.*
33 = तैंतिस *tẽtis.*
34 = चौंतिस *chaũtis.*
35 = पैंतिस *paĩtis.*
36 = छत्तिस *chhattis.*
37 = सैंतिस *saĩtis.*
38 = अड़तिस *aṛ'tis.*
39 = उनचालिस *un'chális.*
40 = चालिस *chális.*
41 = एकतालिस *ěk'tális.*
42 = ब्यालिस *byális.*
43 = तेतालिस *tetális.*
44 = चौआलिस *chaŭális.*
45 = पैतालिस *paĩtális.*
46 = छियालिस *chhiyális.*
47 = सैतालिस *saĩtális.*
48 = अड़तालिस *aṛ'tális.*
53 = तेरपन *těr'pan.*
63 = तिरेसठ *tiraisaṭh.*
100 = सै *sai* or सऽ *sa.*

§ 16. Ordinals.

The ordinals up to 'sixth' are as follows :—

1st = पहिल *pahil* or पहिलऽ *pahila ; obl.* पहिला *pahilá.**

2nd = दोसर *dosar* or दोसरऽ *dŏs'ra ; obl.* दोसरा *dŏs'rá* or दुसरा *dus'rá.**

3rd = तेसर *tesar* or तेसरऽ *těs'ra ; obl.* तेसरा *těs'rá* or तिसरा *tis'rá.**

4th = चौठ *chauṭh* or चौठऽ *chauṭha.*

5th = पचम *pacham* or पचमऽ *pach'ma.*

6th = छठम *chhaṭham* or छठमऽ *chhaṭh'ma.*

The ordinals above 'sixth' are all formed by adding अम *am* or मऽ *'ma* to the cardinals : as दसम *dasam* or दसमऽ *das'ma,* 'tenth ;' पचासम *pachásam* or पचसमऽ *pachas'ma,* 'fiftieth.' The weak forms are rarely used.

---

* The first three ordinals follow pronominal genitives in the formation of oblique forms. See *post,* § 34.

§ 17. Fractional Numbers.

These are—

$\frac{1}{4}$ = पाव *páw* or पा *pá*.

$\frac{1}{3}$ = तेखन्री *tĕkh'ri* or तिरभाग *tir'bhág*.

$\frac{1}{2}$ = आधऽ *ádha*.

$\frac{3}{4}$ = पौन *paun* or तीन पाव *tín páw*.

—$\frac{1}{4}$ = पौने *paune*.

1$\frac{1}{4}$ or +$\frac{1}{4}$ = सावा *sáwá*.

1$\frac{1}{2}$ = डेढ़ *ḍeṛh*.

2$\frac{1}{2}$ = अढ़ाइ *aṛhái*.

+$\frac{1}{2}$ = साढ़े *sáṛhe*.

§ 18. Multiplicatives.

Multiplicatives, such as the English 'twice' and 'thrice,' are not found in this dialect. The Bihárí idiom is illustrated in such phrases as दू सते चौदह *dú sate chaudah*, 'two seven's, fourteen;' छ तिरि अठारह *chha tiri aṭhárah*, 'six three's, eighteen,' which correspond to the English idioms 'seven times two' and 'three times six.' Numbers thus used are called multiplicatives, and differ in some respects from the cardinals. The following are the multiplicative numbers up to 10, including fractions:—

× 1, काँ *kā́*.
× 1$\frac{1}{4}$, सवा *sawá*, समाँ *samā́*, or सवैया *sawaiyá*.
× 1$\frac{1}{2}$, डेओढ़ा *ḍĕoṛhá*.
× 2, दुन्ना *dunná*, दून *dún*, दुगुना *duguná*.
× 2$\frac{1}{2}$, अढ़ैया *aṛhaiyá*.
× 3, तिया *tiyá*, तिरि *tiri*.
× 3$\frac{1}{2}$, हुट्ठा *huṭṭhá*, हुट्ठै *huṭṭhai*.
× 4, चौका *chauká*, चौके *chauke*, चौकै *chaukai*.
× 4$\frac{1}{2}$, ढौंचे *ḍhŏche*, ढौँचऽ *dhaũcha*.
× 5, पचे *pache*.
× 5$\frac{1}{2}$, पहुँचा *pahuṅchá*.

× 6, छक्काँ *chhakkã*, छक्के *chhakke*, छाक *chhák*.
× 7, सते *sate*, सत्ते *satte*.
× 8, अट्ठे *aṭṭhe*.
× 9, नम *nam*, नमाँ *namã*, नाम *nám*.
× 10, दहाँ *dahã*, दहाइ *dahái*, or धाँ *dhã*.

§ 19. Definite Cardinals.

These are as follows:—

एगो *ego*, 'the one;'
दुओ *duo*, दुनो *duno*, दोनो *dono*, 'the two,' 'both;'
तीनो *tíno*, 'the three;'
चारो *cháro*, 'the four;' and so on,

adding ओ *o* to the numerals, after omitting a final short vowel. Example: पाँचो भाइ जौरे छैन्ह *pãchõ bhái jaure chhainh*, 'the five brothers are an undivided family.'

§ 20. Indefinite Cardinals.

The termination ओँ *õ* added to the numbers 'one hundred,' 'one thousand,' and so on, always denotes an indefinite number of these aggregates. In this idiom सैकड़ *saikaṛ* is always substituted for सै *sai*, 'one hundred.' Examples are सैकड़ोँ पेड़ *saik'ṛõ peṛ*, 'hundreds of trees;' हजारोँ *hajárõ*, 'thousands;' लाखोँ *lákhõ*, 'tens of thousands;' हजारोँ अदिमी मरऽलात *hajárõ adimí mar'lát*, 'thousands of men died.'

§ 21. Collective Numerals.

These—viz. जोड़ा *joṛá*, 'a pair,' गण्डा *gaṇḍá*, 'a four'—are the same as in High Hindí.

CHAPTER III.

PRONOUNS.

§ 22. The following tables show the declensional forms of the principal pronouns and pronominal forms.

The declension of pronouns presents some important points of difference from that of nouns, which must be carefully noticed.

While nouns frequently remain unchanged before post-positions, pronouns, with few exceptions, change to some other form, called the *oblique* or *inflected base.*

The accusative singular of pronouns is, with one or two exceptions, never the same as the nominative. In circumstances corresponding to those in which the accusative of a noun takes the nominative form, the accusative of a pronoun usually takes the oblique form without any post-position.

The genitive forms of pronouns ending in र *r* and न *n* are also to be noticed. They have all oblique forms ending in रा *rá* or ना *ná*, for which see § 34.

Pronouns have the same form, whether referring to masculine or feminine nouns. With the exception of the pronouns of the second person, they all want the vocative case.

§ 23. Pronouns of the First Person and of the Second Person Non-Honorific.

These pronouns have each two forms—a shorter and a longer. The shorter form in the singular is rarely used except in poetry.

हमें *hamẽ*, 'I.'

Singular.

	Shorter form.	*Longer form.*
Nom.	*Wanting.*	हमें *hamẽ* or हम्मै *hammai.*
Acc.	मोरा[1] *morá* or मोरा कै *morá kai.*	हमरा[1] *ham'rá* or हमरा कै *ham'rá kai.*
Instr.	मोरा सैँ *morá saı̃.*	हमरा सैँ *ham'rá saı̃.*
Dat.	मोरा लै *morá lai.*	हमरा लै *ham'rá lai.*
Abl.	मोरा सैँ *morá saı̃.*	हमरा सैँ *ham'rá saı̃.*
Gen.	मोरठ *mora,* (fem.) मोरी *morí.*	हमरठ *ham'ra,* (fem.) हमरी *ham'rí.*
Loc.	मोरा मेँ *morá mẽ.*	हमरा मेँ *ham'rá mẽ.*
Voc.	*Wanting.*	*Wanting.*

[1] मोरो *moro* and हमरो *ham'ro* may be used for मोरा *morá* and हमरा *ham'rá* in an emphatic sense: thus हमरो दठ *ham'ro da,* 'give to me also.' In poetry a shorter oblique form, मोहि *mŏhi,* instead of मोरा *morá,* is sometimes found.

Plural.

A periphrastic plural is formed as in the case of substantives, but from the oblique form; thus nom. हमरा आरहिन *ham'rá ár'hin,* हमरा सभै *ham'rá sabhai,* हमरा सब *ham'rá sab,* हमरा सन्ही *ham'rá sanhí,* or हमरा लोग *ham'rá log,* and so on.

तोँ *tõ*, 'thou.'

Singular.

	Shorter form.	*Longer form.*
Nom.	*Wanting.*	तोँ *tõ* or तोहेँ *tohẽ.*
Acc.	तोरा[1] *torá* or तोरा कै *torá kai.*	तोह॰रा[1] *tŏh'rá* or तोह॰रा कै *tŏh'ra kai.*
Instr.	तोरा सैँ *torá saĩ.*	तोह॰रा सैँ *tŏh'rá saĩ.*
Dat.	तोरा लै *torá lai.*	तोह॰रा लै *tŏh'rá lai.*
Abl.	तोरा सैँ *torá saĩ.*	तोह॰रा सैँ *tŏh'rá saĩ.*
Gen.	तोरऽ *tora*, (fem.) तोरी *torí.*	तोह॰रऽ *tŏh'rá*, (fem.) तोह॰री *tŏh'rí.*
Loc.	तोरा मेँ *torá mẽ.*	तोह॰रा मेँ *tŏh'rá mẽ.*
Voc.	*Wanting.*	हे तोँ *he tõ.*

[1] तोरो *toro* and तोह॰रो *tŏh'ro* may be used for तोरा *torá* and तोह॰रा *tŏh'rá* in an emphatic sense: thus तोह॰रो देखै छी *tŏh'ro dekhai chhí*, 'I see you also.' In poetry, a shorter oblique form, तोहि *tŏhi* instead of तोरा *torá*, is sometimes found.

Plural.

A periphrastic plural is formed as in the case of substantives, but from the oblique form: thus, nom. तोरा आर॰हिन *torá ár'hin*, तोरा सभै *torá sabhai*, तोरा सब *torá sab*, तोरा सन्ही *torá sanhí*, तोह॰रा लोग *tŏh'rá log*, and so on; so also तोह॰रा आर॰हिन *tŏh'rá ár'hin*, &c.

§ 24. Pronoun of the Second Person Honorific and Reflexive Pronoun.

अप॰ने *ap'nĕ*, 'your honor.'

Nom. sing. अप॰ने *ap'nĕ*, आप॰ने *áp'nĕ*, or अप॰नै *ap'naĭ*; obl. sing. अप॰ने *ap'nĕ*, अप॰नै *ap'naĭ*, अप॰ना *ap'ná*, or अप॰नऽ *ap'na*. Declined throughout regularly like a substantive.

अपन्ने *ap'ne*, 'self.'

Nom. sing. अपन्ने *ap'nĕ*, आपन्ने *áp'nĕ*, or अपन्नै *ap'naĭ*; obl. sing. अपन्ने *ap'nĕ*, अपन्नै *ap'naĭ*, अपन्ना *ap'ná*, अपन्नउ *ap'na*, अपन्नहि *ap'nahi*. Declined regularly throughout the singular, except in the genitive singular, which is अपन्नउ *ap'na*, (fem.) अपन्नी *ap'ní*. In the plural it is regular except in the genitive, which is आपुसउ केरउ *ápusa kera*, and in the locative, which is आपुसउ में *ápusa mẽ*.

§ 25. Demonstrative Pronouns.

These are (1) the proximate demonstrative ई *í*, 'this,' and (2) the remote demonstrative ऊ *ú*, 'that.'

Like the personal pronouns, they have each two forms, a shorter and a longer.

ई *í*, 'this.'

Singular.

	Shorter form.	*Longer form.*
Nom.	ई *í*, हई *haí*, है *hai*, इहै *ihai*, or एँ *ãi*.	*Wanting.*
Acc.	एहि[1] (कै) *ĕhi* (*kai*).	एकन्रा[2] (कै) *ĕk'rá* (*kai*).
Instr.	एहि सँ *ĕhi sãi*.	एकन्रा सँ *ĕk'rá sãi*.
Dat.	एहि लै *ĕhi lai*.	एकन्रा लै *ĕk'rá lai*.
Abl.	एहि सँ *ĕhi sãi*.	एकन्रा सँ *ĕk'rá sãi*.
Gen.	एहि केरउ *ĕhi kera*.	एकन्रउ *ĕk'ra*, (fem.) एकन्री *ĕk'rí*.
Loc.	एहि में *ĕhi mẽ*.	एकन्रा में *ĕk'rá mẽ*.

[1] Or ईथि *íthi*, and so throughout.

[2] Or हेकन्रा *hĕk'rá*, and so throughout.

Plural.

As in the case of the personal pronouns, a periphrastic plural can be formed: thus, nom. ई सभै *í sabhai*, &c., obl. ई सभ *í sabhai*, एकन्रा सभै *ĕk'rá sabhai*, &c., and so on.

The forms given above are all non-honorific. When an honorific sense is implied, the following forms are used :—

Singular Honorific.

	Shorter form.	*Longer form.*
Nom.	इनी *iní* or हिनी *hiní*.	*Wanting.*
Acc.	इनी[1] (कै) *iní* (*kai*).	इन॰का[2] (कै) *in'ká* (*kai*).
Instr.	इनी सैँ *iní sa̐i*.	इन॰का सैँ *in'ká sa̐i*.
Dat.	इनी लै *iní lai*.	इन॰का लै *in'ká lai*.
Abl.	इनी सैँ *iní sa̐i*.	इन॰का सैँ *in'ká sa̐i*.
Gen.	इनी केरऽ *iní kera*.	इन॰करऽ *in'kara*, (fem.) इन॰करी *in'karí*.
Loc.	इनी मेँ *iní mẽ*.	इन॰का मेँ *in'ká mẽ*.

[1] Or हिनी *hiní*, and so throughout.

[2] Or इन्ह॰का *inh'ká*, हिन॰का *hin'ká*, or हिन्ह॰का *hinh'ká*, and so throughout.

Plural.

Periphrastic plural इन्ह सभै *inh sabhaï*, &c. ; obl. इन्ह सभै *inh sabhai*, इन॰का सभै *in'ká sabhai*, &c.

ऊ *u*, 'that.'

The close analogy between the declension of this pronoun and that of ई *i*, 'this,' will be manifest from the following paradigm :—

Singular.

	Shorter form.	*Longer form.*
Nom.	ऊ *ú*, हऊ *haú*, हौ *hau*, or वैँ *wa̐i*.	*Wanting.*
Acc.	ओहि[1] (कै) *ŏhi kai*.	ओक॰रा[2] (कै) *ŏk'rá* (*kai*).
Instr.	ओहि सैँ *ŏhi sa̐i*.	ओक॰रा सैँ *ŏk'rá sa̐i*.
Dat.	ओहि लै *ŏhi la̐i*.	ओक॰रा लै *ŏk'rá lai*.
Abl.	ओहि सैँ *ŏhi sa̐i*.	ओक॰रा सैँ *ŏk'rá sa̐i*.
Gen.	ओहि केरऽ *ŏhi kera*.	ओक॰रऽ *ŏk'ra*, (fem.) ओक॰री *ŏk'ri*.
Loc.	ओहि मेँ *ŏhi mẽ*.	ओक॰रा मेँ *ŏk'rá mẽ*.

[1] Or ऊथि *úthi*, and so throughout.

[2] Or होक॰रा *hŏk'rá*, and so throughout.

Plural.

The plural is the same as the singular. As in the case of substantives, periphrastic plural can be formed : thus, nom. ऊ सभै *ú sabhai*, &c. ; obl. ऊ सभै *ú sabhai*, ओकऽरा सभै *ŏk'rá sabhai*, &c., and so on.

The forms given above are all non-honorific. When an honorific sense is implied, the following forms are used :—

Singular Honorific.

	Shorter form.	*Longer form.*
Nom.	उनी *uní* or हुनी *huní*.	*Wanting.*
Acc.	उनी[1] (कै) *uní* (*kai*).	उनऽका[2] (कै) *un'ká* (*kai*).
Instr.	उनी सँ *uní sãĩ*.	उनऽका सँ *un'ká sãĩ*.
Dat.	उनी लै *uní lai*.	उनऽका लै *un'ká lai*.
Abl.	उनी सँ *uní sãĩ*.	उनऽका सँ *un'ká sãĩ*.
Gen.	उनी केरऽ *uní kera*.	उनऽकरऽ *un'kara*, (fem.) उनऽकरी *un'karí*.
Loc.	उनी मँ *uní mẽ*.	उनऽका मँ *un'ká mẽ*.

[1] Or हुनी *huní*, and so throughout.

[2] Or उन्हऽका *unh'ká*, हुनऽका *hun'ká*, or हुन्हऽका *hunh'ká*, and so throughout.

Plural.

Periphrastic plural उन्ह सभै *unh sabhai*, &c. ; obl. उन्ह सभै *unh sabhai*, उनऽका सभै *un'ká sabhai*, &c.

NOTE.—In the above two demonstrative pronouns the shorter form may be used either adjectivally or substantivally, but the longer form can only be used as a substantive, and never as an adjective.

§ 26. Correlative Pronouns.

These are (1) the relative pronoun जे *je*, 'who ;' (2) the correlative pronoun से *se*, 'that ;' and (3) the interrogative pronoun के *ke*, 'who ?'

The close analogy between their forms should be noted. Like the personal and demonstrative pronouns, they have each a shorter and a longer form.

It is not necessary to give their declension in full, as it is on exactly the same lines as that of the demonstrative pronouns. I shall therefore give only the nominative, genitive, and general oblique forms for the non-honorific singular.

Relative.

जे *je*, 'who.'

Singular Non-Honorific.

	Shorter form.	*Longer form.*
Nom.	जे *je* or जैँ *jaĩ*.	*Wanting.*
Gen.	जेहि केरठ *jèhi kera.*	जेकऽरठ *jĕk'ra.*
Obl.	जेहि *jĕhi.*	जेकऽरा *jĕk'rá.*

Singular Honorific

Nom. जिनी *jini.*

Correlative.

से *se*, 'that.'

Singular Non-Honorific.

	Shorter form.	*Longer form.*
Nom.	से *se* or तैँ *taĩ*.	*Wanting.*
Gen.	तेहि केरठ *tĕhi kera.*	तेकऽरठ *tĕk'ra.*
Obl.	तेहि *tĕhi.*	तेकऽरा *tĕk'rá.*

Singular Honorific.

Nom. तिनी *tini.*

Interrogative.

के *ke*, 'who ?'

Singular Non-Honorific.

	Shorter form.	*Longer form.*
Nom.	के *ke.*	*Wanting.*
Gen.	केहि केरऽ *kĕhi kera.*	केकऽरऽ *kĕk'ra.*
Obl.	केहि *kĕhi.*	केकऽरा *kĕk'rá.*

Singular Honorific.

Nom. किनी *kiní.*

Other optional forms and plurals as in the demonstrative pronouns.

NOTE.—In the above correlative pronouns the shorter form may be used either adjectivally or substantivally, but the longer form can only be used as a substantive, and never as an adjective. As in the case of the demonstrative pronouns, the non-honorific plural is formed by adding सभ *sabh.*

§ 27. Interrogative Pronoun.

Substantival.

की *kí*, 'what ?'

This pronoun is really a neuter form of के *ke,* and can only refer to inanimate things. Its plural is the same as that of के *ke.*

Singular.

Nom. की *kí.*
Obl. कथी *kathí.*

Declined regularly like a substantive. Its dative, कथी लै *kathí lai,* for what ?' is used as an adverb, meaning 'why ?'

§ 28. Indefinite Pronouns.

कोय *koy*, 'anyone,' 'some one.'

This is declined throughout the singular only.

Singular.

Nom. कोय *koy* or कोइ *koï*.
Obl. कोय *koy*, केकरहौ *kĕkar'haŭ*, केकरौ *kĕk'raŭ*, or केकरो *kĕk'rŏ*.

Declined regularly like a substantive, except the genitive, which is केकरो *kĕk'rŏ*.

Plural.

Wanting.

§ 29. कुछु *kuchhu*, 'anything,' 'something.'

Declined regularly like a substantive in the singular. It has for its oblique form कुछु *kuchhu* or कथू *kathú*. The plural is wanting.

§ 30. The indefinite pronoun सभ *sabh*, सभै *sabhai*, or सब *sab*, 'all,' 'every one,' is declined regularly like a substantive. When plurality is to be emphasised, it has an oblique plural form सभनि *sabhani* : thus, सभ० केर० *sabha kera* 'of all,' *taken as a whole ;* but सभनि केर० *sabhani kera*, 'of all,' *taken severally*.

§ 31. The indefinite pronouns जेकोय *jekoy*, 'whoever,' जेकुछु *jekuchhu*, 'whatever,' are compounds, and are declined regularly like the latter of their component parts : thus, acc. sing. जे केकरो कै *je kĕk'rŏ kai*, जे कुछु कै *je kuchhu kai ;* instr. जे केकरो सँ *jĕ kĕk'rŏ saँ*, &c.

The indefinite pronominal adjective कै *kai* or कैक *kaik* signifies 'several.' It is also used as an interrogative, meaning 'how many ?'

§ 32. Derivative Pronominal Forms.

The following table gives the more usual pronominal adjectives and adverbs in a succinct form.

		PRONOUN.	Manner.	
			Pron. Adj.	Pron. Adv.
Demonstrative ...	Proximate ...	ई *í*, 'this' ...	एहिनठ *ěhina*, ऐन्हठ *ainha*, 'of this kind.'	एना *ená*, हेना *hená*, एहन्नाइ *ěh'náï*, 'thus.'
	Remote ...	ऊ *ú*, 'that' ...	ओहिनठ *ŏhina*, औन्हठ *aunha*, 'of that kind.'	ओना *oná*, होना *honá*, ओहन्नाइ *ŏh'náï*, 'in that way.'
Relative		जे *je*, 'who' ...	जैहिनठ *jaĭhina*, जैन्हठ *jainha*, 'of what kind.'	जेना *jená*, जेहन्नाइ *jěh'-náï*, 'in what way.'
Correlative		से *se*, 'that' ...	तैहिनठ *taĭhina*, तैन्हठ *tainha*, 'of that kind.'	तेना *tená*, तेहन्नाइ *těh'-náï*, 'in that way.'
Interrogative		के *ke*, 'who?' ...	कैहिनठ *kaĭhina*, कैन्हठ *kainha*, 'of what kind?'	केना *kená*, केहन्नाइ *kěh'-náï*, 'in what way?'

* कँठियाँ *kăṅṭhiyá̃* does not mean 'where?,' as might be expected, but 'to what several places?' टियाँ *tena ṭhiyá̃*, and कोनऽ ठियाँ *kona ṭhiyá̃*.

Pron. adj. of Quantity.	Pron. adv. of Time.	Pron. adv. of Place.	Pron. adv. of Direction.
एतै *ĕtai*, एतन्ना *ĕt'ná*, एतन्वाय *ĕt'wáy*, 'this much.'	अबे *abĕ* or आबे *ábĕ*, 'now.'	ऐठियाँ *aĭṭhiyã́*, हिँयाँ *hĩyã́*, 'here.'	इन्दे *indĕ*, हिन्दे *hindĕ*, or इन्ने *innĕ*, 'hither.'
ओतै *ŏtai*, ओतन्ना *ŏt'ná*, ओतन्वाय *ŏt'wáy*, 'that much.'	*Wanting.*	वैठियाँ *waĭṭhiyã́*, हूँआँ *hũã́*, 'there.'	उन्दे *undĕ*, हुन्दे *hundĕ*, or उन्ने *unnĕ*, 'thither.'
जेतै *jĕtai*, जेतन्ना *jĕt'ná*, जेतन्वाय *jet'wáy*, 'how much.'	जबे *jabĕ*, 'when.'	जैठियाँ *jaĭṭhiyã́*, जहाँ *jahã́*, 'where.'	जिन्दे *jindĕ*, जिन्ने *jinnĕ*, 'whither.'
तेतै *tĕtai*, तेतन्ना *tĕt'ná*, तेतन्वाय *tĕt'wáy*, 'so much.'	तबे *tabĕ*, 'then.'	तैठियाँ *taĭṭhiyã́*, तहाँ *tahã́*, 'there.'	तिन्दे *tindĕ*, तिन्ने *tinnĕ*, 'thither.'
केतै *kĕtai*, केतन्ना *kĕt'ná*, केतन्वाय *kĕt'wáy*, 'how much?'	कबे *kabĕ*, 'when?'	कहाँ *kahã́*,* 'where?'	किन्दे *kindĕ*, किन्ने *kinnĕ*, 'whither?'

Other adverbs of place are एनऽ ठियाँ *ena ṭhiyã́*, ओनऽ ठियाँ *ona ṭhiyã́*, जेनऽ ठियाँ *jena ṭhiyã́*, तेनऽ

§ 33. Adjectival Pronouns.

The following sentences are designed to show the use of the various pronouns, both adjectivally and substantivally. Before doing so it is best to note here that colloquially the oblique forms एह *ĕh*, ओह *ŏh*, जेह *jĕh*, तेह *tĕh*, and केह *kĕh*, are frequently written and pronounced ई *í*, ऊ *ú*, जे *je*, ते *te*, and के *ke* respectively.

NOTE that while जे *je* and से *se* are used either as adjectives or substantives in both the nominative and oblique cases, के *ke* cannot be used as an adjective at all. When used as an adjective, के *ke* always becomes कौन *kaun* in the nominative and कौनऽ *kauna*, (fem.) कौनी *kauní*, in the oblique cases. कोय *koy* may also become कौन्हों *kaunhŏ* or कौनों *kaunŏ* when used as an oblique adjective.

(1) जे ऐलऽ छलऽ, से गेलै, *je aila chhala, se gelai* : 'he who had come, went.'

(2) जे लोग ऐलऽ छलात, से लोग गेलात, *je log aila chhalát, se log gelát* : 'the men who had come, went.'

(3) जेकऽरऽ खेत, तेकऽरऽ धान, *jĕk'ra khet, tĕk'ra dhán* : 'he who owns the field, owns the paddy.'

(4) जे लोगऽ केरऽ खेत, ते लोगऽ केरऽ धान, *je loga kera khet, te loga kera dhán* : 'the man who owns the field, owns the paddy.'

(5) के छलै *ke chhalai?* 'who was it?'

(6) ऊ कौन लोग छिकै *ú kaun log chhikai?* 'what caste is he?'

(7) केकऽरऽ घोड़ा छिकै *kĕk'ra ghoṛá chhikai?* 'whose is the horse?'

(8) कौनऽ लोगऽ केरऽ घोड़ा छिकै *kauna loga kera ghoṛá chhikai?* 'to what people does the horse belong?'

(9) की छिकै *kí chhikai?* 'what is it?'

(10) की गाछ छिकै *kí gáchh chhikai*, 'what tree is it?'

(11) कथी मेँ पानि आनऽले छऽ *kathí mẽ páni án'lĕ chha?* 'in what have you brought the water?'

(12) कौनऽ लोटा मेँ पानि आनऽले छऽ *kauna loṭá mẽ páni án'lĕ chha?* 'in what *loṭá* have you brought the water?'

(13) कोय नहीँ ऐलै *koy nahí ailai*, 'no one came.'

(14) कोय लरका नहीँ ऐलै *koy lar'ká nahí ailai*, 'no boy came.'

(15) ऊ गाँवऽ मेँ केकर्रो कुछु नहीँ छै *ú gắwa mẽ kĕk'rŏ kuchhu nahí chhai*, 'in that village no one has anything.'

(16) ऊ गाँवऽ केरऽ कोय बनियाँ सेँ कुछु नहीँ मिलतै *ú gắwa kera koy baniyắ sãi kuchhu nahí mil'tai*, 'in that village nothing will be got from any shopkeeper.'

(17) ऊ औखधऽ कै कथू मेँ धरै होतै *ú aukhadha kai kathú mẽ dharai** *hotai*, 'it will be (necessary) to put that medicine into something.'

(18) कौन्हों तरह से *kaunhŏ tarah sai*, 'in any way.'

(19) कैक अदमी ऐलै *kaik ad'mí ailai*, 'several men came,' or 'how many men came?'

§ 34. The Pronominal Oblique Genitive.

The following are examples of pronominal genitives which end in र *r* or न *n*, and which have an oblique form ending in रा *rá* or ना *ná*. These oblique forms occur for all pronominal genitives ending in र *r*, and are used with nouns in any form except that of the nominative singular or plural:—

Direct Genitive.	Meaning.	Oblique form.
मोरऽ *mora.*	'My.'	मोरा *morá.*
हमरऽ *ham'ra.*	'My.'	हमरा *ham'rá.*
तोरऽ *tora.*	'Thy.'	तोरा *torá.*
तोहरऽ *tŏh'ra.*	'Thy.'	तोहरा *tŏh'rá.*
अपनऽ *ap'na.*	'Own.'	अपना *ap'ná.*
एकरऽ *ĕk'ra.*	'Of this.'	एकरा *ĕk'rá.*
ओकरऽ *ŏk'ra.*	'Of that,' 'his.'	ओकरा *ŏk'rá.*
जेकरऽ *jĕk'ra.*	'Whose.'	जेकरा *jĕk'rá.*
तेकरऽ *tĕk'ra.*	'His.'	तेकरा *tĕk'rá.*
केकरऽ *kĕk'ra.*	'Whose?'	केकरा *kĕk'rá.*

* Dative of the verbal noun.

The following examples will show the use of the genitive in—(*a*) its direct form, (*b*) its oblique form :—

a.—GENITIVES AGREEING WITH NOUNS IN THE NOMINATIVE FORM, *i.e.* DIRECT GENITIVES.

ओक॰री बहू कैहिन॰ सुन्दर छै *ŏk'ri bahú kaihina sundar chhai*, 'how beautiful his wife is !'

केक॰र॰ बेटा छै *kĕk'ra beṭá chhai ?* 'whose son is he ?'

हम॰र॰ धन्धा बिगर॰तै *ham'ra dhandhá bigar'tai*, 'my profession will be ruined.'

ओक॰र॰ कान॰ब॰ सुनि कै *ŏk'ra kán'ba suni kĕ*, 'on hearing her lamentations.'

ओक॰र॰ एक॰रार लिख॰ *ŏk'ra ĕk'rár likha*, 'write a bond to that effect' (*lit.* of that).

अप॰न॰ सभै धन उड़ाय कैं, भिखारी होय गेल॰ छेलै *ap'na sabhai dhan uṛáy kaĩ bhikhári hoy gela chhĕlai*, 'having wasted all his substance, he had become poor.'

b.—GENITIVES AGREEING WITH NOUNS NOT IN THE NOMINATIVE FORM, *i.e.* OBLIQUE GENITIVES.

ओक॰रा चढ़े केर॰ घोड़ा *ŏk'rá chaṛhĕ kera ghoṛá*, 'his riding-horse' (*lit.* the horse of his riding).

ऊ ओक॰रा फुल॰वारी मेँ ऐलै *ú ŏk'rá phul'wárí mẽ ailai*, 'he came into *his* (some one else's) garden.'

हम॰रा सिर॰की मैँ *ham'rá sir'kí mẽ*, 'in my hovel.'

तोह॰रा घर॰ मैँ *tŏh'rá ghara mẽ*, 'in your house.'

तोह॰रा हथ॰वा सैँ *tŏh'rá hath'wá sãĩ*, 'from thy hand.'

हम॰रा दर॰वाजा सैँ ओक॰र॰ दर॰वाजा बाँस भरि दूर छै *ham'rá dar'wájá sãĩ ŏk'ra dar'wájá bãs bhari dúr chhai*, 'his doorway is a rod distance from mine.

गिर॰हस्त अप॰ना जीह॰ मैँ कहल॰कै *gir'hast ap'na jíhá mẽ kahal'kai*, 'the husbandman said in his heart.'

Sometimes, by the vulgar, the direct form is used instead of the oblique, but the oblique form is never used instead of the direct. It should be observed, moreover, that in South Bhagalpúr these rules are by no means universally followed. The direct form is the rule, and the oblique the exception.

DIVISION II.

CONJUGATION.

CHAPTER IV.

INTRODUCTORY.

§ 35. It must be noted with respect to the following paradigms that colloquially the plural is commonly used in the place of the singular: thus तोँ छ *tõ chha*, 'you are,' is commonly used instead of तोँ छेँ *tõ chhẽ*, 'thou art,' which is the more correct form (see § 46a).

NOTE also that there is great laxity colloquially in regard to gender. The forms given for the feminine are only those which are specially confined to that gender; but instead of these, the masculine forms are often used colloquially. In the following paradigms when the masculine and feminine forms coincide, the latter are not given. As a matter of fact feminine forms are rarely used, masculine ones being preferred, even when the subject of the verb is feminine.

§ 36. With regard to the spelling of the various tense-forms, it must be noted that ऐ *ai* and औ *au* are frequently written अइ *aï* and अउ *aü* respectively: thus such forms as देखै *dekhai* and देखिऔन्ह *dĕkhiaunh* are often written देखइ *dĕkhaï* and देखिअउन्ह *dĕkhiaünh*. It has not been thought necessary to put both these varieties of spelling into the paradigms: hence only देखै *dekhai*, देखिऔन्ह *dĕkhiaunh*, *&c.*, will be found therein. With regard to this and to the shortening of ante-penultimate vowels, see General Introduction, §§ 34—37.

Every plural form ending in न्ह *nh* can also be spelt as ending in न *n* : thus गिर॰लैन्ह *gir'lainh* or गिर॰लैन *gir'lain*. Only the fuller form in न्ह *nh* will be given in the paradigms.

When a stem terminates in the letter ब *b* and is followed by a termination beginning with ह *h*, the final ब *b* of the stem and the initial ह *h* of the termination generally coalesce into भ *bh*. Thus देखब॰हो *dĕkhab'ho* becomes देख॰भो *dĕkh'bho*.

§ 37. Conjugational System.

The conjugation of the verb √ देख *dekh*, 'see,' being given in full, it is not necessary to give here the details of conjugation at length.

§ 38. There are three moods—the Indicative, Conjunctive, and Imperative. These may again be divided into *simple tenses*—formed from the root direct, and *periphrastic tenses*—formed with the aid of auxiliary verbs added to the present or past participle, or to the conjugated preterite indicative.

§ 39. The *simple tenses* are as foll vs :—

INDICATIVE.	CONJUNCTIVE.	IMPERATIVE.
Preterite.	Present.	Present.
Future.	Preterite.	

Of these, the present imperative is always the same as the present njunctive.

§ 40. The *periphrastic tenses* are as follows :—

a) From the present participle, direct or indirect form—

Indicative—

Definite present	with auxiliary	present.
Imperfect	"	preterite.
Durative future	"	future.

Conjunctive—

Future	with auxiliary	present	conjunctive.
Durative present	„	preterite	„

b) From the past participle: direct form in the neuter verb, oblique form in the active verb—

Indicative—

Perfect	with auxiliary	present.
Pluperfect	„	past.
Future exact	„	future.

Conjunctive—

Future exact	with auxiliary	present	conjunctive.
Preterite	„	preterite	„

Concerning the use of the auxiliary in tenses formed from the past participle, see General Introduction, p. 13, cl. (4).

§ 41. The Simple Tenses.

The personal terminations are nearly the same for all these tenses. They are added to a tense-stem, the formation of which will be described afterwards. They are nearly the same for all tenses.

These terminations are given in the following table. It will be observed that there are many optional forms of terminations for each person. They are all used with nearly equal frequency. They should be carefully committed to memory.

It must be noted that the termination अ *a* of the 2nd plural masculine is pronounced with a peculiar drawl, something like the English word 'awe.' Thus, देखअ *dekh*'awe.'

Table showing the General Personal Terminations.

Person.	Singular.		Plural.	
	Masculine.	Feminine.	Masculine.	Feminine.
1st	आँ *á*, आँव *áw*, आओँ *áõ*.		इऐ *iai*, इऔ *iau*. इऐन्ह *iainh*, इऔन्ह [*iaunh*. इहैन्ह *ihainh*, इहौन्ह [*ihaunh*.	
2nd	ए *e*, ऐँ *ẽ*, ऐ *ai*, ऐँ *ãi*, ॰है *'hai*, ॰हैँ *'hãi*.		अ *a*, ॰हो *'ho*, ॰हौ *'hau*, ॰हैन्ह *'hainh*.	
3rd	ए *e*, ऐ *ai*, औ *au*.		आत *át*, ऐन्ह *ainh*, औन्ह *aunh*.	ईत *ít*.

The first person is often used honorifically in the sense of the second person: thus देखाँव *dekháw*, 'see !'

§ 42. These terminations are added to various tense-stems, and it is by these tense-stems that the tenses are distinguished. The formation of each tense-stem will be given separately under the heading of each tense, and the conjugation of each tense will now be described in the order in which they will subsequently be given in the conjugation of the model verb √ देख *dekh*, 'see.' Terminations in आत *át* and ईत *ít* are in the south of the district spelt आथ *áth* and ईथ *íth*.

§ 43. The Preterite Indicative.

The stem of this tense is formed by adding अल *al* or इल *il* to the root. To this the terminations in § 41 are added. Thus √ देख *dekh*, 'see,' preterite stem देखल *dekhal* or देखिल *dekhil*, to which the terminations are added: thus देख॰लाँ *dĕkh'lá* or देखिलाँ *dĕkhilá*, 'I saw.' This tense has in the case of transitive verbs the following terminations instead of those given in § 41:— अक *ak*, ॰कऽ *'ka*, ॰कै *'kai*, or ॰कौ *'kau* for the third person singular masculine; ॰की *'kí* for the third person singular feminine; ॰कात *kát*, ॰कैन्ह *'kainh*, or ॰कौन्ह

'kaunh for the third person plural masculine; and ऽकीत *'kít* for the third person plural feminine. In the case of neuter verbs the terminations in § 41 are taken, and also आ *á* may be used in the second singular masculine, and in the third singular masculine it may drop all terminations altogether.

In addition to the above, the second plural feminine of both transitive and neuter verbs ends in ई *í*.

§ 44. The Future Indicative.

This tense has two stems—one for the first and second persons, and one for the third person. The first stem is formed by adding अब *ab* or इब *ib* to the root; the second is the root itself.

The following are the terminations of this tense. All should be added to the root direct.

After certain vowels, *e.g.* आ *á*, the stem termination may be एब *ĕb* instead of अब *ab*.

Terminations of the Future.

Person.	Singular.		Plural.	
	Masculine.	Feminine.	Masculine.	Feminine.
1st	ऽबौँ *'baũ*.		ऽब॰ *'ba*, ऽबै *'bai*, ऽबौ *'bau*, ऽभैन्ह, ऽभौन्ह, *'bhainh*,* *'bhaunh*.*	
2nd	ऽबे *'be*, ऽबेँ *'bẽ*. ऽबै *'bai*, ऽबैँ *'baĩ*. ऽभै *'bhai*,* ऽभैँ *bhaĩ*.*		ऽब॰ *'ba*. ऽभो *'bho*,* ऽभौ *'bhau*.*	
3rd	ऽत॰, *'ta*, ऽतै *'tai*, ऽतौ *'tau*.	ऽती *'tí*.	ऽतात *'tát*, ऽतैन्ह, ऽतौन्ह, *'tainh*, *'taunh*.	ऽतीत *'tít*.

* These are contractions for ऽब है *'b hai*, ऽब हैं *'b haĩ*, &c.

§ 45. The Present Conjunctive and Imperative.

In this tense the terminations are added to the root itself: thus देखिऐ *dĕkhiai*, 'let me see.' The terminations are those given in § 41, except that in the first person masculine singular it takes ओं *õ*, औं *aũ*, इहौं *ihaũ*, and in the second person masculine singular imperative it optionally takes no termination whatever.

In the plural it may in the first person masculine also take the termination इअ *ia*. In the third person it takes अथ *ath* instead of आत *át*.

The feminine is the same as the masculine.

§ 46. The Preterite Conjunctive.

In this tense the stem termination causes some apparent irregularities in combining with the personal terminations. The easiest way of finding the forms is to add the following terminations direct to the root. The masculine in this tense is the same as the feminine.

Person.	Singular.	Plural.
1st	॰ताँ *'tā̃*, ॰ताँव *'tā̃w*, ॰ताओं *'táõ*, ॰तियाँ *'tiyā̃*, ॰तिहाँ *'tihā̃*.	॰तिऐ *'tiai*, ॰तिऔ *'tiau*, ॰तिऐन्ह *'tiainh*, ॰तिऔन्ह *'tiaunh*, ॰तिहैन्ह *'tihainh*, ॰तिहौन्ह *'tihaunh*.
2nd	॰तिहा *'tihá*, ॰तिहै *'tihai*, ॰तिहैँ *'tihaĩ*.	॰तिअ *'tia*, ॰तिहठ *'tiha*, ॰तिहो *'tiho*, ॰तिहौ *'tihau*.
3rd	॰तिहै *'tihai*, ॰तिहौ *'tihau*, ॰तिऐ *'tiai*, ॰तै *'tai*, ॰तौ *'tau*.	॰तिहैन्ह *'tihainh*, ॰तिहौन्ह *'tihaunh*, ॰तैन्ह *'tainh*, ॰तौन्ह *'taunh*.

§ 46a. The Use of the Various Verbal Terminations.

It will be noticed that each person has many terminations, but they do not all mean exactly the same thing. At the same time it must be noted that this multiplicity of verbal forms is partly due to local and personal circumstances—an inhabitant of one place using one set of forms, and an inhabitant of another, another. This is due to the want of a literature, which would fix each verbal form in its proper and exact shade of meaning. The following instructions will help to explain approximately the more customary uses of the forms.

In the first place it must be noted that in South Bhagal'púr number is continually disregarded, verbs in the singular form being used with plural subjects, and *vice versâ*. Thus, take **देखलꣿकꣿ** *dĕkhal'ka,* which is properly third singular preterite. The following examples show that it can be used both in a singular and in a plural sense :—

(Singular) **ऊ हमꣿरा नदीक काता मेँ देखलꣿकꣿ** *ú ham'rá nadík kátá mẽ dĕkhal'ka,* 'he saw me beside the river.'

(Plural) **ऊ सभ हमꣿरा नदी केरꣿ कछारा मेँ देखलꣿकꣿ** *ú sabh ham'rá nadí kera kachhárá dĕkhal'ka,* 'they saw me on the bank of the river.'

So also **देखलꣿकात** *dĕkhal'kát* (properly 3rd plural) may be used as a singular ; viz. **ऊ देखलꣿकात** *ú dĕkhal'kát,* 'he saw,' and **ऊ सभ देखलꣿकात** *ú sabh dĕkhal'kát,* 'they saw.' It may be asked, then, why these terminations have been divided into singular and plural. The answer is twofold, —first, that though no longer used in their proper sense, the terminations were originally singular and plural as written, and in songs (which always conserve an older form of the language) they are so used to the present day. Secondly, at the present day there is this important difference in their use,—singular terminations (especially in the second and third persons) are always used non-honorifically, and plural terminations honorifically, as regards the subject ; thus, **ऊ देखलꣿकꣿ** *ú dĕkhal'ka* (singular) means 'he (that humble person) saw,' but **ऊ देखलꣿकात** *ú dĕkhal'kát* (plural) 'he (that respectable person) saw.' In the first person, however, this distinction has been lost, and singular and plural are used indiscriminately.

There is another way of looking at a verbal form, and that is the relation it bears to the object. There is nothing like this in any European language ; so it requires more careful exemplification in the present case. For the purposes of the present explanation a sentence may be divided into subject, verb, and object. The object may be direct or remote. Thus, in 'the king gave a village to the bráhman,' 'the king' is the subject, 'gave' is the verb, 'a village' is the direct object, and 'the bráhman' is the remote object. So in 'the child fell on the ground,' for the purposes of the present explanation 'the ground' may be considered as the remote object. In European grammar the form of a verb depends on the subject, *i.e.*, we say that it agrees with its subject in number and person, but the object (direct or remote) has no effect at all on the form of the verb. In Bihárí, on the contrary, the selection of the verbal form to be used largely depends upon the object. Thus, while in Europe we must say that the verb agrees with its subject in number and person, in Bihár we must say that it agrees with its subject, and also with its object, in honour and person.

The following are approximately the rules on this point :—

(*a*) The terminations ending in औ *au* are used when the object (direct or remote) is in the second person and is considered inferior to the speaker. If, however, the termination is pronounced with a drawl, something like *a-o*, the object is mentioned with some, but not great, respect.

Exception.—If the verb itself is in the second person, the object may be in the first or third person.

(*b*) The terminations ending in औन्ह *aunh* are used when the object (direct or remote) is in the second person and is spoken of with respect.

(*c*) The terminations ending in ऐ *ai* are used when the object (direct or remote) is in the first or third person and is considered inferior to the subject.

(*d*) The terminations ending in ऐन्ह *ainh* are used generally when the object (direct or remote) is mentioned with great respect. In this case the object may be in the first, second, or third person.

The following examples will make the above clear :—

हमेँ तोर॰ बैरी छेलिऔ *hamẽ tora bairí chhĕliau*, '(You fool), I was your enemy.' (Here the direct object, 'your enemy,' being inferior and in the second person, a termination ending in औ *au* is used.)

हमेँ तोह॰र॰ पोथी बिहान॰ देख॰बौ *hamẽ tŏh'ra pothi bihána dĕkh'bau*, 'I will see your book (my humble friend) to-morrow.'

जौँ तोहेँ हम॰रा मारि डाल॰तिहैँ, तबे ऊ मौँती तोरा हाथ ऐतिहौ, *jŏ tohẽ ham'rá mári ḍál'tihaĩ, tabĕ ú mŏtí torá háth aĩtihau*, 'If you had killed me, the pearl would have come into your hand (you fool)?'

तोह॰रा गाड़ी मेँ की माल छौ *tŏh'rá gáṛí mẽ kí mál chhau?* '(My humble friend), what goods are in your cart?'

अबे जाहौ, आज साँझ कैँ तोह॰र॰ पाती देख॰बौ *abĕ jáhau, áj sãjh kaĩ toh'ra páti dĕkh'bau* (pronounced *dĕkh'ba-o*), 'Go now, sir; I will see your letter this evening.'

देखल॰हौ कुकुर नहीँ भागे सक॰लै *dĕkhal'hau kukur nahí bhágĕ sak'lai?* 'Did you see the dog (inferior), how it could not run away?' (Here, although the object is in the third person, still a termination ending in औ *au* is used, because the subject is in the second person.)

जबे तोहेँ हम॰रा छोड़ि देबै, तबे कह॰भौन्ह *jabĕ tohẽ ham'rá chhoṛi debai, tabĕ kah'bhaunh*, 'When you will let me (your humble servant) go, then I will tell you (your honour).'

तौँ ओक॰रा चाकर॰ कै देख॰ले छै *tõ ŏk'rá chákara kai dekh'lĕ chhai?* 'Have you (my humble friend) seen his servant?' (Here both subject and object are non-honorific.)

देखल॰हौ मुर॰ता ननुआ कै कँहिन॰ भारी चट॰कन खीँचि के मारल॰कै *dĕkhal'hau Mur'tá nanuá kai kaĩhina bhári chaṭ'kan khĩchi kĕ máral'kai?* 'Did you see how Mur'tá gave a severe slap to the child?' (Here the object, 'the child,' is inferior.)

हमेँ आप॰ने कै देख॰बैन्ह *hamẽ áp'nĕ kai dĕkh'bainh*, 'I will see your honour.' Here the object is mentioned with great respect.)

आपन्ने हमन्रा नेँदा कै देखन्लाँ *áp'nĕ ham'rá nĕdá kai dĕkh'lá̃*, 'Did your honour, see my child?' (Here the first person of the verb is used honorifically instead of the second person, and no special reference being made to the person of or respect due to the object, the form देखन्लिऐ *dĕkh'liai* is not used.)

रे छौँड़ा, हमन्रऽ बही देखन्ले छै? *re chhaũṛá, ham'ra bahí dĕkh'lĕ chhai?* 'Ho! you boy, there, have you seen my book?' (Here the subject is non-honorific, and there is no reference to the object.)

मजिस्टर साहेब हमन्रा देखलन्कात *Majisṭar Sáhĕb ham'rá dĕkhal'kát*, 'His Honor the Magistrate saw me.' (Here the subject is honorific, and no reference is made to the honour of the object.)

हो काका, देखन्लऽ मोहनऽ केरी बहू केना के हँकैलन्की *ho káká, dĕkh'la Mŏhana kerí bahú kená kĕ hãkaĭl'kí?* 'Hallo, uncle, did you see how Mohan's wife called me?' (Here no special reference is made to the honour of the object.)

CHAPTER V.

AUXILIARY VERBS.

§ 47. There are two classes of auxiliary verbs—the *defective* and the *complete*.

§ 48. There is only one *defective auxiliary verb* in use in this dialect,—that derived from the √ अछ *achh*.

This is used only in the present and preterite tenses, and always in this dialect loses its initial vowel. It has in the present tense two forms,—a weak (*e.g.* छी *chhī*, 'I am') and a strong (*e.g.* छिकों *chhikõ*, 'I am'). In the preterite tense it is used only in the weak form (*e.g.* छलों *chhalõ*, 'I was').

§ 49. The *complete auxiliary verb* is formed from the √ हो *ho* 'become,' which is conjugated through all moods and tenses. Its preterite is never used as an auxiliary, but only as a verb substantive, meaning 'I became.'

§ 50. Defective Auxiliary Verb.

√ अछ *achh*, 'be.'

Present : *'I am,' &c.*

WEAK FORM.

Person.	SINGULAR.	PLURAL.
	Masculine and Feminine.	Masculine and Feminine.
1st	*Not used.*	छी, छिअ, छिऐ. छिऔ, *chhí, chhia, chhiai, chhiau,* छिऐन्ह, छिऔन्ह, *chhiainh, chhiaunh,* छिहैन्ह, छिहौन्ह *chhihainh, chhihaunh.*
2nd	छे, छेँ, छै, छैँ, *chhe, chhẽ, chhai, chhaĩ,* छहै, छहैँ. *chhahai, chhahaĩ.*	छ, छहो, छहौ, *chha, chhaho, chhahau,* छहैन्ह *chhahainh.*
3rd	छे, छै. छौ, *chhe, chhai, chhau.* छत *chhat* (irregular).	छैन्ह छौन्ह *chhainh, chhaunh,* छथ छथीन, छथून *chhath, chhathín, chhathún.*

§ 51. Strong Form.

Not used as an auxiliary, but only as a verb substantive.

Person.	Singular.	Plural.
	Masculine and Feminine	Masculine and Feminine.
1st	छिकों, छिकौँ, छिकिहौँ. *chhikõ, chhikaũ, chhikihaũ.* छिकाँ, छिकाँव, छिकाओँ. *chhikā̃, chhikā̃w, chhikáõ.*	छिकिअ, छिकिऐ, छिकिऔ, *chhikia, chhikiai, chhikiau,* छिकिऐन्ह, छिकिऔन्ह, *chhikiainh, chhikiaunh.* छिकिहैन्ह, छिकिहौन्ह, *chhikihainh, chhikihaunh.*
2nd	छिके, छिकेँ, छिकै, छिकैँ. *chhike, chhikẽ, chhikai, chhikaĩ.* छिकऽहै, छिकऽहैँ *chhik'hai, chhik'haĩ.*	छिकऽ *chhika.* छिकऽहो, छिकऽहौ. *chhik'ho, chhik'hau.* छिकऽहैन्ह *chhik'hainh.*
3rd	छिके, *chhike,* छिकै, छिकौ *chhikai, chhikau.*	छिकथ *chhikath.* छिकैन्ह, छिकौन्ह. *chhikainh, chhikaunh.*

§ 52. Preterite : '*I was,*' *&c.*

Person.	Singular.		Plural.	
	Masculine.	Feminine.	Masculine.	Feminine.
1st	छलाँ, छलाँव, *chhalá̃,** *chhalá̃w,* छलाओँ *chhaláõ.*		छलिऐ, छलिऔ, *chhaliai, chhaliau,* छलिऐन्ह, छलिऔन्ह, *chhaliainh, chhaliaunh,* छलिहैन्ह, छलिहौन्ह, *chhalihainh, chhalihaunh.*	
2nd	छला, छले, छलैँ, *chhalá, chhale, chhalẽ,* छलै, छलैँ, *chhalai, chhalaĩ,* छल॰है. छल॰हैँ. *chhal'hai, chhal'haĩ.*	छली *chhalí.*	छल॰, छल॰हो, *chhala, chhal'ho,* छल॰हौ, छल॰हैन्ह. *chhal'hau, chhal'hainh.*	छलीँ *chhalĩ.*
3rd	छल॰ *chhala,* छले *chhale,* छलै, छलौ. *chhalai, chhalau.*	छली *chhalí.*	छलात, *chhalát,* छलैन्ह, छलौन्ह. *chhalainh, chhalaunh.*	छलीत *chhalít.*

* In the southern parts of the district this is also spelled छिलाँ *chhilá̃* or छेलाँ *chhĕlá̃,* and so throughout.

§ 53. The Complete Auxiliary Verb.

√ हो *ho*, '*be*,' '*become*'

INDICATIVE MOOD.

(*a*)—Preterite: '*I became*,' *&c.*

NOTE.—This tense is never used as an auxiliary, छलूँ *chhalū̃* (see above) being used instead.

Person.	Singular.		Plural.	
	Masculine.	Feminine.	Masculine.	Feminine.
1st	होलौं *holā̃*.*		होलिऐ *hŏliai*.	
2nd	होलेँ *holẽ*.	होली *holī*.	होलह *hola*.	होलीं *holī̃*.
3rd	होलह *hola*.	होली *holī*.	होलात *holát*.	होलीत *holīt*.

* Or होअलौं *hoalā̃*, and so throughout.

Optional forms as in छलूँ, *chhalū̃*.

§ 54. (*b*)—Future: '*I shall be*,' *&c.*

Person.	Singular.		Plural.	
	Masculine.	Feminine.	Masculine.	Feminine.
1st	होबौं *hobaũ*.		होबह, होबै, होबौ, *hoba*, *hobai*, *hobau*, होभैन्ह, होभौन्ह. *hŏbhainh*, *hŏbhaunh*.	
2nd	होबे, होबेँ, होबै, *hobe*, *hobẽ*, *hobai*, होबैँ, होभै, होभैँ. *hobaĩ*, *hŏbhai*, *hobhaĩ*.		होबह, होभो, होभौ. *hoba*, *hŏbho*, *hŏbhau*.	
3rd	होतह, होतै, होतौ. *hota*, *hotai*, *hotau*.	होती *hotī*.	होतैन्ह, होतौन्ह, *hotainh*, *hotaunh*, होतात, *hotát*.	होतीत *hotīt*.

CONJUNCTIVE MOOD.

§ 55. (*c*)—Present: '(*If*) *I be*,' *&c.*

Person.	SINGULAR. Masculine and Feminine.	PLURAL. Masculine and Feminine.
1st	होओं, होअौं, होइहौं. *hoõ*, *hoaũ*, *hoihaũ*.	होइअ, होइऐ, होइअौ, *hoïa*, *hoïai*, *hoïau*, होइऐन्ह, होइअौन्ह, *hoïainh*, *hoïaunh*, होइहैन्ह, होइहौन्ह, *hoïhainh*, *hoihaunh*.
2nd	होए, होएँ, होऐ, होऐँ. *hoë*, *hoẽ*, *hoai*, *hoãi*.	होअ *hoa*.
	होहै *hohai*, होहैँ *hohãi*.	होहो *hoho*, होहौ *hohau*.
	हो *ho*.	
3rd	होए *hoë*,	होअथ *hoath*.
	होऐ *hoai*, होअौ *hoau*.	होऐन्ह, *hoainh*, होअौन्ह, *hoaunh*.

§ 56. (*d*)—Preterite: '*(If) I had been*,' *&c.*

Person.	SINGULAR.	PLURAL.
	Masculine and Feminine.	Masculine and Feminine.
1st	होताँ *hotā́*, होताँव *hotā́w*. होताओँ, होतियाँ. होतिहाँ. *hŏtáŏ*, *hŏtiyā́*, *hŏtihā́*.	होतिऐ, होतिऔ, होतिऐन्ह, होतिऔन्ह, *hŏtiaï*, *hŏtiau*, *hŏtiainh*, *hŏtiaunh*, होतिहैन्ह *hŏtihainh*, होतिहौन्ह *hŏtihaunh*.
2nd	होतिहा, होतिहै, होतिहैँ. *hŏtihá*, *hŏtihai*, *hŏtihaĩ*.	होतिअ, होतिहऽ. होतिहो, होतिहौ. *hŏtia*, *hŏtiha*, *hŏtiho*, *hŏtihau*.
3rd	होतिहै, होतिहौ, होतिऐ. *hŏtihai*, *hŏtihau*, *hŏtiai*. होतै *hotai*, होतौ *hotau*.	होतिहैन्ह, होतिहौन्ह, होतैन्ह, होतौन्ह. *hŏtihainh*, *hŏtihaunh*, *hotainh*, *hotaunh*.

§ 57. Imperative Mood.

Present: '*Let me see*,' *&c.*

The same as the present conjunctive.

Precative Forms.

Non-honorific—

होइहौ *hoïhau*, हूअ *húa*.

Honorific—

होइअ *hoia*, होइहऽ *hoïha*, होहिहैँ *hŏhihaĩ*, 'be good enough to be'

The periphrastic tenses are quite regular, and need not be given.

§ 58. Present Participle, '*being.*'

Singular and Plural.

होतऽ *hota ;* obl. होते *hotĕ* or होतै *hotaĭ.*

Past Participle, '*been.*'

होलऽ *hola.*

Conjunctive Participle, '*having been.*'

होय के *hoy kĕ.*

Infinitive, '*to be.*'

होब *hob.*

CHAPTER VI.

THE REGULAR ACTIVE VERB.

§ 59. There is only one conjugation of active verbs, if we except a few irregular verbs to be noted further on. The conjugation of neuter verbs differs from that of active verbs only in certain of the past tenses, and these will be treated of in a future page. Verbs whose roots end in vowels also exhibit slight variations, which will be explained at the proper place. For the sake of uniformity the tenses are given in the same order, and under the same names, as those in Dr. Hoernle's grammar.

Reference is again made to General Introduction, §§ 34 to 36, with regard to the changes of the root-vowel.

§ 60. √ देख *dekh*, 'see.'

PRESENT PARTICIPLE: देख॰लठ *dĕkh'la.*

PAST PARTICIPLE: देख॰तठ *dĕkh'ta.*

Simple Tenses.

INDICATIVE MOOD.

§ 61. (*a*)—Preterite: '*I saw*,' *&c.*

Person.	Singular.		Plural.	
	Masculine.	Feminine.	Masculine.	Feminine.
1st	देख॰लाँ, देख॰लाँव. *dĕkh'lā́*,* *dĕkh'lā́w*. देख॰लाओँ *dĕkh'láõ*.		देख॰लिऐ *dĕkh'liai*, देख॰लिऔ *dĕkh'liau*, देख॰लिऐन्ह *dĕkh'liainh*, देख॰लिऔन्ह *dĕkh'liaunh*, देख॰लिहैन्ह *dĕkh'lihainh*, देख॰लिहौन्ह *dĕkh'lihaunh*.	
2nd	देख॰ले, देख॰लेँ, *dĕkh'le*, *dĕkh'lẽ*. देख॰लै, देख॰लैँ, *dĕkh'lai*, *dĕkh'lãĩ*, देखल॰है, देखल॰हैँ. *dĕkhal'hai*, *dĕkhal'hãĩ*.	देख॰ली. *dĕkh'lí*.	देख॰लऽ *dĕkh'la*, देखल॰हो *dĕkhal'ho*, देखल॰हौ *dĕkhal'hau*, देखल॰हैन्ह *dĕkhal'hainh*.	देख॰लीँ *dĕkh'lí*.
3rd	देख॰लक *dĕkh'lak*. देखल॰कऽ *dĕkhal'ka*. देखल॰कै *dĕkhal'kai*, देखल॰कौ *dĕkhal'kau*.	देखल॰की. *dĕkhal'kí*.	देखल॰कात *dĕkhal'kát*, देखल॰कैन्ह *dĕkhal'kainh*, देखल॰कौन्ह *dĕkhal'kaunh*.	देखल॰कीत *dĕkhal'kít*.

* Or देखिलाँ *dĕkhilā́*, and so throughout.

§ 62. (*b*)—Future: '*I shall see,*' *&c.*

erson.	SINGULAR.		PLURAL.	
	Masculine.	Feminine.	Masculine.	Feminine.
t	देख॰बौँ *dĕkh'baũ.**		देख॰बऽ, *dekh'ba,* देख॰बै, देख॰बौ, *dĕkh'bai, dĕkh'bau,* देख॰भैन्ह, देख॰भौन्ह. *dĕkh'bhainh, dĕkh'bhaunh.*	
nd	देख॰बे देख॰बेँ. *dĕkh'be, dĕkh'bẽ.* देख॰बै, देख॰बैँ. *dĕkh'bai, dĕkh'baĩ.* देख॰भै, देख॰भैँ. *dĕkh'bhai, dĕkh'bhaĩ.*		देख॰बऽ *dĕkh'ba.* देख॰भो *dĕkh'bho.* देख॰भौ *dĕkh'bhau.*	
rd	देख॰तऽ *dĕkh'ta.* देख॰तै, देख॰तौ, *dĕkh'tai, dĕkh'tau,* देख॰तऽ *dĕkh'ta.*	देख॰ती *dĕkh'tī.*	देख॰तात *dĕkh'tát.* देख॰तैन्ह, देख॰तौन्ह, *dĕkh'tainh, dĕkh'taunh.*	देख॰तीत *dĕkh'tīt.*

* Or देखिबौँ *dĕkhibaũ*, and so throughout.

CONJUNCTIVE (CONDITIONAL) MOOD.

§ 63. (*c*)—Present : '(*If*) *I see*,' rarely '*I see*,' or '*I shall see*,' *&c.*

Person.	SINGULAR. Masculine and Feminine.	PLURAL. Masculine and Feminine.
1st	देखोँ, देखौँ, देखिहौँ. *dekhõ, dekhãũ, dĕkhihãũ.*	देखिअ, देखिऐ, देखिऔ, देखिऐन्ह, *dĕkhia, dĕkhiai, dĕkhiau, dĕkhiainh,* देखिऔन्ह, देखिहैन्ह, देखिहौन्ह. *dĕkhiaunh, dĕkhihainh, dĕkhihaunh.*
2nd	देखे, देखेँ. *dekhe, dekhẽ.* देखै, देखैँ, देख॰है, देख॰हैँ. *dekhai, dekhãĩ, dĕkh'hai, dĕkh'hãĩ.*	देखऽ, देख॰हो, देख॰हौ, *dekha, dĕkh'ho, dĕkh'hau,* देख॰हैन्ह *dĕkh'hainh.*
3rd	देखे *dekhe.* देखै, देखौ. *dekhai, dekhau.*	देखथ *dekhath,* देखैन्ह, देखौन्ह, *dekhainh, dekhaunh.*

§ 64. (*d*)—Preterite: '(*If*) *I had seen,*' *&c.*

Person.	Singular. Masculine and Feminine.	Plural. Masculine and Feminine.
1st	देख॰ताँ, देख॰ताँव, देख॰ताओँ, *dĕkh'tā̃, dĕkh'tā̃w, dĕkh'táõ,* देख॰तियाँ, देख॰तिहाँ. *dĕkh'tiyā̃, dĕkh'tihā̃.*	देख॰तिऐ, देख॰तिऔ, *dĕkh'tiai, dĕkh'tiau,* देख॰तिऐन्ह, देख॰तिऔन्ह, *dĕkh'tiainh, dĕkh'tiaunh.* देख॰तिहैन्ह, देख॰तिहौन्ह. *dĕkh'tihainh, dĕkh'tihaunh.*
2nd	देख॰तिहा, देख॰तिहै, देख॰तिहैँ, *dĕkh'tihá, dĕkh'tihai, dĕkh'tihaĩ.*	देख॰तिअ, देख॰तिहऽ, *dĕkh'tia, dĕkh'tiha,* देख॰तिहो, देख॰तिहौ. *dĕkh'tiho, dĕkh'tihau.*
3rd	देख॰तिहै, देख॰तिहौ, देख॰तिऐ, *dĕkh'tihai, dĕkh'tihau, dĕkh'tiai,* देख॰तै, देख॰तौ. *dĕkh'tai, dĕkh'tau.*	देख॰तिहैन्ह, देख॰तिहौन्ह, *dĕkh'tihainh, dĕkh'tihaunh,* देख॰तैन्ह, देख॰तौन्ह. *dĕkh'tainh, dĕkh'taunh.*

NOTE.—The word छल *chhal* may optionally be added to any of the above forms in the south of the district: thus देख॰ताँ छल *dĕkh'tā̃ chhal.*

IMPERATIVE MOOD.

§ 65. (*e*)—Present.—Same as present conjunctive. 2nd sing., also देख *dekh.*

Precative Forms.

Non-honorific—

2nd person: देखिहौ *dĕkhihau.*

Honorific—

2nd person: देखिअ *dĕkhia*, देखिहऽ *dĕkhiha*, देखिहैँ *dekhihaĩ.*

(B)—Periphrastic Tenses.

INDICATIVE MOOD.

§ 66. In the following paradigms the optional forms of the auxiliary verbs will not all be given, as taking up too much valuable space. For similar reasons feminine forms are generally omitted. When not given, they only differ from the masculine in assuming the feminine form of the auxiliary verb.

§ 67. √(g)—Definite Present: '*I am seeing,*' '*I see,*' *&c.*

Person.	Singular.	Plural.
1st	*Not used.*	देखै छी *dekhai chhí.*
2nd	देखै छँ *dekhai chhẽ.*	देखै छ० *dekhai chha.*
3rd	देखै छै *dekhai chhai.*	देखै छैन्ह *dekhai chhainh.*

§ 68. There being no special feminine forms of the auxiliary verb, the feminine is the same as the masculine.

Any optional form of the present of the weak defective auxiliary verb may be used; thus, first plural देखै छिऐ *dekhai chhiai.* The word देखै *dekhai* is only an old form of the present participle, देखैत *dekhait,* with the final त *t* dropped. Some people contract this tense to देखिछी *děkhichhí,* &c. Compare the Ban'gálí colloquial देख्‌छि *děkh'chhi* instead of देखितेछि *děkhitechhi,* 'I see.'

§ 69. (*i*)—Imperfect : '*I was seeing.*'

Person.	Singular.	Plural.
1st	देखै छलाँ *dekhai chhalá̃.*	देखै छलिऐ *dekhai chhaliai.*
2nd	देखै छलैँ *dekhai chhalẽ.*	देखै छलऽ *dekhai chhala.*
3rd	देखै छलऽ *dekhai chhala.*	देखै छलात *dekhai chhalát.*

To form the feminine, use feminine forms of the auxiliary verb; thus, 2nd singular देखै छली *dekhai chhalí.*

Any optional form of the preterite of the defective auxiliary verb may be used.

§ 70. (*j*)—Durative Future '*I shall be seeing,*' *&c.*

Person.	Singular.	Plural.
1st	देखन्ते होबौँ *děkh'tě hobaũ.*	देखन्ते होबऽ *děkh'tě hoba.*
2nd	देखन्ते होबेँ *děkh'tě hobẽ.*	देखन्ते होबऽ *děkh'tě hoba.*
3rd	देखन्ते होतै *děkh'tě hotai.*	देखन्ते होतात *děkh'tě hotát.*

To form the feminine, use feminine forms of the auxiliary verb; thus, 3rd singular देखन्ते होती *děkh'tě hotí.*

Any optional form of the future of the complete auxiliary verb may be used throughout.

Some people use रहन्बौँ *rah'baũ*, 'I shall remain,' instead of होबौँ *hobaũ*, and so throughout.

§ 71. (k)—Perfect : '*I have seen*,' &c.

Person.	Singular.	Plural.
1st	*Not used.*	देख॰ले छी *dĕkh'lĕ chhí.*
2nd	देख॰ले* छेँ *dĕkh'lĕ chhĕ̃.*	देख॰ले छऽ *dĕkh'lĕ chha.*
3rd	देख॰ले छै *dĕkh'lĕ chhai.*	देख॰ले छैन्ह *dĕkh'lĕ chhainh.*

* Or देख॰ने *dĕkh'nĕ* or देख॰लै *dĕkh'laĭ*, and so throughout.

The feminine is the same as the masculine, as in the definite present.

As in the definite present, any optional form of the present of the defective auxiliary verb may be used: thus, first plural देख॰ले छिऐ *dĕkh'lĕ chhiai*, and so on.

§ 72. (l)—Pluperfect : '*I had seen*,' &c.

Person.	Singular.	Plural.
1st	देख॰ले* छलोँ *dĕkh'lĕ chhalŏ̃.*	देख॰ले छलिऐ *dĕkh'lĕ chhaliai.*
2nd	देख॰ले छलेँ *dĕkh'lĕ chhalĕ̃.*	देख॰ले छलऽ *dĕkh'lĕ chhala.*
3rd	देख॰ले छलऽ *dĕkh'lĕ chhala.*	देख॰ले छलात *dĕkh'lĕ chhalát.*

* Or देख॰ने *dĕkh'nĕ* or देख॰लै *dĕkh'laĭ*, and so throughout.

To form the feminine, use feminine forms of the auxiliary, as in the imperfect.

Any optional form of the preterite of the defective auxiliary verb may be used.

§ 73. (*m*)—Future Exact: '*I shall have seen*,' '*I may have seen*,' *&c.*

Person.	Singular.	Plural.
1st	देख॰ले* होबौँ *dĕkh'lĕ hobaũ.*	देख॰ले होबऽ *dĕkh'lĕ hoba.*
2nd	देख॰ले होबेँ *dĕkh'lĕ hobẽ.*	देख॰ले होबऽ *dĕkh'lĕ hoba.*
3rd	देख॰ले होतै *dĕkh'lĕ hotai.*	देख॰ले होतात *dĕkh'lĕ hotát.*

* Or देख॰ने *dĕkh'nĕ* or देख॰लै *dĕkh'laĭ*, and so throughout

To form the feminine, use feminine forms of the auxiliary verb, as in the durative future.

Any other form of the future of the complete auxiliary verb may be used instead throughout.

CONJUNCTIVE (CONDITIONAL) MOOD.

§ 74. (*n*)- Future Conditional: '(*If*) *I be seeing*,' *&c.*

Person.	Singular.	Plural.
1st	देख॰ते होऔँ *dĕkh'tĕ hoaũ.*	देख॰ते होइअ *dĕkh'tĕ hoia.*
2nd	देख॰ते होएँ *dĕkh'tĕ hoẽ.*	देख॰ते होअ *dĕkh'tĕ hoa.*
3rd	देख॰ते होऐ *dĕkh'tĕ hoai.*	देख॰ते होआत *dĕkh'tĕ hoát.*

To form the femioine, use feminine forms of the auxiliary verb.

Some people use रहौँ *rahaũ* instead of होऔँ *hoaũ*, and so throughout.

Any other form of the present conjunctive of the complete auxiliary verb may be used instead throughout.

§ **75.** (*o*)—**Durative Present Conditional :** '(*If*) *I were seeing,*' &c.

Person.	Singular.	Plural.
1st	देखन्ते होताँ *dĕkh'tĕ hotā̆.*	देखन्ते होतिऐ *dĕkh'tĕ hŏtiai.*
2nd	देखन्ते होतिहैँ *dĕkh'tĕ hŏtihai̐.*	देखन्ते होतिअ *dĕkh'tĕ hŏtia.*
3rd	देखन्ते होतै *dĕkh'tĕ hotai.*	देखन्ते होतैन्ह *dĕkh'tĕ hotainh.*

To form the feminine, use feminine forms of the auxiliary verb.

Any other form of the preterite conditional of the complete auxiliary verb may be used instead throughout.

§ **76.** (*p*)—**Future Exact Conditional :** '(*If*) *I have seen,*' &c.

Person.	Singular.	Plural.
1st	देखन्ले* होयौँ *dĕkh'lĕ hoau̐.*	देखन्ले होइअ *dĕkh'lĕ hoia.*
2nd	देखन्ले होएँ *dĕkh'lĕ hoĕ.*	देखन्ले होअ *dĕkh'lĕ hoa.*
3rd	देखन्ले होऐ *dĕkh'lĕ hoai.*	देखन्ले होआत *dĕkh'lĕ hoát.*

* Or देखन्ने *dĕkh'nĕ* or देखन्लै *dĕkh'laĩ*, and so throughout.

To form the feminine, use feminine forms of the auxiliary verb.

Any other form of the present conjunctive of the complete auxiliary verb may be used instead throughout.

§ 77. (*q*)—Preterite Conditional : '(*If*) *I had seen*,' *&c.*

Person.	Singular.	Plural.
1st	देख॰ले* होताँ *dĕkh'lĕ hotā̆.*	देख॰ले होतिऐ *dĕkh'lĕ hŏtiai.*
2nd	देख॰ले होतिनैँ *dĕkh'lĕ hŏtinăĭ.*	देख॰ले होतिअ *dĕkh'lĕ hŏtia.*
3rd	देख॰ले होतै *dĕkh'lĕ hotai.*	देख॰ले होतैन्ह *dĕkh'lĕ hotainh.*

* Or देख॰ने *dĕkh'nĕ* or देख॰लै *dĕkh'laĭ*, and so throughout.

To form the feminine, use feminine forms of the auxiliary verb.

Any other form of the preterite conditional of the complete auxiliary verb may be used instead throughout.

78. Participles.

ADJECTIVAL.

Present, 'seeing' . . . देख॰त॰ *dĕkh'ta ;* fem. देख॰ती *dĕkh'ti ;* obl. देख॰ते *dĕkh'tĕ* or देख॰तै *dĕkh'taĭ.*

Past, 'seen' . . . . . देख॰ल॰ *dĕkh'la ;* fem. देख॰ली *dĕkh'li ;* obl. देख॰ले *dĕkh'lĕ* or देख॰लै *dĕkh'laĭ.*

CONJUNCTIVE.

'Having seen' . . . . देखि के *dekhi kĕ*, देखि कै *dekhi kaĭ.*

§ 79. Infinitives or Verbal Nouns, *'to see,' 'the act of seeing.'*

Nominative	Oblique.
देख *dekh,** देखि *dekhi.*	देखे *dĕkhĕ* or देखैँ *dekhaĭ.*
देख॰लऽ *dĕkh'la.*	देख॰ला *dĕkh'lá.*
देख॰बऽ *dĕkh'ba.*	*Not used.*

§ 80. Noun of Agency, *'one who sees.'*

देख॰निहार *dĕkh'nihár* or देख॰वैया *dĕkh'waiyá.*

---

* This form of the verbal noun is always the same as the root.

CHAPTER VII.

THE REGULAR NEUTER VERB.

§ 81. This verb differs from the active verb only in the formation of certain of the tenses formed from the past participle. The three more usual of these tenses are here given; the conjugation of the rest of the verb can be learnt from the conjugation of the √ देख *dekh*.

NOTE that throughout the periphrastic tenses of the neuter verb, in which the past participle occurs, the past participle takes the direct form गिरऽलऽ *gir'la* (fem. गिरऽली *gir'lī*), and not the form गिरऽले *gir'lĕ*, which might be expected: thus हमें गिरलऽ होबौँ *hamẽ girala hobaũ*, 'I shall have fallen,' and not हमें गिरऽले होबौँ *ham gir'lẽ hobaũ*.

§ 82. √ गिर *gir*, 'fall.'

PAST PARTICIPLE: गिर॰ल० *gir'la*; fem. गिर॰ली *gir'li*.

INDICATIVE MOOD.

§ 83. Preterite: '*I fell*,' *&c.*

Person.	Singular.		Plural.	
	Masculine.	Feminine.	Masculine.	Feminine.
1st	गिर॰लाँ, गिर॰लाँव, *gir'lā́*, *gir'lā́w*, गिर॰लाओँ *gir'láõ*.		गिर॰लिऐ, गिर॰लिऔ, *gir'liai*, *gir'liau*, गिर॰लिऐन्ह, गिर॰लिऔन्ह, *gir'liainh*, *gir'liaunh*, गिर॰लिहैन्ह *gir'lihainh*, गिर॰लिहौन्ह *gir'lihaunh*.	
2nd	गिर॰ला, गिर॰ले, गिर॰लेँ, *gir'lá*, *gir'le*, *gir'lẽ*, गिर॰लै, गिर॰लैँ, *gir'lai*, *gir'lãi*. गिरल॰है, गिरल॰हैँ, *giral'hai*, *giral'hãi*.	गिर॰ली *gir'li*.	गिर॰ल० *gir'la*. गिरल॰हो, गिरल॰हौ, *giral'ho*, *giral'hau*, गिरल॰हैन्ह *giral'hainh*.	गिर॰लीँ *gir'li*.
3rd	गिर॰ल० *gir'la*, गिर॰लै *gir'lai*, गिर॰लौ *gir'lau*.	गिर॰ली *gir'li*.	गिर॰लात *gir'lát*, गिर॰लैन्ह *gir'lainh*, गिर॰लौन्ह *gir'launh*.	गिर॰लीत *gir'lit*.

§ 84. (*k*)—Perfect: '*I have fallen,*' *&c.*

Person.	Singular.		Plural.	
	Masculine.	Feminine.	Masculine.	Feminine.
1st	*Not used.*	*Not used.*	गिरऽलऽ छी *gir'la chhí.*	गिरऽली छी *gir'lí chhí.*
2nd	गिरऽलऽ छँ *gir'la chhẽ.*	गिरऽली छँ *gir'lí chhẽ.*	गिरऽलऽ छऽ *gir'la chha.*	गिरऽली छऽ *gir'lí chha.*
3rd	गिरऽलऽ छै *gir'la chhai.*	गिरऽली छै *gir'lí chhai.*	गिरऽलऽ छैन्ह *gir'la chhainh.*	गिरऽली छैन्ह *gir'lí chhainh.*

Any optional form of the present of the weak defective auxiliary verb may be used: thus, गिरलऽ छियै *girala chhiai*, &c.

§ 85. (*l*)—Pluperfect : '*I had fallen,*' *&c.*

Person.	Singular.		Plural.	
	Masculine.	Feminine.	Masculine.	Feminine.
1st	गिर॰लठ छलाँ *gir'la chhalā̃.*	गिर॰ली छलाँ *gir'lí chhalā̃.*	गिर॰लठ छलिऐ *gir'la chhaliai.*	गिर॰ली छलिऐ *gir'lí chhaliai.*
2nd	गिर॰लठ छलैँ *gir'la chhalē̃.*	गिर॰ली छली *gir'lí chhalí.*	गिर॰लठ छलठ *gir'la chhala.*	गिर॰ली छलीँ *gir'lí chhalī̃.*
3rd	गिर॰लठ छलठ *gir'la chhala.*	गिर॰ली छली *gir'lí chhalí.*	गिर॰लठ छलात *gir'la chhalát.*	गिर॰ली छलीत *gir'lí chhalít.*

Any optional form of the preterite of the second auxiliary verb may be used

CHAPTER VIII.

VOCALIC ROOTS.

§ 86. Many verbs have roots ending in vowels, and the junction of the root with the termination frequently causes some slight apparent irregularity.

For this reason the following examples are given of the conjugation of verbs having roots ending in vowels. They are here conjugated in the masculine gender, and through the four radical and participial tenses. From these the periphrastic tenses can easily be formed. It has not been thought necessary to give the conjugation in full for each person.

With regard to the shortening of the root-vowel, see General Introduction, § 36.

§ 87. Example of a verb whose root ends in आ *á* :—

The conjugation of these verbs should be carefully studied, as an important class of active and causal verbs follows it.

In the preterite indicative these verbs insert a junction vowel or semivowel between the root and the ल *l* of the termination ; thus ख* + इ + लाँ *kha* + *i* + *lá̃* or खैलाँ *khailá̃*, 'I ate,' where इ is the junction vowel, and प* + य़् + लाँ *pa* + *y'* + *lá̃*, or पैलाँ *pailá̃*, 'I got,' where य *y* is the junction semivowel. As will be subsequently seen, the same peculiarity exists in other tenses besides the preterite.

---

* With regard to the shortening of the root-vowel and contraction of concurrent vowels, see General Introduction, §§ 34, 36.

All verbs which take इ *i* or य *y* in the preterite indicative insert इ *i* or य *y* in the future, in the past participle, and in that form of the 3rd singular preterite which is the same as the past participle.

§ 88. The first verbal noun, or root, of these verbs sometimes ends in आब *áb* or आव *áw*, and sometimes in आ *á*, according to the following rule :—

1) All active (including causal) roots end in आब *áb* or आव *áw* : thus पाब *páb* or पाव *páw*, 'obtain ;' obl. पाबे *pábě* or पावे *páwě*.

Exception.—The √ खा *khá*, 'eat,' although active, ends in आ *á*.

2) All neuter roots end in आ *á* : thus अघा *aghá*, 'satiate ;' obl. अघाए *agháě*.

Exceptions.—The √ गाब *gáb*, 'sing,' and √ आब *áb*, 'come,' though neuter, end in आब *áb* or आव *áw*.

Verbs whose roots end in आब *áb* or आव *áw* may optionally insert a ब *b* or व *w* in the present conjunctive, but not those whose roots end in आ *á*.

Note also that all verbs whose roots end in आब *áb* or आव *áw* may drop the ब *b* or व *w* and be declined like simple verbs in आ *á*.

§ 89. √ पा *pá*, 'get.'

INFINITIVE (1ST FORM): पावि *páwi*, पाब *páb*, पाव *páw*, or पा *pá* ; obl. पाबे *pábé*, पावे *páwě*, or पाए *páě*.

(But from √ खा *khá* ; dir. खाइ *kháï* or खा *khá* ; obl. only खाए *kháě*.)

(2ND FORM): पायल॰ *páyala*, पाइल॰ *páïla*, or पैल॰ *paila* ; obl. पैला *pailá*. (See General Introduction, § 37.)

PRES. PART. पायत॰ *páy'ta*, पाइत॰ *páïta*, or पैत॰ *paita*.

INDICATIVE MOOD.

Person.	Preterite.		Future.	
	Singular.	Plural.	Singular.	Plural.
1st	पैलाँ *pailã́.**	पैलियै *paĭliai.*	पैबौँ *paibaũ.*†	पैबऽ *paiba.*‡
2nd	पैलेँ *pailẽ.*	पैलऽ *paila.*	पैबेँ *paibẽ.*†	पैबऽ *paiba.*†
3rd	पैल॰कऽ *paĭl'ka.*	पैल॰कात *paĭl'kát.*	पैतऽ *paita.*§	पैतात *paitát.*§

* Often written पय॰लाँ *pay'lã́* or पइ॰लाँ *païlã́*, and also, incorrectly, पाय॰लाँ *páy'lã́.*

† Often written पय॰बौँ *pay'baũ* or पइबौँ *païbaũ*, &c.

‡ Often written पाय॰बऽ *páy'ba* or पाइबऽ *páïba.*

§ Often written पाय॰तऽ *páy'ta*, पय॰तात *pay'tát*, and also, incorrectly, पाय॰तात *páy'tát.*

The definite present is पाय॰छी *páy'chhí*, 'I get.'

CONDITIONAL MOOD.

Person.	Present.		Preterite.	
	Singular.	Plural.	Singular.	Plural.
1st	पाबौँ or पाऔँ *pábaũ** or *páaũ.*	पाबिअ or पैअ *pábia* or *paia.*	पैताँ *paitã́.*†	पैतिऐ *paĭtiai.*
2nd	पाबेँ or पाएँ *pábẽ* or *páẽ.*	पाबऽ or पाअ *pába* or *páa.*	पैतिहैँ *paĭtihaĩ.*	पैतिअ *paĭtia.*
3rd	पाबै or पाऐ *pábai* or *páai.*	पाबथ or पाथ *pábath* or *páth.*	पैतै *paitai.*	पैतैन्ह *paitainh.*

* Or पावौँ *páwaũ*, and so throughout; but from खा *khá* and other roots ending in आ *á* the forms are only—

Sing.—(1) खाऔँ *kháaũ*, (2) खाएँ *kháẽ*, (3) खाऐ *kháai*;
Plur.—(1) खैअ *khaia*, (2) खाअ *kháa*, (3) खाथ *kháth*, and not खाबौँ *khábaũ*, &c.

† Often spelt पय॰ताँ *pay'tã́* or पइ॰ताँ *païtã́*, and incorrectly पाय॰ताँ *páy'tã́.*

90. Example of a verb whose root ends in ई í:—

√पी pí, 'drink.'

INFINITIVE (2ND) FORM: पीअलऽ *piala* or पीलऽ *píla*; obl. पीला *pílá*, 'to drink.'

PRES. PART. पीतऽ *píta*.

INDICATIVE MOOD.

Person.	PRETERITE.		FUTURE.	
	Singular.	Plural.	Singular.	Plural.
1st	पीलाँ *pílã́*.	पिलिऐ *piliai*.	पीबौँ *píbaũ*.	पीअबऽ *píaba* or पीबऽ *píba*.
2nd	पीलेँ *pílẽ*.	पीलऽ *píla*.	पीबेँ *píbẽ*.	पीबऽ *píba*.
3rd	पिलऽकै *pil'kai*.	पिलऽकात *pil'kát*.	पीतऽ *píta*.	पीतात *pítát*.

CONDITIONAL MOOD.

Person.	PRESENT.		PRETERITE.	
	Singular.	Plural.	Singular.	Plural.
1st	पीऔँ *píaũ*.	पिबिऐ *pibiai*.	पीताँ *pítã́*.	पितिऐ *pitiai*.
2nd	पीएँ *píẽ*.	पीअ *pía*.	पितिहैँ *pitihãĩ*.	पितिअ *pitia*.
3rd	पीऐ *píai*.	पीअथ *píath*.	पीतै *pítai*.	पीतैन्ह *pítainh*.

§ 91. **Example of a verb whose root ends in ऊ *ú* :—**

√ चू *chú*, 'drip.'

INFINITIVE (2ND FORM) : चूअलऽ *chúala* or चूलऽ *chúla*, 'to drip.'

PRES. PART. चूतऽ *chúta.*

INDICATIVE MOOD.

Person.	Preterite.		Future.	
	Singular.	Plural.	Singular.	Plural.
1st	चूलाँ *chúlā̃.*	चुलिऐ *chuliai.*	चूबौँ *chúbaũ.*	चूअबऽ *chúaba* or चूबऽ *chúba.*
2nd	चूलेँ *chúlẽ.*	चूलऽ *chúla.*	चूबेँ *chúbẽ.*	चूबऽ *chúba.*
3rd	चूलऽ *chúla.*	चूलात *chúlát.*	चूतै *chútai.*	चूतात *chútát.*

CONDITIONAL MOOD.

Person.	Present.		Preterite.	
	Singular.	Plural.	Singular.	Plural.
1st	चूऔँ *chúaũ.*	चूइऐ *chúiai.*	चूताँ *chútā̃.*	चुतिऐ *chutiai.*
2nd	चूएँ *chúẽ.*	चूअ *chúa.*	चुतिहेँ *chutihẽ.*	चुतिअ *chutia.*
3rd	चूऐ *chúai.*	चूअथ *chúath.*	चूतै *chútai.*	चूतैन्ह *chútainh.*

§ 92. Example of a verb whose root ends in ओ *o*:—

√ रो *ro*, 'weep.'

INFINITIVE (2ND FORM): रोअबऽ *roala* or रोबऽ *rola*, 'to weep.'
PRES. PART. रोतऽ *rota*.

INDICATIVE MOOD.

Person.	PRETERITE.		FUTURE.	
	Singular.	Plural.	Singular.	Plural.
1st	रोलाँ *rolā́*.*	रोलिऐ *rŏliai*.	रोबौं *robaũ*.	रोअबऽ *roäba* or रोबऽ *roba*.
2nd	रोलैं *rolẽ*.	रोलऽ *rola*.	रोबैं *robẽ*.	रोबऽ *roba*.
3rd	रोलऽ *rola*.	रोलात *rolát*.	रोतऽ *rota*.	रोतात *rotát*.

* Or रोअलाँ *roalā́* and so throughout.

3rd singular present रोऐ छै *roai chhai* or रोय्छै *roy'chhai*.

CONDITIONAL MOOD.

Person.	PRESENT.		PRETERITE.	
	Singular.	Plural.	Singular.	Plural.
1st	रोऔं *roaũ*.	रोइऐ *roiai*.	रोताँ *rotā́*.	रोतिऐ *rŏtiai*.
2nd	रोएँ *roẽ*.	रोअ *roa*.	रोतिहैं *rŏtihā̃*.	रोतिअ *rŏtia*.
3rd	रोऐ *roai*.	रोअथ *roath*.	रोतै *rotai*.	रोतैन्ह *rotainh*.

For further examples of verbs of this class, see conjugation of √हो *ho*, § 53 & ff. This root √रो *ro* is not much used in South Bhagalpúr, the √कान *kán* being preferred. It is, however, given as an example for the sake of uniformity with the other grammars of this series

CHAPTER IX.

IRREGULAR VERBS,

§ 93. The verbs √ जा *já*, 'go,' and √ हो *ho*, 'become,' are irregular in their preterite tense indicative. The conjugation of √ जा *já* is therefore given in that tense only. The conjugation of √ हो *ho* has been already given in § 53 and ff., and is not given here. The √ मर *mar*, 'die,' √ कर *kar*, 'do,' and √ धर *dhar*, 'seize' or 'place,' which are irregular in most Bihárí dialects, are regular in South Bhagalpúr.

The verbs √ दे *de*, 'give,' and √ ले *le*, 'take,' are more or less irregular throughout all the tenses. The verb √ दे *de* is therefore given conjugated throughout the four radical and participial tenses. The verb √ ले *le* is conjugated precisely like the verb √ दे *de*.

§ 94. The √ कर *kar*, 'do,' and √ धर *dhar*, 'seize' or 'place,' are conjugated regularly. It will be noticed that as we approach Ban·gál these verbs become regular, while in Western Bihár (see the earlier parts of this series of grammars) they are irregular. So also they are regular in standard Ban·gálí: thus, करिलाम *karilám*, 'I did.' In some of the Ban·gálí dialects, however, they follow the usage of Western Bihár, in being irregular, *e.g.*, Ran·g'púr कैल्लाम *kaĭllám*, 'I did,' धैल्लाम *dhaĭllám*, 'I seized.' So also Ran·gpúri मैल्लाम *maĭllám*, 'I died.'

§ 95. The √ मर *mar*, 'die,' is declined regularly.

§ 96. √ जा *já*, 'go.'

This root is conjugated like √ खा *khá* in all tenses but the preterite indicative, which is therefore here given. (See § 87 and ff.) With it is given the same tense of √ आब *áb*, 'come,' for the sake of comparison. The conjugation of √ आब *áb* is quite regular, following √ पाब *páb*, 'obtain,' except that the 3rd sing. pret. ind. is आयल० *áyala* or ऐल० *aila*, and the 3rd plur. of the same tense ऐलात *ailát*, it being a neuter and not a transitive verb.

VERBAL NOUN (2ND FORM): आयल० *áyala* or ऐल० *aila*.	जायल० *jáyala*, जैल० *jaila*, or गेल० *gela*.
PRES. PART. ऐत० *aita*.	जैत० *jaita*.
PAST PART. आयल० *áyala* or ऐल० *aila*.	गेल० *gela*.

Person.	√ आब *áb*, PRETERITE INDICATIVE.		√ जा *já*, PRETERITE INDICATIVE.	
	Singular.	Plural.	Singular.	Plural.
1st	ऐलाँ *ailā̃*.	ऐलिऐ *ăliai*.	गेलाँ *gelā̃*.	गेलिऐ *gĕliai*.
2nd	ऐलैं *ailẽ*.	ऐल० *aila*.	गेलैं *gelẽ*.	गेल० *gela*.
3rd	आयल० *áyala* or ऐल० *aila*.	ऐलात *ailát*.	गेल० *gela*.	गेलात *gelát*.

§ 97. √ दे *de*, 'give.'

VERBAL NOUN { 1st FORM: द० *da*, दे *de*, or दै *dai*; obl. देव० *dewa*.
2ND FORM: देल० *dela*, 'to give.' }

PRES. PART. देत० *deta*.

PAST PART. देल० *dela*.

INDICATIVE MOOD.

Person.	PRETERITE.		FUTURE.	
	Singular.	Plural.	Singular.	Plural.
1st	देलाँ *delā̃*.	देलिऐ *dĕliai*	देबौँ *debaũ*.	देब० *deba*.
2nd	देलैं *delẽ*.	देल० *dela*.	देबैं *debẽ*.	देब० *deba*.
3rd	देलन्कै *dĕl'kai*.	देलन्कात *dĕl'kát*.	देत० *deta*.	देतात *detát*.

CONDITIONAL MOOD.

Person.	PRESENT.		PRETERITE.	
	Singular.	Plural.	Singular.	Plural.
1st	दौँ, दीहौँ, *daũ*, *díhaũ*, or दीऔँ *díaũ*.	दीऐ *díai*.	देताँ *detá̃*.	देतिऐ *dĕtiai*.
2nd	दे, दैँ, दै, दैँ, *de*, *dẽ*, *dai*, *daĩ*, or देहीँ *dehĩ*.	दअ *da*, दिअ *dia*, दहो *daho*, or देहो *deho*.	देतिहैँ *dĕtihaĩ*.	देतिअ *dĕtia*.
3rd	दै *dai*, दीऐ *díai*.	दैन्ह *dainh*.	देतै *detai*.	देतैन्ह *detainh*.

PRECATIVE: दीहअ *díha*.

Similarly is conjugated the √ ले *le*, 'take,' the letter लअ *la* being substituted for the letter द *da* throughout.

CHAPTER X.

THE PASSIVE VERB.

§ 98. The passive verb is formed by conjugating the verbal noun ending in अलऽ *ala* with the verb √ जा *já*, 'go:' thus देख॰लऽ जैलऽ *dĕkh'la jaila*, 'to be seen.' This verbal noun is not altered for gender, number, person, or tense, only the verb जैलऽ *jaila* being conjugated. Thus—

Indicative Preterite Masculine: *'I was seen,' &c.*

Person.	Singular.	Plural.
1st	देख॰लऽ गेलाँ *dĕkh'la gelá̃.*	देख॰लऽ गेलिऐ *dĕkh'la gĕliai.*
2nd	देख॰लऽ गेलेँ *dĕkh'la gelẽ.*	देख॰लऽ गेलऽ *dĕkh'la gela.*
3rd	देख॰लऽ गेलै *dĕkh'la gelai.*	देख॰लऽ गेलात *dĕkh'la gelát.*

§ 99. This verbal noun in अलऽ *ala* must be carefully distinguished from the past participle having the same termination. The former even in irregular verbs is sometimes quite regular, so that we have verbal nouns such as जैलऽ *jaila* beside past participles like गेलऽ *gela*. At the same time it must be remembered that the verbal noun can also take the form of the past participle as well as its proper form: so that we may have गेलऽ *gela* as a verbal noun as well as जैलऽ *jaila*. An example of an irregular passive verb is जैलऽ जै छै *jaila jai chhai* (impersonal), 'it is gone'—*tium est;* but, used in the sense of the potential, 'it can go.' When neuter verbs are used in the passive voice, they are always used in an impersonal potential sense: thus, हमरा सैँ चल॰लऽ नहिँ जै छै *ham'rá sãi chal'la nahĩ jai chhai*, 'by me it cannot be gone,' *i.e.* 'I cannot go.'

§ 100. Another common form of the passive is made by adding to the direct form of the first variety of the verbal noun the verb पर॰लऽ *par'la*, 'to fall;' the whole then forms an intensive compound. (See § 114.)

An example of this form is—

> कुछु कुछु जानि परै छै *kuchhu kuchhu jáni parai chhai*, 'a little is evident.'

§ 101. The Potential Passive Voice.

This voice is formed in the same manner as the causal verb (see § 103). It has a potential force, intimating not so much that a thing *is* done, as that it *can be* done. An example of its use is—

> ई तो कोय एक तरह केरऽ अद्‌मी देखाय दै छै *í to koy ĕk tarah kera ad'mí dĕkháy dai chhai*, 'this (fellow) appears (*lit.* is seen) to be a man of strange habit.'

§ 102. The Periphrastic Passive Voice.

A very common kind of passive voice is formed by placing the verb √आब *áb* after the first or shortest form of a verbal noun in the locative case: thus देखे मँ ऐलऽ *dekhĕ mẽ aila*, 'the coming into seeing,' *i.e.* 'to be seen.' The person by whom the action is done is put in the oblique genitive form of the noun or pronoun when there is one: thus तोरा सभै हम्‌रा देखे मँ ऐलऽ *torá sabhai ham'rá dekhĕ mẽ aila*, 'you came into my seeing,' 'you were seen by me.' The following example shows a verb in this voice conjugated in the preterite indicative masculine :—

Singular.	Plural.
1. देखे मँ ऐलाँ *dekhĕ mẽ ailā̃*.	1. देखे मँ ऐलिऐ *dekhĕ mẽ aĭliaí*.
2. देखे मँ ऐलैँ *dekhĕ mẽ ailẽ*.	2. देखे मँ ऐलऽ *dekhĕ mẽ aila*.
3. देखे मँ ऐलऽ *dekhĕ mẽ aila*.	3. देखे मँ ऐलात *dekhĕ mẽ ailát*.

EXAMPLE.—हम्‌रा आर्‌हिन तोह्‌रा देखै मँ ऐ छिऐ *ham'rá ár'hin tŏh'rá dekhaĭ mẽ ai chhiai*, 'we are seen by you.'

CHAPTER XI.

CAUSAL VERBS.

§ 103. A causal verb is formed by adding आ *á* to the root of the simple verb, and a double causal by adding वा *wá* or बा *bá*. The stems thus formed are conjugated exactly like verbs whose roots end in आ *á* (see § 87)—that is, like the √ पा *pá*, taking आब *áb* or आव *áw* in the first verbal noun, the present conjunctive, and present participle. (See § 88.)

Simple Verb.	Causal.	Double Causal.
√ उठ *uṭh*, 'rise.'	उठा *uṭhá*, 'raise.'	उठ॰वा *uṭh'wá*, 'cause [to raise.'
√ कह *kah*, 'say.'	कहा *kahá*, 'cause [to speak.'	कह॰वा *kah'wá*, 'cause [to cause to speak.'
√ नुक *nuk*, 'be hidden.'	नुका *nuká*, 'hide.'	नुक॰वा *nuk'wá*, 'cause [to hide.'
√ पक *pak*, 'be cooked.'	पका *paká*, 'cook.'	पक॰वा *pak'wá*, 'cause [to cook.'
√ मिल *mil*, 'meet.'	मिला *milá*, 'mix.'	मिल॰वा *mil'wá*, ['cause to mix.'
√ सुन *sun*, 'hear.'	सुना *suná*, 'tell.'	सुन॰वा *sun'wá*, 'cause [to tell.'

§ 104. If the simple root contains a long vowel it is shortened, viz. आ *á* to अ *a*, ई *í* to इ *i*, ऊ *ú* to उ *u*, ए *e* to ऎ *ĕ*, ओ *o* to ऒ *ŏ*, ऐ *ai* to ऐ *ăi*, and औ *au* to औ *ău*.

Similarly, if a root ends in a double consonant, it is made single: thus—

Simple Verb.	Causal.	Double Causal.
जाग *jág*, 'be awake.'	जगा *jagá*, 'awaken.'	जगवा *jag'wá*, 'cause to awake.'
पाक *pák*, 'be cooked.'	पका *paká*, 'cook.'	पकवा *pak'wá*, 'cause to cook.'
जीत *jít*, 'conquer.'	जिता *jitá*, 'cause to conquer.'	जितवा *jit'wá*, 'cause to cause to conquer.'
सीख *síkh*, 'learn.'	सिखा *sikhá*, 'teach.'	सिखवा *sikh'wá*, 'cause to teach.'
पी *pí*, 'drink.'	पिआ *piá*, 'cause to drink.'	पिअवा *piawá*, 'cause to cause to drink.'
भीज *bhíj*, 'wet.'	भिजा *bhijá*, 'moisten.'	भिजवा *bhij'wá*, 'cause to moisten.'
घूर *ghúr*, 'be turned.'	घुरा *ghurá*, 'turn.'	घुरवा *ghur'wá*, 'cause to turn.'
बूड़ *búṛ*, 'sink.'	बुड़ा *buṛá*, 'immerse.'	बुड़वा *buṛ'wá*, 'cause to immerse.'
सूत *sút*, 'sleep.'	सुता *sutá*, 'put to sleep.'	सुतवा *sut'wá*, 'cause to put to sleep.'
देख *dekh*, 'see.'	देखा *dĕkhá*, 'show.'	देखवा *dĕkh'wá*, 'cause to show.'
बैस *bais*, 'sit.'	बैसा *baĭsá*, 'seat.'	बैसवा *baĭs'wá*, 'cause to sit.'
दौड़ *dauṛ*, 'run.'	दौड़ा *daŭṛá*, 'to be run.'	दौड़वा *daŭṛ'wá*, 'cause to cause to run.'
नुक्क *nukk*, 'be hidden.'	नुका *nuká*, 'hide.'	नुकवा *nuk'wá*, 'cause to hide.'

Note in connection with the above :—

Simple Verb.	Causal.
√ कह *kah*, 'speak'	कहला *kah'lá*, also regular.
√ खा *khá*, 'eat'	खवा *khawá*.
√ पी *pí*, 'drink'	पिला *pilá*, also regular.

§ 105. Some primitive neuter verbs, having a monosyllabic root enclosing a short vowel, form the first causal by simply lengthening that vowel. The double causal is formed in the usual way, *e.g.*—

Simple Verb.	Causal.
√ कट *kat*, 'be cut'	काट *kát*, 'cut.'
√ बंध *bandh*, 'be tied'	बाँध* *bãdh* or बान्ह *bánh*, 'tie.'
√ लद *lad*, 'be loaded'	लाद *lád*, 'load.'
√ खिंच *khiñch*, 'be dragged'	खींच* *khích*, 'drag.'

§ 106. Sometimes a cognate diphthong is substituted for the long vowel, *e.g.*—

खुल *khul*, 'be open.'	खोल *khol*, 'open.'
घुर *ghur*, 'melt.' (*Neut.*)	घोर *ghor*, 'melt.' (*Act.*)

§ 107. The verb √ निकल *nikal* or निकस *nikas*, 'come out,' makes its causal निकाल *nikál* or निकास *nikás*, 'take out,' on the analogy of the above. So also √ पसर *pasar*, 'be scattered,' makes पसार *pasár*, 'scatter,' 'extend;' √ससर *sasar*, 'slip,' ससार *sasár*, 'cause to slip;' √ उपर *upar*, 'be rooted up,' उपार *upár*, 'root up;' and √ उखर *ukhar*, 'be rooted up,' उखार *ukhár*, 'root up.'

* When the vowel is lengthened, *anuswár* becomes *a unásik*. (Compare General Introduction, § 28.)

§ 108. The following are irregular :—

Simple Verb.	Causal.	Double Causal.
✓ अट *aṭ*, 'be stopped.'	आर *ár*, 'stop.'	अरा *ará*.
✓ फट *phaṭ* or फाट *pháṭ*, ['be torn.'	फार *phár*, 'tear.'	फरा *phará*.
✓ छूट *chhúṭ*, 'be separated.'	छोर *chhor* or छार *chhár*, ['separate.'	छोरा *chhŏrá*.
✓ जूट *júṭ*, 'be joined.'	जोर *jor*, 'join.'	जोरा *jŏrá*.
✓ टूट *ṭúṭ*, 'be broken.'	तोर *tor*, 'break.'	तोरा *tŏrá*.
✓ फूट *phúṭ*, 'be burst.'	फोर *phor*, 'burst.'	फोरा *phŏrá*.
✓ बिक्क *bikk*, 'be sold.'	बेच *bech* or बिका *biká*, ['sell.'	बेचा *běchá*.
✓ रह *rah*, 'remain.'	राख *rákh* or रक्ख *rakkh*, ['place.'	रखा *rakhá*.
✓ मर *mar*, 'die.'	मार *már* or मुआ *muá*, 'cause to die,' 'kill.'	मरवा *mar'wá*, ['cause to kill.'

CHAPTER XII.

COMPOUND VERBS.

§ 109. Compound verbs are either intensives, potentials, completives, frequentatives, desideratives, continuatives, staticals, inceptives, permissives, or acquisitives.

§ 110. Compound verbs may be classed as—(1) those formed with the verbal noun and (2) those formed with the participles.

(1) Those formed with the verbal noun are—

a) Intensives.
b) Potentials.
c) Completives.
d) Frequentatives.
e) Desideratives.
f) Inceptives.
g) Permissives.
h) Acquisitives.

(2) Those formed with the participles—

a) Continuatives.
b) Staticals.

Class I.—Compounds formed with the Verbal Noun.*

§ 111. There are three varieties of the verbal noun—

a) In अ *a* (silent) or इ *i*, oblique form ए *ĕ* or ऐ *aĭ*; as देख *dekh* or देखि *dekhi*, obl. देखे *dekhĕ* or देखै *dekhaĭ*.

b) In ॰लऽ *'la*, oblique form ॰ला *'lá*; as देख॰लऽ *dĕkh'la*, obl. देख॰ला *dĕkh'lá*.

c) In ॰बऽ *'ba*, oblique form wanting; as देखब *dekhab*.

The direct first form in अ *a* (silent) is always the same as the root.

* Much of the succeeding matter is based on Kellogg's Hindí Grammar.

Compound verbs are either formed with the direct form of the first or second variety of the verbal noun, or with the oblique form of the first variety.

§ 112. *Intensives* are formed with the direct form of the first variety; *Frequentatives* are always, and *Desideratives* are sometimes, formed with the direct form of the second variety; *Potentials, Completives,* and *Desideratives,* and *Inceptives, Permissives,* and *Acquisitives,* are always, formed with the oblique form of the first variety.

§ 113. *Intensive* compounds intensify or otherwise modify the meaning of the verb whose root stands first in the compound. They are formed by adding to a verbal noun of the first variety in the direct form one of certain other verbs, which latter verb in conjunction with the verbal noun is then conjugated as usual. This second conjugated member does not, however, retain its separate character and significance, but only modifies, in accordance with the general idea which it embodies, the meaning of the unconjugated verbal noun to which it is annexed. Examples are—

√फैँक *phẽk*, 'throw.'	फैँक (or फैँकि) देल० *phẽk* (or *phẽki*) *dela*, 'to throw away.'
√तोर *tor*, 'break.'	तोर (or तोरि) डाल॰ल० *tor* (or *tori*) *ḍál̤'la*, 'to break in pieces.'
√बन *ban*, 'be made.'	बन (or बनि) ऐल० (or जैल०) *ban* (or *bani*) *aila* (or *jaila*), 'to be completed.'
√खा *khá*, 'eat.'	खा (or खाइ) जैंल० *khá* (or *kháï*) *jaila* 'to eat up.'
√बोल *bol*, 'speak.'	बोलि उठ॰ल० *boli uṭh'la*, 'to speak suddenly.'
√काट *káṭ*, 'cut.'	काटि लेल० *káṭi lela*, 'to cut for oneself.'
√राख *rákh*, 'place.'	राखि लेल० *rákhi lela*, 'to lay by.'

§ 114. The auxiliary verbs usually employed to form intensives are—

√दे *de*,	'give,'	implying	*intensity.*
√डाल *ḍál*,	'throw,'	"	*violence.*
√आब *áb*,	'come,'	"	*completion.*
√जा *já*,	'go,'	"	*completion.*
√पर *par*,	'fall,'	"	*chance.*
√उठ *uṭh*,	'rise,'	"	*suddenness.*
√ले *le*,	'take,'	"	*reflexiveness.*

परब *parab* is also used in intensive compounds to form passives of transitive verbs. (See § 100.)

§ 115. *Potentials* are formed by adding to the oblique form of the first verbal noun of any verb the verb सकब *sakab*, 'to be able,' which may then be conjugated throughout. Examples are—

बोले सकऽबऽ *bolĕ sak'ba*, 'to be able to speak.'

हौ दौड़े सकै छै *hau dauṛi sakai chhai*, 'he can run.'

हमें जाए सकऽबऽ *hamẽ jáĕ sak'ba*, 'I shall be able to go.'

जौं हौ सब आए सकै *jaũ hau sab áĕ sakai* 'if they are able to come.'

हमें नहीं जाए सकै छी *hamẽ nahĩ jáĕ sakai chhí*, 'I cannot go.'

§ 116. *Completives* are formed by adding to the same form of the verbal noun of a verb the verb चुकऽबऽ *chuk'ba*, 'to be finished,' which may then be conjugated throughout. This compound denotes the *completion* of the act denoted by the primary member of the compound. Examples are—

ऊ खाए चुकऽलऽ *ú kháĕ chuk'la*, 'he has done eating.'

जबे हौ खाए चुकऽतऽ *jabĕ hau kháĕ chuk'ta*, 'when he shall have eaten.'

ऊ तऽ जाए चुकऽलऽ छै *ú ta jáĕ chuk'la chhai*, 'he is indeed already gone.'

§ 117. *Frequentatives* are formed by affixing to the direct form of the second variety of the verbal noun of any verb the verb करऽबऽ *kar'ba*, 'to do,' which may then be used in any tense. Examples are—

> ऐलऽ करऽ *aila kara*, 'come often,' *lit.* 'do the act of coming.'
>
> हमेँ सास्त्र कै पढ़ऽलऽ करै छी *hamẽ sást'r kai paṛh'la karai chhí*, 'I am in the habit of reading the shástras.'
>
> तोरा सन्ही हमऽरऽ सब बात मानऽलऽ करऽ *torá sanhí ham'ra sab bát mán'la kara*, 'always obey my words.'
>
> तोँ सभै कहिने एना करऽलऽ करै छऽ *tõ sabhai kahine ená kar'la karai chha*, 'why do you always do so?'
>
> ऊ जैलऽ करै छै *ú jaila karai chhai*, 'he often goes.'

§ 118. *Desideratives* are formed sometimes like frequentatives, with the direct form of the verbal noun in ऽलऽ *'la*, substituting the verb चाहऽबऽ *cháh'ba*, 'to wish,' for करऽबऽ *kar'ba* as the second or conjugated member. They denote primarily *desire* to do the action expressed of the principal member; secondarily, the *immediate futurity* of that action. An example is—

> ऊ बोलऽलऽ चहऽछै *ú bŏl'la chah'chhai*, 'he wishes to speak.'
>
> घड़ी बजऽलऽ चहऽछै *gharí baj'la chah'chhai*, 'the clock is on the point of striking.'

Desiderative compounds with the verbal noun in लऽ *la* are rare. More often the principal verb is put in the oblique form of the first variety of the verbal noun with or without the dative postposition लै *lai*. Examples are—

> ऊ बोलेँ लै (or बोलेँ) चाहै छै *ú bolĕ lai* (or *bolĕ*) *cháhai chhai*, 'he wishes to speak.'

घड़ी बाजै (or बाजै लै) चाहै छलठ *ghaṛí bájaĭ* (or *bájaĭ lai*) *cháhai chhala*, 'the clock was about to strike.'

ऊ जाए चाहै छै *ú jáĕ cháhai chhai*, 'he wishes to go.'

ऊ मरै (or मरै लै) चाहै छै *ú maraĭ* (or *maraĭ lai*) *cháhai chhai*, 'he is at the point of death.'

The desiderative compound in the precative form is idiomatically used to express obligation or duty. Examples are—

ई पोथिया कै पढ़ऽलठ चहिअ *í pŏthiyá kai paṛh'la chahia*, '(one) ought to read this book' (*lit.* 'be good enough to wish to read').

हुँआँ जाए लै चहिअ *hŭă jáĕ lai chahia*, 'it is right for you (*i.e.* you ought) to go there.'

§ 119. *Inceptives* are formed by using the inflected form of the first variety of the verbal noun in construction with the verb लागऽबठ *lág'ba*, 'to be joined,' 'to begin,' and denote the action of the verbal noun as *beginning*. Examples are—

ऊ कहै लगऽलै *ú kahaĭ lag'lai*, 'he began to say.'

हौ मारे लगऽलठ *hau márĕ lag'la*, 'he began to beat.'

बाघ खाए लगऽलठ *bágh kháĕ lag'la*, 'the tiger began to eat.'

§ 120. *Permissives* are formed by combining the same form of the verbal noun with the verb देबठ *deba*, 'to give,' and express *permission* to do the act denoted by the verbal noun. Examples are—

हमऽरा जाए दे *ham'rá jáĕ de*, 'let me go.'

हमऽरा बोलै दे *ham'rá bolaĭ de*, 'be good enough to let me speak.'

वँ ओकऽरा खाए देलऽकै *wăĭ ŏk'rá kháĕ dĕl'kai*, 'he allowed him to eat.'

§ 121. *Acquisitives* are the exact converse of the preceding, and are formed in the same way, substituting पाएल *páĕl*, 'to get,' for देल *del*. Examples are—

तोहेँ हुँआँ नहीँ जाए पैभेँ *tohĕ hŭă nahí jáĕ paĭbhĕ*, 'you will not obtain permission to go there.'

हम्मै बैसै नहीँ पैलाँ *hammai baisaĭ nahí pailă*, 'I was not allowed to sit.'

Class II.—Compounds formed from the Participles.

§ 122. *Continuatives* are formed by combining the oblique form of the past participle of any verb with the verb जैब॰ *jaiba*, 'to go,' or the oblique form of the present participle with the verb रह॰ब॰ *rah'ba*, 'to remain.' It must be remembered that in the case of neuter verbs the oblique form of the past participle is the same as the direct: thus, गिर॰ल॰ *gir'la*, obl. गिर॰ल॰ *gir'la*; while in the case of active verbs it is formed by adding ए *ĕ*: thus, देख॰ल॰ *dekh'la*, obl. देख॰ले *dĕkh'lĕ*, often pronounced देख॰ने *dĕkh'nĕ*. The present participle always has its oblique form in ॰ते *'tĕ* or ॰तै *'taĭ*, both in active and neuter verbs: thus, देख॰त॰ *dĕkh'ta*, obl. देख॰ते *dĕkh'tĕ* or देख॰तै *dĕkh'taĭ*; गिर॰त॰ *gir'ta*, obl. गिर॰ते *gir'tĕ* or गिर॰तै *gir'ta*.

The compound with जैब॰ *jaiba* expresses *steady progression*, and with रह॰ब॰ *rah'ba* the *continuance* of a complete action. Examples—

ऊ लिख॰ले जै छै *ú likh'lĕ jai chhai*, 'he is going on writing.'

ऊ लड़िकी सभै पढ़॰ने जै छलै *ú laṛiki sabhai paṛh'nĕ jai chhalai*, 'those girls were going on reading.'

पानी बह॰ल॰ जै छै *páni bah'la jai chhai*, 'the water keeps flowing away.'

ऊ गैते रह॰छै *ú gaitĕ rah'chhai*, 'she continues singing.'

नदी केर॰ धार बह॰ते रहै छै *nadi kera dhár bah'tĕ rahai chhai*, 'the stream of the river keeps flowing on.'

तों सभै कहिने हस॰ते रहै छ॰ *tõ sabhai kahine has'tĕ rahai chha*, 'why do you keep laughing?'

Closely connected with the above is a common combination in which the past participle in its direct form, and changing in gender according to the subject, takes the first place and a verb of motion the second place. Examples are—

एक बाघ घुर॰ल॰ फिरै छलै *ĕk bágh ghur'la phirai chhalai*, 'a tiger was prowling about.'

नौंड़ी चल॰ली जै छली *nãüṛí chal'li jai chhalí*, 'the girl was going along.'

§ 123. ***Staticals*** denote motion in a state of doing anything. They are formed by combining a verb of motion with a past participle in its direct form. Examples are—

ऊ कनऽलऽ होलऽ आबै छै *ú kan'la hola ábai chhai* 'he comes weeping.'

एक जनाना गैली आबै छली *ek janáná gailí ábai chhalí*, 'a woman was coming singing.'

DIVISION III.

INDECLINABLES

§ 124. See General Introduction.

APPENDIX.

THE following conversation and fables are in the dialect of the southern portion of South Bhagal'púr. A translation will be found in the General Introduction. It should be remembered that the dialect of this locality differs slightly from that of the country round the town of Bhagal'púr. See §§ 3, 52, &c.

A.—CONVERSATION BETWEEN TWO VILLAGERS.

१ प्रश्न. कह०, भाय, कहाँ सैँ आवै छ०।

उत्तर. आस॰पासे केर० गाँव० सैँ आवै छिअ ॥

२ प्र. ऊँआँ सैँ कहिया चल॰ल० छेला।

उ. भोरे केर० चल॰ल० छिअ ॥

३ प्र कथी ले ऊँआँ गेल० छेला।

उ. ऊँआँ हम॰र० खेत छै, ओक॰रा देखै ले गेल० छेलिऐ ॥

४ प्र. ओक॰रा मेँ की बुन॰ने छ०।

उ. खाली राहार बुन॰ने छिऐ।

५ प्र. कह०, भाय, अब॰रिक चास० केर० सूरत की छै।

उ. हे। चास० केर० हाल की पूछै छ०। पानि बर॰सै बिनु बऊत हर॰ज होलै।

६ प्र. आज काल अप॰ने केर० भाय नहीँ देखि पड़ै छत।

उ. हम॰र० भाय आज काल किला मेँ नौकर छत। घर जल॰दी नहीँ आवै छथ ॥

७ प्र. अप॰ने केर० बड़॰की गाय केर० की हाल छै।

उ. ऊ आज काल गाभिन छै। मगर अधार नहीँ मिल॰ला सैँ टूटि गेली छै ॥

८ प्र कै महीना सैँ गाभिन छै।

उ. होलै त० आठ महीना। पर पेट ओक॰र० कुछु उंच० नहीँ देखाय दै छै ॥

९ प्र. कोराम छै कि अखनि नहीँ।

उ. हँ, कुछु कुछु जानि पड़ै छै ॥

१० प्र. हे कै बियान छिकै, आरो केत्ते दूध करै छै।

उ. ई अठ्वाँ बियान छिकै, दू अँढ़ाइ सेर दूध एक॰ साँझ॰ मेँ करै छै॥

११ प्र. हम्रा एक बक्री लेना * छै। अपन्ना केर॰ गाँव॰ मेँ मिलन्तै।

उ. हम्रा गाँव॰ मेँ बक्री आवै छै। मगर मोल बहुत करै छै॥

१२ प्र. अपन्ने केरी बक्री की होलौन।

उ. हमेँ चरै लै ओक्रा गाँव॰ हौँ पर छोड़्ने रहै छिऐ॥

१३ प्र. कुछु दूध करै छै।

उ. चिल्का सभैक पौए भरि होय जायछै॥

१४ प्र. केतारी रोप्ले छ॰ कि नहीँ।

उ. केतारी तो रोप्ने छिऐ। मगर ओक्रा मेँ कुछु गुन नहीँ छै॥

१५ प्र. अपन्ने केर॰ हिँयाँ बरद्हा मोट मँगन्नी मिलै सकै छै।

उ. कहिने नहीँ। छिंट्ल॰ हो जैला सेँ लै लीह॰॥

१६ प्र. अपन्ने केर॰ हिँयाँ कै मोट चलै छै।

उ. तीन मोट तो लध्ले † छिऐ॥

१७ प्र. अपन्ने के आम॰ केर॰ बगीचा कुछु फरै छै, कि नहीँ।

उ. ई दफे तो बद्री सेँ गाछ॰ सभै मेँ लाही लागि गेलै। नहीँ तो बड्डी होयछेलै॥

१८ प्र. थोड़ आम हम्रो ‡ अचार॰ लै दीह॰।

उ. जबे अपन्ने केर॰ मन चाहै, आवि कै तोड़्वाय लीह॰॥

१९ प्र. अपन्ने केर॰ लर्का कुछु पढ़ै छै कि नहीँ।

उ. हाँ। गुरू के हिँयाँ जायछै। अच्छर तो चिन्हि गेल॰ छै। आज काल थोड़ा पढ़ै छै॥

२० प्र. इस्कूल॰ मेँ कहिने नहीँ जाय दै छ॰।

उ. कुछु सिखि ले, तबे भेजि देबै॥

---

* See General Introduction, § 47.

† Perf. from √लाध.

‡ Emphatic for हम्रा, 'to me also.'

२१ प्र. हम्हूँ* अप॰ना लर॰का कैँ इस्कूल॰ मैँ भेजो लै चाहै छिऐ।

उ. अच्छा, हम॰रा लर॰का केर॰ साथे ओक॰रो† भेजि दीहो॥

B.—FABLES.

पहिल॰ कथा।

एक मुरगा गोब॰र॰ केर॰ ढेर॰ कैँ गोड़॰ सैँ उटकि रह॰ल॰ छेलै। संजोग॰ ओक॰रा मैँ सैँ बड़॰ छेन॰ मोँती निकलि ऐलै। मुरगा बोल॰लै, वाह, केहन॰ रङ्ग रूप आरो चमक दमक छै। जौहरी एक॰रा पैतिऐ, तँ बड़ी खुसी होतिऐ। पर हम॰र॰ पेट॰ केर आगिन एक॰रा सैँ नहीँ बुझैतै। हाय, एको चाउर॰ केर॰ दाना हम॰रा हाथ॰ ऐतिऐ, तो से मोँती सैँ बढ़ि के होतिऐ। ई बात सच्चे छै।

जे चीज अप॰ना काम॰ मैँ नहीँ आवे, ऊ चीज जरि जाय।

दोस॰र॰ कथा।

गरीब॰ केर॰ पुछ॰ब॰, आरो गोसाँय केर॰ जवाब देब॰।

एक गरीब कोय पूरा गोसाँय सैँ पुछ॰लकै, कि हमँ तो भूखे मरै छी, आरो हम॰र॰ परोसी गद्दी तकिया पर रात दिन सुख चैन करै छै। ओक॰रा मैँ केहन॰ गुन छै, जे भग॰वान ओक॰रा नेहाल कर॰लकै, आरो हम॰रा गरीब कर॰लकै। ई सुनि के, गोसाँय जवाब देलकै, बाबा, तोँहँ ई नहीँ सुनने छ॰।

राम झरोखा पर बैठि के सभे केर॰ हाज॰री लै छै।
जैहिन॰ जेक॰र॰ कमाय, तैहिन॰ तेक॰रा दै छै॥

तेस॰र॰ कथा।

देस बिदेस फिरै केर॰ गुन।

कोय भला आद॰मी एक गोसाँय सैँ कह॰लकै, महाराज, देस देस आरो गाँव गाँव बुल॰ला सैँ की गुन छै। एक॰ ठियाँ रहि कै पर॰मेसर॰ मैँ लौ कहिने नहीँ लगावै छ॰,

---

* Emphatic for हमँ, 'I also.'

† Emphatic for ओक॰रा, 'him also.'

आरो कोय मण्ड॰ मैँ बैठि के परन्मेसर॰ केर॰ गुन कहिने नहीँ गावै छ॰। जोगी जी कहलन्कै कि, बाबा, ई सभै सचे छै। पर तोँ ई कहानी नहीँ सुनन्ने छ॰।

बहन्ल॰ पानि साफ होयन्छै, आरो बान्हन्ल॰ पानि गँधायन्छै। साधु जन कै बुलन्ला सैँ अच्छा। कलङ्क नहीँ लगावे कोय।

चौठ॰ कथा।

एक दिन जाड़ा केर॰ दिन॰ मैँ कोय बड़ा अदन्मी केर॰ घर॰ मैँ आगिन लागि गेलै। सभै चीज बिखै जरि कै खाख होय गेलै। ऊ बाहर॰ मैँ खड़ा होय कै पछन्ताय रहिछ॰ छेलै। कि एक गरीब परोसी जाड़ा केर॰ मारन्ल॰, थर थर काँपन्ल॰, घर॰ सैँ निकलि ऐलै, आरो आगिन तापे लगन्लै। तबे ऊ धनन्बान बोलन्लै, वाह, वाह।

केकन्हो घर जरै, कोय तापै।

पचन्म॰ कथा।

बान्हन्ल॰ लकन्ड़ी सभै आरो खुलन्ल॰ लकन्ड़ी सभै।

एक गिरन्हस्त॰ केर॰ लड़िका सभै अपन्ना मैँ बड़ी लड़ाइ झगन्ड़ा करै छेलै। बात॰ सैँ बड़ी समुझैलन्कै, पर कोय कुछु नहीँ मनलन्कै। तबे गिरन्हस्त अपन्ना जीह॰ मैँ कहलन्कै कि, जोँ एकन्रा सभै कै कुछु करि कै देखाइऐ तबे चाहिय कि कुछु समुझि जाए। एक दिन ऊ अपन्ना बेटा सभै कैँ बोलैलन्कै, आरो कहलन्कै, कि थोड़॰ लकन्ड़ी हमन्रा आगू मैँ लै आने। ऊ लकन्ड़ी सभै कै वैँ गिरन्हस्त एक रस्सी सैँ कस्सि कै बान्हलन्कै। फेर एक एक लड़िका सैँ कहलन्कै कि, रस्सी मत् खोल॰, आरो लकन्ड़ी सभै कै तोरि डाल॰। हर एकै जोर करलन्कै, पर कुछु नहीँ होलै। फेर गिरन्हस्त खोलि कै एक एक लकन्ड़ी देलन्कै। तबे ऊ सभै ओकन्रा झट पट तोरि डललन्कै। तबे ओकन्रा सभै केर बाप कहलन्कै कि, बेटा, जोँ तोँहैँ सभै बान्हन्ला लकन्ड़ी केर॰ ढब॰ सैँ अपन्ना मैँ मिलन्ल॰ रह॰, तोँ सभै दुस्मन॰ केर॰ दाँत खट्टा करन्बे। आरो जबे फरक भेल॰, तबे जानिह॰ कि खराब भेल॰।

फरक भेल॰, से बिगड़न्ल॰।

छठ॰मऽ कथा ।

ऊँड़ार आरो भेड़ा केर॰ मेल ।

एक बाजि ऊँड़ार सभै भेड़ा सभै सेँ कह॰लाय पठैल॰कै कि, आव॰, हम॰रा आर तोह॰रा आर अपन्ना मेँ मेल करि लिअ । कहिने अपन्ना मेँ लड़िअ, आरो एक दोस॰रा केर॰ आस॰रा मेँ पियास॰ल॰ रहिअ । ई पाजी कुत्ता सभै लड़ाइ केर॰ जड़ छिकै । एना होँ सहो खनि भूकि भूकि कै हम॰रा भड़॰काय॰छै । आरो हम॰रा आर कै तोरा आर सेँ लड़ाय॰छै । इन॰का हम॰रा पास पठाय दे, फेर कैहिन॰ झग॰ड़ा छै । हम॰रा तोरा मेँ सभै दिन पियार आरो मेल रह॰तै । तबे तोह॰र॰ एको बाल खराब नहीँ होतौन । गँवार भेड़ा ई बद॰मास ऊँड़ार॰ केर॰ बात मानि लेल॰कै, आरो कुत्ता सभै कै ऊँड़ार॰ केर॰ पास पठाय देल॰कै । पहिला त॰ ऊँड़ार सभै कुत्ता सभै कै खाय गेलै । फेर भेड़ा सभै केर॰ पीछू दौड़॰लै, आरो थोड़॰वाय हो दिन॰ मेँ भेड़ा सभै कै ओ खाय गेलै । सच्चे छै ।

बैरी सदाय धोखा दै छै । ऊ बड़ी गँवार छै, जे बैरी कै सच्चा समुझै छै ॥

सात॰म॰ कथा ।

बाघ ऊँड़ार आरो चीता ।

एक बाजि बाघ ऊँड़ार आरो चीता अपन्ना मेँ ई ठह॰रैल॰कै कि सभै मिलि कै सिकार मारौँ । फेर अपन्ना मेँ बाँटि लौँ । ई ठानि कै जङ्ग॰ल॰ मेँ दौड़ धूप करै लग॰लै, आरो जबे एक बड़॰ हेन॰ कार॰ हरिन मारि लेल॰कै, तबे बाघ बोल॰लै कि, आब॰, एक॰रा बाँट॰, आरो झट तीन टुक॰ड़ा करि डलल॰कै, आरो गरजि कै बोल॰लै कि, पहिल॰ टुक॰ड़ा तो हमेँ लेबौँ, कहिने कि हमेँ जङ्ग॰ल॰ केर॰ राजा छिकाँ, आरो दोस॰र॰ टुक॰ड़ा ओ हमौँ लेबौँ, कहिने कि हमेँ एक॰रा मारै मेँ बड़ी दौड़ धूप कर॰ने छिऐ । आरो तेस॰र॰ टुक॰ड़ा इहै धरल छै, देखिअ तो केक॰र॰ मग॰दूर छै, जेँ हम॰रा आगू सेँ उठाय लै जाए । ई सुनि कै चीता आरो ऊँड़ार दुम दबाय कै भग॰लै, आरो बाघ हरिन॰ कैँ अकसरे खाय गेलै । ई कहानी सच्चे छै ।

जेक॰री लाठी, ओक॰री भैँस ।

आठ॰मऽ कथा ।

माँटी आरो पित॰रऽ केरऽ घैला केरऽ बात॰चित ।

एक बाजि काँही नद्दी मेँ बोहऽ ऐलै । तबे एक पित॰रऽ केरऽ घैलऽ आरो एक माँटी केरऽ घैलऽ भाँसि चल॰लै । पित॰रऽ केरऽ घैलऽ माँटी केरऽ घैला सेँ कहल॰कै कि, हम॰रा साथे लग॰लऽ चलऽ, तबे हमेँ तोरा बचाय लेबौँ । माँटी केरऽ घैलऽ बोल॰लै कि, ई अप॰ने बड़ी अच्छा बात कहिलाँव । हमेँ अप॰ना केरऽ भला मान॰बऽ आरो सभै दिन गुन गाय॰बऽ । पर सच पूछऽ, तैँ हम॰रा ई डर छै कि, काँही पाऽनि केरऽ लह॰रऽ केरऽ धक्का सेँ अप॰ने केरऽ लग जाय रहिअ । कहिने कि जोँ अप॰ने सेँ हमेँ दूर रहिअ, तोँ एना हौँ हिल॰लऽ भुल॰लऽ कन्हौ किनारा पर जाय लाग॰बऽ । पर जोँ अप॰ने सेँ मैंट होअलऽ, आरो कभी भुल॰ला सेँ टक्कर लागि गेलऽ, तैँ हम॰रऽ पेट फाटि जैतै । सच्चे छै ।

बड़ा सेँ आस रखिअ, पर पास नहीँ जैअ ।

नौमऽ कथा ।

एक मुन॰सी बजारऽ मेँ बैठि कै चिट्ठी लिखि रह॰लऽ छेलै । एक पर॰देसी ऐलै आरो बोल॰लै कि, मुन॰सी जी, की लिखै छऽ । मुन॰सी जी जवाब देल॰कै कि, भाइ, चिट्ठी लिखै छिअ । वेँ कहल॰कै कि, हम॰रो सलाम लिखि दीहऽ । मुन॰सी जी कहल॰कै कि, नहीँ अर॰जी लिखै छिअ । उ कहल॰कै कि, हम॰रो सही करि दीहऽ । मुन॰सी ओक॰ताय कै बोल॰लै कि, तमस्सुक लिखै छिअ, उ बोल॰लै कि, हम॰रो गवाही लिखि दीहऽ । मुन॰सी सोचल॰कै कि, ई तो कोय एक अजब तरह केरऽ अद॰मी देखाय दै छै । पुछल॰कै कि, अप॰ने केरऽ नाम की छिकै । उ हँस॰लै, आरो बोल॰लै, हम॰रऽ नाम छिकै, मानऽ चाहे नहीँ मानऽ, हमेँ तोरऽ पछभा छिकिहौन्ह ।

दस॰मऽ कथा ।

एक अद॰मी केरऽ घरऽ मेँ राति केरऽ बक्ति मेँ आगिन लागि गेलै । उ तो अप॰नऽ बाल बच्चा सभै लै कै भग॰लै, आरो नौक॰रऽ सभै कैँ हुकुम देल॰कऽ कि,चीज बिखे निकासैँ । एत॰ना हीँ मेँ आगिन बड़ी पसरि गेलै, सौँसे घर धूँआँ धक्कर होय गेलै । नौकर बोल॰लै कि, जी, हमेँ की की निकासिअ । तबे उ बड़ऽ अद॰मी हुस॰तैलै आरो कहल॰कै कि बाबा आगिन लागै छेनी घरऽ मेँ, जे निक॰सै, से भाग ।

एगारहऽम॰ कथा।

एक गमारीन गोआरिन माथा पर दही केर॰ हँड़िया धरि के चलऽली जाय छेलै। चलऽते चलऽते ओकऽरा जीह॰ मेँ ई अभिलाख उठऽलै कि, हँ, अच्छा, ई दही कैँ बेँचऽबै आरो पैसा सैँ आम मोल लेबै। कुछु आम हमऽरा जिम्मा छै, सभे मिलाय कै तीन से सैँ कुछु बढ़ि जैतै, एकऽरा मेँ कुछु सड़ि पचि जैतै, पर, हौं, अढ़ाइ सऽ त॰ बचऽबै करऽतै, आरो ओकऽरा मेँ सैँ जे कुछु बचि कै निकसऽतै ओकऽर॰ अच्छा भाव उठऽतै। तो सुखऽराती मेँ एक हरा साड़ी लेब॰। हँ हँ, हरा साड़ी हमऽरा आँग॰ मेँ अच्छा सोभऽतै। आरो, बस, हमैँ तोँ हरा ही साड़ी लेबै, आरो ओकऽरा पीन्हि कै मेला जैबै, आरो खूब ऐँठि जूँठि कै अपऽना गहऽना, आरो कपऽड़ा केर॰ सोभा, आरो मुँह॰ केर॰ चमक झलक देखैबै आरो चाल॰ चाल॰ मेँ से से ऐँठ ऐँठऽबै। ई मन॰ मेँ करि के ऊ गमारीन गोआरिन, जेना चमकि ठमकि कै टेड़ी चाल चलऽली, तेना हौँ दही केर॰ हँड़िया माथा पर॰ सैँ गिरि कै टुकऽड़ा टुकऽड़ा होय गेलै, आरो सभे बनऽल॰ बनैल॰ मनऽसुआ फुराय गेलै।

बारऽम॰ कथा।

चील आरो कौआ।

एक चील्ह॰ के लोल॰ मेँ एक घोँघा छेलै। केतऽनौ धरऽती मेँ उठाय उठाय पटऽकलऽकै, तइओ घोँघा नहीँ भाँगऽलै। तबे एक कौआ ई रास्ता बतैलऽकै कि है घोँघा कैँ लोल॰ मेँ लै कै बड़ी दूर ऊँच॰ उड़ि जाहौ; आरो वहाँ सैँ गिराय दीहौ, तबे घोँघा टूटि जैतौ। चील्ह कहलऽकै कि ई बहुत नीक॰ बात छै, आरो घोँघा कैँ लै कै उड़ऽलै, आरो बड़ी ऊँच॰ दूर जाय कै छोड़ि देलऽकै। जोन्हाएँ घोँघा धरऽती पर गिरऽलै टुकऽड़ा टुकऽड़ा होय गेलै, आरो कौआ ओकऽर॰ गुद्दा खाय गेलै। थोड़ा देर॰ मेँ चील्ह हेँठ उतरऽलै, तबे खोलऽरा * कैँ छोड़ि कुछु नहीँ पैलऽकै।

तेरऽम॰ कथा।

खट्टा अँगूर।

एक लोमऽड़ी कोय फुलऽवारी मेँ गेलै। देखलऽकै कि अँगूर॰ सभे केर॰ थौक॰ पकऽल॰ टटिया मेँ लटकि रहऽल॰ छै, कि जेकऽरा सैँ रस टपकि रहऽल॰ छै, आरो कोय

---

* Or खोलऽसा।

जोगनियौं नह्यौं छै। ई देखि कै ओक॰रा मुँह॰ मैं पानि भरि ऐलै। बहुत तरह सैं उछल॰लै कुद॰लै, पर अँगूर॰ केर॰ थौक॰ तक नहीं पहुँचे सक॰लै। जबे कोन्हों तरह सैं दाव नहीं लग॰लै, तबे एना बकलि बकलि चल॰लै कि खट्टा अँगूर॰ कैं कौनैं खाय।

चौद॰म॰ कथा।

एक किमियागर कोय अद॰मी सैं कहल॰कै कि, जौं तोहें कुछु चाँदी हम॰रा हाँ आने, तबे हमैं एक ऐन्ह॰ जड़ी लगावौं कि तुरन्ते ओ हौं चाँदी केर॰ सोना होय जैतौ। ऊ सोझ॰ सादा अद॰मी ओक॰रा धोखा पट्टी मैं आवि गेल॰, आरो काहूँ सैं पैंच॰ उधार करि कै हू से रुपैया केर॰ चाँदी ओ हौं रसायनी कैं आनि देल॰कै। रसायनी ओ हौं राति मैं बिछौना उठाय कै काहीं चलल॰ गेलै। अबे ऊ बेचारा बिर्पत्तक मार॰लै ऊ बद॰माश॰ रसायनी केर॰ खोज॰ मैं दौड़ धूप करे लग॰लै। जङ्गले जङ्गले खोजि मार॰लै, पर ओहि रसायनी केर॰ काहीं पता नहीं लग॰लै। ओक॰रा ई तरह सैं घब॰राल॰ देखि कै, एक अद॰मी कहल॰कै कि, तोह॰रा ई भूल होअलौन्ह, कि वैं बद॰माश गोसाँय केर॰ फन्दा मैं फसि गेल॰है। अबे पछ॰तैला सैं आरो ओक॰रा खोज॰ मैं दौड़ धूप कर॰ला सैं कुछु नहीं होतौन। ई बात पर हमैं एक बात तोह॰रा सुनाय छिओन्ह, जेक॰रा सदाय याद राखे ले चहिय।

पन्द्र॰म॰ कथा।

एक चिड़िया कोय गिर॰हस्त॰ केर॰ फुल॰वारी मैं जाय कै, काँच॰ पक॰ल॰ फल सभे केर॰ सभे काटि आयल॰ करे छेलै। गिर॰हस्त सदाय ओक॰रा खोज॰ मैं छेलै। एक दिन अँगूर॰ केर॰ टटिया पर जाल लगाय कै ओक॰रा पक॰ड़ल॰कै, आरो मारे ले चह॰लकै। चिरिया गिर॰हस्त॰ सैं कहल॰कै कि, जौं तोहें हम॰रा छोड़ि दे, तबे हमैं ई भलाय केर॰ बद॰ला मैं तोह॰रा तीन बात बताय दीहौन्ह, कि जेक॰रा मैं तोह॰रा बहुत भल॰ हौतौन्ह। गिर॰हस्त कहल॰कै कि तौं पहिले बताय दे, तबे हमैं तोह॰रा छोड़ि देबौं। चिड़िया ओक॰रा तीन बात कह॰लकै, एक तँ इहे कि, दुस॰मन जे अप॰ना काबू मैं आवि जाय, तबे छोड़े ले नहीं चहिय। दुस॰र॰ जे बात अकिल॰ मैं नहीं आवे, ओक॰रा मानै ले नहीं चहिय। तेस॰र॰ गेल॰ होल॰ चीज॰ ले पछ॰तावे ले नहीं चहिय। ओर चौठा॰

एक बात आरो छै, कि अबे तोहँ हम॰रा छोड़ि देबै, तबे कहिभौन्ह। गिर॰हस्त ई बात॰ कैँ सुनि कै, जेन्ह कह॰ने छेलै बेहे कर॰लकै, आरो ऊ छोडि चिड़िया कैँ छोड़ि देल॰कै। तबे चिड़िया भित्ति पर बैठि कै कहल॰कै कि, हम॰रा पेट॰ मैँ मुरगी केरऽ अण्डा सैँ आो बड़॰ एक मोँती छेलऽ। जोँ तोहँ हम॰रा नहीँ छोड़॰तिहैँ. आरो मारि डाल॰तिहैँ, तबे ऊ मोँती तोरा हाथ ऐतिहौ। गिर॰हस्त पछ॰तावे लग॰लै। ऊ कहल॰कै, रे गँवार, तोँ हम॰र॰ तीनो बात इख॰नी भूलि गेलैँ। कहिने कि हमेँ तोरऽ बैरी छेलियौ, जबे पकड़ि पैले छेलैँ. तबे छोड़े लै की छेलौ। आरो मुरगी केर॰ अण्डा केर॰ बरोबर तेँ हमेँ अप॰नहिँ नहीँ छियै, फेर मुरगी केर॰ अण्डा सैँ बड़ऽ मोती हम॰रा पेट॰ मैँ होअबऽ कबे अकिल मैँ आबे सकै छै। पर तोहँ ए दोँ बात॰ पर भरोसा कर॰ले। आरो अबे तोरा हाथऽ सैँ छूटि गेलाँ, तबे पछ॰तैला सैँ की होतै। एक॰रा सैँ इहै फल निकल॰लछ छै कि, पहिले सैँ हर एक काम॰ के बड़ी सोचि बिचारि कै काम करै ले चहिय। आरो जे काम बिगड़ि जाय, सो फेर पछ॰तैल॰ नहीँ चहिय।

चौल॰भ॰ कथा।

कोय सम॰तानीक॰ के दू बेटा छेलै। जबे ओक॰र॰ बाप मरि गेलै तबे दोनो भाय, ओक॰र॰ धन आपुस॰ मैँ बाँटि लेल॰कै। बड़॰का भाय अप॰न॰ रुपैया पैसा सुख चैन आरो खेल॰ तमासा मैँ उड़ावे लग॰लै, आरो छोट॰का भाय बड़ी मेह॰नत॰ सैँ खरीद बिक॰री करै लग॰लै। एक दिन बड़॰का भाय छोट॰का कैँ ठट्ठा करि कै कहल॰कै कि, भाय, कहिने दिन भरि अनाज तौल॰ल॰ करै छ॰। हम॰रा सङ्ग॰ मैँ रह॰, खा, पीअ, सुख कर॰। बहुत दिन॰ केर॰ बाद, जबे छोट॰का भाय लह॰ना तगादा सैँ बहुत रुपैया जमा करि लेल॰कै, तबे ओक॰र॰ बड़॰का भाय, जे राग रङ्ग आरो खेल तमासा मैँ अप॰न॰ सभे धन उड़ाय कै भिखारी होय गेल॰ छेलै, ओक॰रा डेऊढ़ी पर जाय कै कहे लग॰लै कि, भाय, हमोँ तोह॰रा रहिले ठट्ठा मैँ उड़ैले छेलिऔन्ह, पर जोँ हम्हूँ तोह॰रा नाखि खरीद बिक॰री कर॰तियाँ, आरो अनाज तौलतियाँ, तबे आय पाओ भरि अनाज इमे उमे सैँ माँगि नहीँ खेतियाँ। अन्ने छै।

आस॰कत ऐन्ह॰ कीड़ा छै।
कि धन॰ कैँ धूरा करि डाले छै।

सत॰रम० कथा।

लाल॰चाहा कुत्ता।

कोय कुत्ता नद्दी केर० किनारा पर एक हाड़ पैल॰कै, आरो मुँह० मँ लेल॰कै। जौँ पर॰छाँय अप॰न० पानि मेँ देखल॰कै, समुझल॰कै कि दोसर॰ हाड़ छिकै। मारे लालच॰ मुँह खोलल॰कै, कि ओक॰रा ओ पानि सँ निकाल्लौँ। ज हाड़ जे मुँह० मँ छेलै, से हो गिरि पड़॰लै। सच्चे छै।

माँछी बैठ॰लै दूध० मँ, पाँख गेलै लपटाय। हाय मलल॰कै आरो माथ० धुनल॰कै। लालच बड़ी बैजाय।

Reg. No. 12943J—480+30—28-2-87.

SEVEN

GRAMMARS

OF THE DIALECTS AND SUBDIALECTS OF THE

BIHARI LANGUAGE.

SPOKEN IN THE PROVINCE OF BIHAR, IN THE EASTERN PORTION OF THE NORTH-WESTERN PROVINCES, AND IN THE NORTHERN PORTION OF THE CENTRAL PROVINCES.

PART VIII.

MAITHIL-BAN·GÁLÍ DIALECT

OF CENTRAL AND WESTERN PURANIYÁ.

Compiled under orders of the Government of Bengal.

By GEORGE A. GRIERSON, B.C.S.,
JOINT-MAGISTRATE OF PATNA.

CALCUTTA:
PRINTED AT THE BENGAL SECRETARIAT PRESS.
1887.

CONTENTS.

INTRODUCTION.

§ 1. The following grammar treats of the dialect of Central, Northern, and Western Puraniyá (Purniah). This dialect is founded on the archaic North Maithilí dialect spoken in North Darbhangá and the Supaul subdivision of Bhagalpúr. A grammar and reading-book of Northern Maithilí has been published by the Asiatic Society of Bengal.* Towards Central Puraniyá this dialect shows a distinct tendency towards Ban·gálí. The dialect of Eastern Puraniyá is a variety of Ban·gálí.

§ 2. The alphabet and rules for spelling will be found in the General Introduction to this series of grammars, and the remarks therein found are not repeated here.

---

* Introduction to the Maithilí Language of North Bihár. By G. A. Grierson.

	Rs.	A.	P.
Part I, Grammar (extra number, J. A. S. B., 1880)	2	0	0
Part II, Chrestomathy and Vocabulary (extra number, J. A. S. B., 1882)	4	0	0

Published by the Asiatic Society of Bengal.

DIVISION I.

DECLENSION.

CHAPTER I.

NOUNS.

§ 3. For general remarks, see the General Introduction, § 38 and ff.

The following are the post-positions used in declining the noun in this dialect :—

		Power.
Nom.	*Wanting.*	
Acc.	*Wanting* or के *ke.*	
Instr.	से *se* or सेँ *sẽ.*	'By.'
Dat.	के *ke.*	'To.'
Abl.	से *se* or सेँ *sẽ.*	'From
Gen.	क *k*, के *kĕ*, कर *kar*, or केर *ker.*	'Of.'
Loc.	मेँ *mẽ.*	'In.'
Voc.	*Wanting.*	

All these post-positions will only be used in one example, that of घोड़ा *ghoṛá*, 'a horse;' but they can all be used with all nouns.

Except that for the genitive, they can be used with all pronouns. In the genitive singular many pronouns do not take these post-positions, but have other forms subject to special rules.

The plural is the same as the singular.

The following are examples of declension :—

§ 4. (a) Masculine Tadbhavas in आ *á*.

Example of the declension of a *tadbhava** masculine noun in आ *á* :—

घोड़ा *ghoṛá*, 'a horse.'

Short form, { Weak, घोड़ *ghoṛ*. Strong, घोड़ा *ghoṛá*. } Long form,* घोड़वा *ghŏṛ'wá*. Redundant form,† घोड़ौवा *ghŏṛauwá*.

Singular and Plural.

Nom.	घोड़ा [1] *ghoṛá*,	'a horse.'
Acc.	घोड़ा *ghoṛá* or घोड़ा के *ghoṛá ke*,	'a horse.'
Instr.	घोड़ा से *ghoṛá sẽ* or सँ *sẽ*,	'by a horse.'
Dat.	घोड़ा के *ghoṛá ke*,	'to a horse.'
Abl.	घोड़ा से, *ghoṛá se*, सँ *sẽ*,	'from a horse.'
Gen.	घोड़ाक *ghoṛák*, घोड़ा के *ghoṛá kë*, or घोड़ा कर *ghoṛá kar* or केर *ker*,	'of a horse.'
Loc.	घोड़ा मेँ *ghoṛá mẽ*,	'in a horse.'
Voc.	हो घोड़ा *ho ghoṛá !*	'O horse!'

[1] Or घोड़ *ghoṛ*, घोड़वा *ghŏṛ'wá*, or घोड़ौवा *ghŏṛauwá*, and so throughout.

---

* See General Introduction, § 12.

† See General Introduction, §§ 12, 38, and ff.

§ 5. (b) Masculine Nouns ending in Silent Consonants.

Example of the declension of a masculine noun ending in a silent consonant:—

घर *ghar*, 'a house.'

Short form, { Weak, घर *ghar*. Strong, घरा *ghará*. } Long form,* घरऽवा *ghar'wá*. Redundant form,* घरौवा *gharauwá*.

Singular and Plural.

Nom.	घर[1] *ghar*,	'a house.'
Acc.	घर *ghar* or घर के *ghar ke*,	'a house.'
Instr.	घरैँ *gharẽ*, घर से *ghar se*, *&c.*,	'by a house.'
Dat.	घर के *ghar ke*,	'for a house.'
Abl.	घर से *ghar se*, *&c.*,	'from a house.'
Gen.	घरक *gharak*, घर के *ghar kĕ*, *&c.*,	'of a house.'
Loc.	घरे *ghare*, घर में *ghar mẽ*,	'in a house.'
Voc.	हो घर *ho ghar !*	'O house !'

[1] Or घरऽवा *ghar'wá*, घरौवा *gharauwá*, and so throughout.

§ 6. It is not necessary to decline further any nouns in full, as the above examples suffice. All nouns ending in vowels are declined like घोड़ा *ghoṛá*, and all those ending in silent consonants like घर *ghar*. The final syllables of all long and redundant forms may optionally be nasalised by the addition of *anunásik* : thus घोड़ऽवा *ghŏṛ'wá* or घोड़ऽवाँ *ghŏṛ'wá̃* ; घरौवा *gharauwá* or घरौवाँ *gharauwá̃* ; मलिया *maliyá* or मलियाँ *maliyá̃*.

Note, however, that—

(1) Occasionally in the case of masculine nouns ending in a silent consonant we find an instrumental in ऐं *ẽ* and a locative in ए *e* : thus हम बलैँ ले जैब *ham balẽ le jaib*, 'I shall take away by force,' where बलैँ *balẽ* is the instrumental of बल *bal*, 'force ;' घाटे *gháṭe*, 'at a landing stage,' locative of घाट *gháṭ*, 'a landing stage:' so also घरे घरे *ghare ghare*, 'in every house,' 'from house to house.'

* See General Introduction, §§ 12, 38, and ff.

(2) Certain verbal nouns ending in ल *l* have an oblique form in ला *lá:* thus देखल *dekhal*, abl. देखल्ला से *děkh'lá se*, 'from seeing;' also verbal nouns in the form of the root have an oblique form in ए *ě* or ऐ *aĭ:* thus देख *dekh*, dat. देखे के *dekhě ke* or देखै के *dekhaĭ ke*, 'for seeing.' Full particulars concerning these nouns will be found in § 111.

An example of each of the more common forms of nouns follows :—

§ 7. (c) Masculine Tatsamas* in आ *á*.

राजा *raja*, 'a king.'

Short form, राजा *rájá*. Long form,* रजःवा *raj'wá*. Redundant form,* रजौवा *rajauwá*.

§ 8. (d) Masculine Nouns in ई *í*.

माली *málí*, 'a gardener.'

Short form, माली *málí*. Long form,* मलिया *maliyá*. Redundant form,* मलियवा *maliyawá* or मलीवा *malíwá*.

§ 9. (e) Masculine Nouns in ऊ *ú*.

नाऊ *náú*, 'a barber.'†

Short form, नाऊ *náú*. Long form,‡ नउआ *naüá* or नौआ *nauá*. Redundant form,‡ नउअवा *naüawá* or नौअवा *nauawá*.

---

* See General Introduction, §§ 12, 38, and ff., 34 and 36.

† Kellogg in his Hindí Grammar incorrectly gives आँसू *ású* as an example of a feminine noun in ऊ *ú:* it is masculine. आँसू *ású* is not used in Bihárí, लोर *lor* being the word for 'a tear.'

‡ See General Introduction, §§ 12, 38, and ff., 34 and 36.

§ 10. (f) Feminine Nouns in ई *í* and इ *i*.

पोथी *pothí*, 'a book.'

Short form, पोथी *pothí*. Long form,* पोथिया *pŏthiyá*. Redundant form,* पोथियवा *pŏthiyawá* or पोथीवा *pothíwá*.

राति *rati*, 'night.'

Short form, राति *ráti*. Long form,* रतिया *ratiyá*. Redundant form,* रतियवा *ratiyawá* or रतीवा *ratíwá*.

§ 11. (g) Feminine Nouns ending in a Silent Consonant.

बात *bát*, 'a word.'

Short form, बात *bát*. Long form,* बतिया *batiyá*. Redundant form, बतवा *bát'wá*.

§ 12. Periphrastic Plural.

With reference to the statement that the plural forms are the same as the singular, it must be noted that every noun can also form a periphrastic plural by the addition of the words सब *sab*, सिभी *sibhí*, सिबी *sibí*, सी *sí*, or आर *ár*. Thus, nom. plur. घोड़ा सब *ghoṛa sab*, घोड़ा सिबी *ghoṛa sibí*, *&c.*; acc. plur. घोड़ा सब के *ghoṛa sab ke*, घोड़ा सिबी के *ghoṛa sibí ke*, and so on. In the case of rational beings the word लोग *log*, 'people,' may also be used; thus, माली लोग *máli log*, 'gardeners.'

§ 13. Genitival Affixes.

The following examples have been specially designed to exhibit the use of the genitival affixes :—

1.	ई राजाक मन्दिर छिकै. *Í rájάk mandir chhikai.*	'This is the king's temple.'
2.	हम्मे कन्स कर दासीन छिकौँ. *Hamme Kans kar dásín chhikŏ.*	'I am the maid-servant of King Kans.'

* See General Introduction, §§ 12, 38, and ff., 34 and 36.

3. मधुमाछी सिबी केर छुत्ता उड़ि गेलै.
Madhumáchhí sibí ker chuttá uṛi gelai.
'A swarm of bees flew away.'

4. छल्ली के मारैक कुछु दोख नहीं.
Challí ke máraïk kuchhu dosh nahí.
'There is no sin in slaying a deceiver.'

5. मथुरा केर मौगी सब कानन्तैं चल गेलै.
Mathurá ker maugí sab kán'tẽ chal gelai.
'The women of Mathurá departed weeping.'

6. बहुत तरन्हक बात सब सुनल गेलै.
Bahut tar'hak bát sab sunal gelai.
'Matters of many kinds were heard.'

7. अस्फटिक के चारों फटकन्वा टूटि गेलै.
Asphaṭik kĕ chárõ phaṭak'wá ṭúṭi gelai.
'The four gates of crystal broke.'

8. देस देसक राजा ऐलै.
Des desak rájá ailai.
'Kings of all countries came.'

9. ऊ सब माली केर बेटन्वा छिकै.
Ú sab málí ker bĕṭ'wá chhikai.
'They are the sons of the gardener.'

10. हम्मे राजा केर गाम मैं ऐलौं.
Hamme rájá ker gám mẽ ailõ.
'I came into the king's villages.'

11. पण्डित सब केर घर मैं अनेक पोथी छै.
Paṇḍit sab ker ghar mẽ anek pothí chhai.
'There are many books in *paṇḍits'* houses.'

CHAPTER II.

ADJECTIVES.

§ 14. Gender.

See General Introduction, § 42 and ff.

§ 15. Numeral Adjectives.

The cardinals are nearly the same as those in High Hindí. The following are the ones that present points of difference :—

1 = एक *ěk* or एगो *ego*.
2 = दो *do*, दूगो *dúgo*, or दुइ *duí*.
4 = चारि *chári*.
9 = नउ *na*.
15 = पन्नरह *pan'ra*.
27 = सतैस *satais*.

28 = अठैस *aṭhais*.
51 = एकौन *ěkaun*.
52 = बौन *baun*.
57 = सँतौन *sãtaun*.
58 = अँठौन *ãṭhaun*.
100 = सै *sai* or सउ *sa*.

§ 16. Ordinals.

The ordinals up to 'sixth' are as follows :—

1*st* = पहिल *pahil* or पहिलका *pahil'ká* or पहिन्क *pahink*.
2*nd* = दोसर *dosar*.
3*rd* = तेसर *tesar*.
4*th* = चौठा *chauṭhá*, चारिम *chárim*, or चारम *cháram*.
5*th* = पँचवाँ *pãch'wã*.
6*th* = छठवाँ *chhaṭh'wã*.

The ordinals above 'sixth' are all formed by adding वाँ *wã* or ओँ *õ* to the cardinals : as दसवाँ *das'wã* or दसोँ *dasõ*, 'tenth;' पचसवाँ *pachas'wã* or पचासोँ *pachásõ*, 'fiftieth.'

§ 17. Fractional Numbers.

These are—

$\frac{1}{4}$ = पा *pá* or पावे *páwe*.
$\frac{1}{3}$ = तिहै *tihai*.
$\frac{1}{2}$ = आध *ádh*.
$\frac{3}{4}$ or $-\frac{1}{4}$ = पौने *paune*.

$1\frac{1}{4}$ or $+\frac{1}{4}$ = सवा *sawá*.
$1\frac{1}{2}$ = डेढ़ *ḍeṛh*
$2\frac{1}{2}$ = अढ़ै *aṛhai*.
$+\frac{1}{2}$ = साढ़े *sáṛhe*.

§ 18. Multiplicatives.

Multiplicatives, such as the English 'twice' and 'thrice,' are not found in this dialect. The Bihárí idiom is illustrated in such phrases as दो सतेँ चौदह *do satẽ chaudah*, 'two seven's, fourteen;' छउ तिया अठारह *chha tiyá aṭhárah*, 'six three's, eighteen,' which correspond to the English idioms 'seven times two' and 'three times six.' Numbers thus used are called multiplicatives, and differ in some respects from the cardinals. The following are the multiplicative numbers up to 10, including fractions :—

× 1, कँ *kã*.
× $1\frac{1}{4}$, सवाँ *sawã*.
× $1\frac{1}{2}$, डौढ़ा *ḍauṛhá*.
× 2, दूना *duná*.
× $2\frac{1}{2}$, अढ़ैया *aṛhaiyá*.
× 3, तिया *tiyá*.
× $3\frac{1}{2}$, हुट्ठा *huṭṭhá*.
× 4, चौका *chauká*.

× $4\frac{1}{2}$, ढौँचा *dhaũcha*.
× 5, पञ्जा *panjá*.
× $5\frac{1}{2}$, पहुञ्चा *pahuncha*.
× 6, छक्का *chhakká*.
× 7, सतेँ *satẽ*.
× 8, अट्ठैँ *áṭṭhẽ*.
× 9, नवउ *nawa*.
× 10, दहाँ *dahã*.

§ 19. Definite Cardinals.

These are as follows :—

एगो *ego*, 'the one.'

दूओ *dúo*, दुन्नो *dunno*, 'the two,' 'both;'

तीनो *tíno*, 'the three;'

चारिओ *chário*, 'the four;' and so on,

adding ओ *o* to the numerals. Example: पाँचो भाइ जौरे छत *pãchõ bhái jaure chhat*, 'the five brothers are an undivided family.'

§ 20. Indefinite Cardinals.

The termination न्हौँ *nhaũ* or हौँ *haũ* added to the numbers 'one hundred,' 'one thousand,' and so on, always denotes an indefinite number of these aggregates. In this idiom सैकर *saikar* is always substituted for सै *sai*, 'one hundred.' Examples are सैकरन्हौँ पेड़ *saĭk'ranhaũ peṛ*, 'hundreds of trees;' हजारन्हौँ *hajár'haũ*, 'thousands;' लाखन्हौँ *lákh'haũ*, 'tens of thousands;' हजारन्हौँ अदिमी मैलै *hajár'haũ adimí mailai*, 'thousands of men died.'

§ 21. Collective Numerals.

These—viz. जोड़ा *joṛá*, 'a pair,' गण्डा *gaṇḍá*, 'a four'—are the same as in High Hindí.

CHAPTER III.

PRONOUNS.

§ 22. The following tables show the declensional forms of the principal pronouns and pronominal forms.

The declension of pronouns presents some important points of difference from that of nouns, which must be carefully noticed.

While nouns frequently remain unchanged before post-positions, pronouns, with few exceptions, change to some other form, called the *oblique* or *inflected base.*

The accusative singular of pronouns is, with one or two exceptions, never the same as the nominative. In circumstances corresponding to those in which the accusative of a noun takes the nominative form, the accusative of a pronoun usually takes the oblique form without any post-position.

The genitive forms of pronouns ending in र *r* and न *n* are also to be noticed.

Pronouns have the same form, whether referring to masculine or feminine nouns. With the exception of the pronouns of the second person, they all want the vocative case.

§ 23. Pronouns of the First Person and of the Second Person Non-Honorific.

These pronouns have in the singular each two forms—a shorter and a longer. The shorter form is rarely used except in poetry.

हम *ham*, 'I.'

Singular.

	Shorter form.	*Longer form.*
Nom.	*Wanting.*	हम *ham*, हम्मे *hamme*, or हम्में *hammẽ*.
Acc.	मोरा[1] *morá* or मोरा के *morá ke*.	हमरा[1] *ham'rá* or हमरा के *ham'rá ke*.
Instr.	मोरा से *morá se*.	हमरा से *ham'rá se*.
Dat.	मोरा के *morá ke*.	हमरा के *ham'rá ke*.
Abl.	मोरा से *morá se*.	हमरा से *ham'rá se*.
Gen.	मोर *mor*.	हमर *hamar*.
Loc.	मोरा में *morá mẽ*.	हमरा में *ham'rá mẽ*.
Voc.	*Wanting.*	*Wanting.*

[1] मोरो *moro* and हमरो *ham'ro* may be used for मोरा *morá* and हमरा *ham'rá* in an emphatic sense: thus हमरो द॰ *ham'ro da*, 'give to me also.' In poetry a shorter oblique form, मोहि *mŏhi*, instead of मोरा *morá*, is sometimes found. हम *ham* may be used throughout instead of हमरा *ham'rá*.

The plural is the same as the singular. A periphrastic plural is formed as in the case of substantives; thus nom. हमरा सब *ham'rá sab*, हमरा सी *ham'rá si*, or हमरा आर *ham'rá ár*, and so on. हम सब *ham sab* is also used, but not हम सी *ham sí*, &c.

हम्मु *hammu* is used emphatically to mean 'I (we) also.'

तों *tõ*, 'thou.'

Singular.

	Shorter form.	*Longer form.*
Nom.	*Wanting.*	तों *tõ* or तूँ *tû.*
Acc.	तोरा[1] *torá* or तोरा के *torá ke.*	तोहरा[1] *tŏh'rá* or तोहरा के *tŏh'rá ke.*
Instr.	तोरा से *torá se.*	तोहरा से *tŏh'rá se.*
Dat.	तोरा के *torá ke.*	तोहरा के *tŏh'rá ke.*
Abl.	तोरा से *torá se.*	तोहरा से *tŏh'rá se.*
Gen.	तोर *tor.*	तोहर *tohar.*
Loc.	तोरा मेँ *torá mẽ.*	तोहरा मेँ *tŏh'rá mẽ.*
Voc.	*Wanting.*	हो तों *ho tõ.*

[1] तोरो *toro* and तोहरो *tŏh'ro* may be used for तोरा *torá* and तोहरा *tŏh'rá* in an emphatic sense: thus तोहरो देखैछी *tŏh'ro dekhaichhí*, 'I see you also.' In poetry a shorter oblique form, तोहि *tŏhi* instead of तोरा *torá*, is sometimes found.

Plural.

The plural is the same as the singular. A periphrastic plural is formed as in the case of substantives; thus, nom. तोरा सब *torá sab*, तोरा सी *torá sí*, तोरा आर *torá ár*, and so on; so also तोहरा सब *tŏh'rá sab*, &c. तों सब *tõ sab*, तूँ सब *tû sab*, are also used.

§ 24. Pronoun of the Second Person Honorific and Reflexive Pronoun.

अपने *ap'ne*, इहाँ *ihā́*, or अहाँ *ahā́*, 'your honor.'

This pronoun is declined regularly like a substantive: thus—अपने के *ap'nĕ ke*, अपने से *ap'nĕ se*, &c.

The nominative plural is अपन्ने *ap'nĕ log*; or सब *sab* may be used instead of लोग *log*.

अपन्ने *ap'nĕ*, or अपन्हें *apanhĕ̃*, 'self.'

The oblique form of this is अपन्ना *ap'ná*, and it is regularly declined like a substantive except in the genitive, which is आपन *ápan*.

§ 25. Demonstrative Pronouns.

These are (1) the proximate demonstrative ई *í*, 'this,' and (2) the remote demonstrative ऊ *ú*. 'that.'

Like the personal pronouns, they have each two forms, a shorter and a longer.

ई *í*, 'this.'

Singular.

	Shorter form.	*Longer form.*
Nom.	इ *i*, ई *í*, ऐ *ẽ*, or इहाय *iháy*.	*Wanting.*
Acc.	ई (के) *í* (*ke*).	एकन्रा (के) *ĕk'rá* (*ke*).
Instr.	ई से *í se*.	एकन्रा से *ĕk'rá se*.
Dat.	ई के *í ke*.	एकन्रा के *ĕk'rá ke*.
Abl.	ई से *í se*.	एकन्रा से *ĕk'rá se*.
Gen.	ई के *í kĕ*.	एकर *ekar*, or एकन्रा के, केर *ĕk'rá kĕ, ker*.
Loc.	ई मैं, *í mẽ*.	एकन्रा मैं *ĕk'rá mẽ*.

इथी *ithí* may be used instead of ई *í* throughout.

Plural.

The plural is the same as the singular. As in the case of substantives, a periphrastic plural can be formed; thus, ई सब *í sab*, एकन्रा सब *ĕk'rá sab*, and so on.

ऊ *u*, 'that.'

The close analogy between the declension of this pronoun and that of ई *í*, 'this,' will be manifest from the following paradigm:—

Singular.

	Shorter form.	*Longer form.*
Nom.	ऊ *ú*, वेँ *wẽ*, or वहाय *waháy*.	*Wanting.*
Acc.	ऊ (के) *ú* (*ke*).	ओकऽरा (के) *ŏk'rá* (*ke*).
Instr.	ऊ से *ú se*.	ओकऽरा से *ŏk'rá se*.
Dat.	ऊ के *ú ke*.	ओकऽरा के *ŏk'rá ke*.
Abl.	ऊ से *ú se*.	ओकऽरा से *ŏk'rá se*.
Gen.	ऊ के *ú kĕ*.	ओकर *okar* or ओकऽरा के, केर *ŏk'rá kĕ, ker*.
Loc.	ऊ मेँ *ú mẽ*.	ओकऽरा मेँ *ŏk'rá mẽ*.

उथी *uthí* may be used instead of ऊ *ú* throughout.

Plural.

The plural is the same as the singular. As in the case of substantives, a periphrastic plural can be formed; thus nom. ऊ सब *ú sab*, ओकऽरा सब *ŏk'rá sab*, and so on.

NOTE.—In the above two demonstrative pronouns the shorter form may be used either adjectivally or substantivally, but the longer form can only be used as a substantive, and never as an adjective.

§ 26. Correlative Pronouns.

These are (1) the relative pronoun जे *je*, 'who;' (2) the correlative pronoun से *se*, 'that;' and (3) the interrogative pronoun के *ke*, 'who?'

The close analogy between their forms should be noted. Like the personal and demonstrative pronouns, they have each a shorter and a longer form.

It is not necessary to give their declension in full, as it is on exactly the same lines as that of the demonstrative pronouns. I shall therefore give only the nominative, genitive, and general oblique forms for each number

Relative.

जे *je*, 'who.'

Singular and Plural.

	Shorter form.	*Longer form.*
Nom.	जे *je.*	*Wanting.*
Gen.	जे के *je kĕ.*	जेकर *jekar* or जकर *jakar.*
Obl.	जे *je.*	जेकरा *jĕk'rá* or जकरा *jak'rá.*

Correlative.

से *se*, that.'

Singular and Plural.

	Shorter form.	*Longer form.*
Nom.	से *se* or ते *te.*	*Wanting.*
Gen.	ते के *te kĕ.*	तेकर *tekar* or तकर *takar.*
Obl.	ते *te.*	तेकरा *tĕk'rá* or तकरा *tak'rá.*

Interrogative.

के *ke*, 'who?'

Singular and Plural.

	Shorter form.	*Longer form.*
Nom.	के *ke.*	*Wanting.*
Gen.	के के *ke kĕ.*	केकर *kekar* or ककर *kakar.*
Obl.	के *ke.*	केकरा *kĕk'rá* or ककरा *kak'rá.*

NOTE.—In the above correlative pronouns the shorter form may be used either adjectivally or substantivally, but the longer form can only be used as a substantive, and never as an adjective. As in the case of the demonstrative pronouns, the periphrastic plural is formed by adding सब *sab*, सिबी *sibí*, सी *sí*, or आर *ár*.

§ 27. Interrogative Pronoun.

SUBSTANTIVAL.

की *kí*, 'what?'

This pronoun is really a neuter form of के *ke*, and can only refer to inanimate things.

Singular.

Nom. की *kí* or का *ká*.

Obl. कथी *kathí* or किथी *kithí*.

Declined regularly like a substantive. Its dative, कथी के *kathí ke* or किथी के *kithí ke*, or irregularly किथी ले *kithí le* or कथी लेल *kathí lel*, 'for what?' is used as an adverb, meaning 'why?'

§ 28. Indefinite Pronoun.

कोइ *koï*, 'anyone,' 'some one.'

This is declined throughout the singular only.

Singular.

Nom. कोइ *koï*.

Obl. कहु *kathú*, कोनो *kono*, ककरो *kak'ro*, केकरो *kĕk'rŏ*, or केकरहु *kĕkar'hau*. Declined regularly like a substantive, except the genitive, which is केकरो *kĕk'rŏ* or केकरहु *kĕkar'hau*.

§ 29. कुछ *kuchh* or कुछु *kuchhu*, 'anything,' 'something.'

Declined regularly like a substantive. The oblique form is कुछ *kuchh*, कुछु *kuchhu*, or कैथी *kĕthi*.

§ 30. The indefinite pronoun सब *sab* or सभै *sabhai* 'all,' 'every one,' is declined regularly like a substantive. When plurality is to be emphasised, it has an oblique plural form सबनि *sabani*: thus, सब के *sab kĕ* 'of all,' *taken as a whole*; but सबनि के *sabani kĕ*, 'of all,' *taken severally*.

§ 31. The indefinite pronouns जेकोइ *jekoï*, 'whoever,' and जेकुछु *jekuchhu*, 'whatever,' are compounds, and are declined regularly like their component parts: thus, acc. sing. जे केकरो के *je kĕk'rŏ ke*, जे कुछु के *je kuchhu ke*, &c.

The indefinite pronominal adjective केतेक *kĕtĕk* or कै *kai* signifies 'several.' It is also used as an interrogative, meaning 'how many?'

§ 32. Derivative Pronominal Forms.

The following table gives the more usual pronominal adjectives and adverbs in a succinct form.

		Pronoun.	Manner.	
			Pron. Adj.	Pron. Adv.
Demonstrative.	Proximate ...	ई *i*, 'this' ...	अहिन *ahin*, एहनु *ĕhanu*, ईरङ्ग *írang*, or ऐन्ह *ainh*, 'of this kind.'	एहन *ĕhan*, 'thus.'
	Remote ...	ऊ *ú*, 'that' ...	ओहिन *ŏhin*, ओहनु *ŏhanu*, ऊरङ्ग *úrang*, 'of that kind.'	ओहन, *ŏhan*, 'in that way.'
Relative ...	...	जे *je*, 'who' ...	जहिन *jahin*, जेहनु *jĕhanu*, जेरङ्ग *jerang*, 'of what kind.'	जेहन *jĕhan*, 'in what way.'
Correlative ...	...	से *se*, 'that' ...	तहिन *tahin*, तेहनु *tĕhanu*, सेरङ्ग *serang*, 'of that kind.'	तेहन *tĕhan*, 'in that way.'
Interrogative ...	...	के *ke*, 'who?' ...	कहिन *kahin*, केहनु *kĕhanu*, कीरङ्ग *kírang*, 'of what kind?'	केहन *kĕhan*, 'in what way?'

Pron. adj. of **Quantity.**	Pron. adv. of **Time.**	Pron. adv. of **Place.**	Pron. adv. of **Direction.**
एतन्वे *ět'we*, 'this much.'	**एहिया** *ěhiyá*, **एखन** *ěkhan*, or **अबे** *ábe*, 'now.'	**एते** *ěte*, 'here.'	**इन्ने** *inne*, **ईम्हर** *ímhař*, 'hither.'
ओतन्वे *ŏt'we*, 'that much.'	**ओहिया** *ŏhiyá*, **ओखन** *ŏkhan*, 'then.'	**ओते** *ŏte*, 'there.'	**उन्ने** *unne*, **ऊम्हर** *úmhar*, 'thither.'
जेतन्वे *jět'we*, 'how much.'	**जहिया** *jahiyá*, **जखन** *jakhan*, **जबे** *jabe*, 'when.'	**जते** *jate*, 'where.'	**जिन्ने** *jinně*, **जेम्हर** *jemhar*, 'whither.'
तेतन्वे *tět'we*, 'so much.'	**तहिया** *tahiyá*, **तखन** *takhan*, or **तबे** *tabe*, 'then.'	**तते** *tate*, 'there.'	**तिन्ने** *tinně*, **तेम्हर** *temhar*, 'thither.'
केतन्वे *kět'we*, 'how much?'	**कहिया** *kahiyá*, **कखन** *kakhan*, or **कबे** *kabe*, 'when?'	**कते** *kate*, 'where?'	**किन्ने** *kinně*, **कौम्हर** *kimhar*, 'whither?'

§ 33. Adjectival Pronouns.

The following sentences are designed to show the use of the various pronouns, both adjectivally and substantivally.

NOTE that, when used as an adjective, के *ke* always becomes कोन *kon*. की *ki* may also become कोन *kon* in the nominative, and always does so in the oblique cases.

(1) जे ऐल छले, से गेले, *je ail chhalai, se gelai:* 'he who had come went.'

(2) जे अदिमी ऐल छले, से अदिमी गेले, *je adimí ail chhalai, se adimí gelai:* 'the man who had come, went.'

(3) जेकर खेत, तेकर धान, *jekar khet, tekar dhán:* 'he who owns the field, owns the paddy.'

(4) जे अदिमी के खेत, से अदिमी के धान *je adimí kĕ khet, se adimí kĕ dhán:* 'the man who owns the field, owns the paddy.'

(5) के रहे *ke rahe?* 'who was it?'

(6) ऊ कोन अदिमी छिकै *ú kon adimí chhikai?* 'what man is he?'

(7) केकर घोड़ा छिकै *kekar ghoṛá chhikai?* 'whose is the horse?'

(8) कोन अदिमी कर घोड़ा छिकै *kon adimí kar ghoṛá chhikai?* 'to what person does the horse belong?'

(9) की छिकै *kí chhikai?* 'what is it?'

(10) की (or कोन) गाछ छिकै *kí* (or *kon*) *gáchh chhikai?* 'what tree is it?'

(11) किथी मेँ पानि नानल छैँ *kithí mẽ páni nánal chhaĩ?* 'in what have you brought the water?'

(12) कोन लोटा मेँ पानि नानल छैँ *kon loṭá mẽ páni nánal chhaĩ?* 'in what *loṭa* have you brought the water?'

(13) कोइ नहीँ आएल *koï nahí áël,* 'no one came.'

(14) कोइ छौँड़ा नहीँ आएल *koï chhaũṛá nahí áël,* 'no boy came.'

(15) ऊ गाँव मेँ केक॰रो कुछु नहीँ छै *ú gāw mē kĕk'rŏ kuchhu nahī chhai*, 'in that village no one has anything.'

(16) ऊ गाँव के कोइ बनियाँ से कुछु नै मिल॰तै *ú gāw kĕ koï baniyā se kuchhu nai mil'tái*, 'in that village nothing will be got from any shopkeeper.'

(17) ऊ दवाय के केथी मेँ धरे* लगं॰तै *ú dawáy ke kĕthí mē dharĕ* lag'tai*, 'it will be (necessary) to put that medicine into something.'

(18) केतेक पुरुख ऐला *kĕtĕk purukh ailá*, 'several men came,' or 'how many men came?'

§ 34. The Pronominal Oblique Genitive.

In this dialect pronominal genitives have not the oblique form which occurs in other dialects.

---

* Dative of the verbal noun.

DIVISION II.

CONJUGATION.

CHAPTER IV.

INTRODUCTORY.

§ 35. It must be noted with respect to the following paradigms that colloquially the plural is commonly used in the place of the singular: thus तों छऽ *tŏ chha*, 'thou art,' is commonly used instead of तों छैं *tŏ chhĕ*, which is the more correct form. The plural form of some persons, especially the third, is often wanting, or, in other words, the same form is often used both in a singular and in a plural sense.

In Northern and Western Puraniyá, the verb has no forms peculiar to the feminine.

As already observed (§ 1), the language spoken in Northern and Western Puraniyá is in the main Maithilí. It, however, especially in the *sadr* (or central) subdivison, shows a distinct tendency towards Baṅgálí. It will be convenient to note here that the first persons in आँ *ã*, as देख॰लाँ *dĕkh'lã*, and the preterite in तिहाँ *tihã*, as देख॰तिहाँ *dĕkḥ'tihã*, and the other forms from the same stem, as देख॰तिहैं *dĕkh'tihaĩ*, *&c.*, are more used in the *sadr* subdivision; while first persons in ओं *ŏ*, as देख॰लों *dekh'lŏ*, and the preterite conditional in तों *tŏ*, as देख॰तों *dekh'tŏ*, देख॰ता *dĕkh'tá*, *&c.*, are more used in the Ḱráríyá (or northern) subdivision.

§ 36. With regard to the spelling of the various tense-forms, it must be noted that ऐ *ai* and औ *au* are frequently written अइ *aï* and अउ *aü* respectively: thus such forms as देखै *dekhai* and देखौ *dekhau* are often written देखइ *dĕkhaï* and देखउ *dĕkhaü*. It has not been thought necessary to put both these varieties of spelling into the paradigms: hence only देखै

dekhai, देखौ *dekhau*, *&c.*, will be found therein. With regard to this and to the shortening of ante-penultimate vowels, see General Introduction, §§ 34—37

§ 37. Conjugational System.

The conjugation of the verb √ देख *dekh*, 'see,' being given in full, it is not necessary to give here the details of conjugation at length.

§ 38. There are three moods—the Indicative, Conjunctive, and Imperative. These may again be divided into *simple tenses*—formed from the root direct, and *periphrastic tenses*—formed with the aid of auxiliary verbs added to the present or past participle, or to the conjugated preterite indicative.

§ 39. The *simple tenses* are as follows:—

INDICATIVE.	CONJUNCTIVE.	IMPERATIVE.
Preterite.	Present.	Present.
Future.	Preterite.	

Of these, the present imperative is always the same as the present conjunctive.

§ 40. The *periphrastic tenses* are as follows:—

a) From the present participle, direct form—

Indicative—

Definite present	with auxiliary	present.
Imperfect	"	preterite.
Durative future	"	future.

Conjunctive—

Future	with auxiliary	present conjunctive.
Durative present	"	preterite "

b) From the past participle —

Indicative—

Perfect (form II) with auxiliary present.
Pluperfect (form II) „ past.
Future exact (form II) „ future.

Conjunctive—

Future exact (form II) with auxiliary present conjunctive.
Preterite (form II) „ preterite „

c) From the preterite indicative—

Indicative—

Perfect (form I) with auxiliary present.
Pluperfect (form I) „ preterite.
Future exact (form I) „ future.

Conjunctive—

Future exact (form I) with auxiliary present conjunctive.
Preterite (form I) „ preterite „

Concerning the use of the auxiliary in tenses formed from the past participle, see General Introduction, p. 13, cl. (4).

§ 41. The Simple Tenses.

The personal terminations are nearly the same for all these tenses. They are added to a tense-stem, the formation of which will be described afterwards.

The terminations of these three tenses are given in the following table. It will be observed that there are many optional forms of terminations for each person. They are all used with nearly equal frequency. They should be carefully committed to memory.

It must be noted that the termination अ *a* of the 2nd plural masculine is pronounced with a peculiar drawl, something like the English word 'awe.' Thus, देखअ *dekh* 'awe.'

Table showing the Personal Terminations of the Present Conjunctive, the Preterite Indicative, and the Preterite Conjunctive.

Person.	Singular.	Plural.
1st	ऊँ *ú*, ओँ *õ*, औँ *aũ*, आँ *ã*.	ई *ï*, इऐ *iai*, इऔ *iau*.
2nd	आ *á*, ए *e*, ऐं *ẽ*, ऐँ *aĩ*.	अ *a*, हक *hak*.
3rd	ऐ *ai*, ऐक *aik*, औ *au*, औक *auk*.	अत *at*,* औन *aun*.*

The first person is often used honorifically in the sense of the second person: thus आबोँ *ábõ*, 'come.'

§ 42. These terminations are added to various tense-stems, and it is by these tense-stems that the tenses are distinguished. The formation of each tense-stem will be given separately under the heading of each tense, and the conjugation of each tense will now be described in the order in which they will subsequently be given in the conjugation of the model verb √ देख *dekh*, 'see.'

§ 43. The Preterite Indicative.

The stem of this tense is formed by adding अल *al* or इल *il* to the root. To this the terminations in § 41 are added. Thus √ देख *dekh*, 'see,' preterite stem देखल *dekhal* or देखिल *dekhil*, to which the terminations are added: thus देखलूँ *děkh'lú* or देखिलूँ *děkhilú*, 'I saw.' इल *il* is principally used in Central Puraniyá. In the third person singular this tense takes either the terminations in § 41 or else the following:—क्कै *'kai*, क्कैक *'kaik*, क्कौ *'kau*,

---

* The forms only occur in the auxiliary verb √अछ *achh*, 'be.' In the case of other verbs, the singular terminations are used for both numbers.

ऽकौक *'kauk*. Thus, देखलऽकै *dĕkhal'kai*, 'he saw,' गिरलऽकै *giral'kai*, 'he fell.' Moreover—

(*a*) In *transitive verbs*, it may also take the termination अक *ak*. Thus,—देखऽलक *dĕkh'lak* 'he saw.'

(*b*) In the case of *neuter verbs*, it may also either take no termination at all, *e.g.* गिरल *giral*, 'he fell,' or take ऽका *ká*: thus गिरलऽका *giral'ká*, 'he fell.' The first is sometimes made into a feminine form, इ *i*: thus गिरलि *girali*, 'she fell.'

§ 44. The Future Indicative.

This tense has two stems—one for the first and second persons, and one for the third person. The first stem is formed by adding अब *ab* or इब *ib* to the root; the second is the root itself.

The following are the terminations of this tense. All should be added to the root direct.

Terminations of the Future.

Person.	Singular.	Plural.
1st	ऽबै *'bai*, ऽबौ *'bau*, ऽबों *'bŏ̃*, ऽबौं *'baũ*.	अब *ab*, ऽबी *'bi*.
2nd	ऽबा *'bá*, ऽबे *'be*, ऽबें *'bẽ*, ऽबैं *'baĩ*, ऽभें *'bhẽ*, ऽमें *'mẽ*.	ऽबऽ *'ba*, ऽबहक *'bahak*.
3rd	अत *át*, ऽतै *'tai*, ऽतौ *'tau*, इत *it*, इतै *itai*, इतौ *itau*.	

इबै *ibai*, इबौ *ibau*, &c., may be used instead of ऽबै *'bai*, ऽबौ *'bau*, &c. Sometimes an irregular second person plural in ईहक *íhak* or ईहहक *íhahak* is found, *e.g.* देखीहक *dĕkhíhak* or देखीहहक *dĕkhíhahak*, 'you will see.'

§ 45. The Present Conjunctive and Imperative.

In this tense the terminations are added to the root itself: thus देखू *dekhû*, 'let me see.' The terminations are those given in § 41. Besides these, this tense may in the third person singular take ए *e*. It also optionally takes no termination whatever in the second and third persons.

In the plural it may in the second person also take the termination ऽहैन *'hain.*

§ 46. The Preterite Conjunctive.

In this tense अत *at* or ऽतिह *'tih* or ऽति *'ti* is added to the root to form the stem. The personal terminations in § 41 are then added: thus देखऽताँ *dĕkh'tā̃* or देखऽतिहाँ *dĕkh'tihā̃* or देखऽतियाँ *dĕkh'tiā̃*, '(if) I had seen.'

In the third person singular it may drop the usual terminations and end in ऐत *ait* or ऽतिहा *'tihá*, added simply to the root. In the first person plural masculine it optionally takes the termination ऽतिहैँ *'tihãĩ* or ऽतिहैन *'tihain*, added directly to the root. It also forms a peculiar periphrastic third person, which will be noted in § 64.

§ 46a. The Use of the Various Verbal Terminations.

It will be noticed that each person has many terminations, but they do not all mean exactly the same thing. At the same time it must be noted that this multiplicity of verbal forms is partly due to local and personal circumstances—an inhabitant of one place using one set of forms, and an inhabitant of another, another. This is due to the want of a literature, which would fix each verbal form in its proper and exact shade of meaning. The following instructions will help to explain approximately the more customary uses of the forms.

In the first place it must be noted that in the Maithilí dialect generally number is continually disregarded, verbs in the singular form being used with plural subjects, and *vice versâ*. In the third person the singular is almost always used instead of the plural. The only exception is in the case of √ अछ *achh*, see § 41. **Thus take** देखऽलक *dĕkh'lak*, which is properly third singular preterite. The following examples show that it can be used both in a singular and in a plural sense:—

Singular.—वँ हमऱा नद्दी कर कञ्छा पर देखऱ्लक, *wẽ ham'rá naddí kar kańchhá par děkh'lak,* 'he saw me on the bank of the river.'

Plural.—वँ सिभी हमऱा नद्दी कर कञ्छा पर देखऱ्लक *wẽ sibhi ham'rá naddí kar kańchhá par děkh'lak,* 'they saw me on the bank of the river.'

So also छौन *chhaun* (properly 3rd plural) may be used as a singular, viz. वँ छौन *wẽ chhaun*, 'he is,' as well as वँ सिबी छौन *wẽ sibi chhaun,* 'they are.' It may be asked, then, why these terminations have been divided into singular and plural. The answer is twofold,—first, that though no longer used in their proper sense, the terminations were originally singular and plural as written, and in songs (which always conserve an older form of the language) they are so used to the present day. Secondly, at the present day there is this important difference in their use,—singular terminations (especially in the second and third persons) are always used non-honorifically, and plural terminations honorifically, as regards the subject: thus तोँ देखऱ्लेँ *tõ děkh'lẽ* (singular) means 'you (that humble person) saw,' but तोँ देखऱ्लऽ *tõ děkh'la* (plural) 'you (that respectable person) saw.' In the first person, however, this distinction has been lost, and singular and plural are used indiscriminately.

There is another way of looking at a verbal form, and that is the relation it bears to the object. There is nothing like this in any European language; so it requires more careful exemplification in the present case. For the purposes of the present explanation a sentence may be divided into subject, verb, and object. The object may be direct or remote. Thus, in 'the king gave a village to the bráhman,' 'the king' is the subject, 'gave' is the verb, 'a village' is the direct object, and 'the bráhman' is the remote object. So in 'the child fell on the ground,' for the purposes of the present explanation 'the ground' may be considered as the remote object. In European grammar the form of a verb depends on the subject, *i.e.*, we say that it agrees with its subject in number and person, but the object (direct or remote) has no effect at all on the form of the verb. In Bihárí, on the contrary, the selection of the verbal form to be used largely depends upon the object. Thus, while in Europe we must say that the verb agrees with its subject in number and person, in Bihár we must say that it agrees with its subject, and also with its object, in honour and person.

The following are approximately the rules on this point :—

(*a*) The terminations ending in औ *au* are used when the object (direct or remote) is in the second person and is considered inferior to the speaker.

(*b*) The word छौन *chhaun* is used when the object (direct or remote) is in the second person and is spoken of with respect.

(*c*) The terminations ending in ऐ *ai* are used when the object (direct or remote) is in the first or third person and is considered inferior to the subject.

(*d*) The terminations ending in ऐन *ain* are used generally when the subject (direct or remote) is mentioned with great respect. In this case the object may be in the first or third person.

The following examples will make the above clear :—

हम तोहर पोथी बिहान देखऽबौ *ham tohar pothi bihán dĕkh'bau*, 'I will see your book (my humble friend) to-morrow.' (Here the direct object, 'your book,' being inferior and in the second person, a termination ending in औ *au* is used.)

तोर एको बाल टेढ़ नहीँ होतौ *tor eko bál ṭeṛh nahĩ hotau*, 'Not a single one of your hairs (my humble friends) will be bent.'

ढोका टूटि जैतौ *ḍoká ṭúṭi jaitau*, 'The cockle will smash (for you).'

तोरा से ई चूकत भेलौ *torá se í chúkat bhelau*, 'You have made this mistake' (*lit.* by you has this mistake taken place).

कहिया ध्यान मेँ आबै सकैछौ *kahiyá dhyán mẽ ábaĭ sakaichhau*, 'How can it ever get into your credence?'

जौँ तोँ हमऽरा मारि डालऽतिहेँ, तऽ ऊ मोती तोर हाथ लगऽतिहौ *jaũ tõ ham'rá mári ḍál'tihẽ, ta ú moti tor háth lag'tihau*, 'If you had killed me, the pearl would have come (my humble friend) into your hand.'

तोह्‌रा गाड़ी मेँ की माल छौ *tŏh'rá gáṛi mẽ ki mál chhau?* '(My humble friend), what goods are in your cart?'

देस देस आरो गाँ गाँ फिरे से की लाभ छौन *des des arò gẵ gẵ phirĕ se ki lábh chhaun*, 'What profit is there to you (respected sir) in wandering about from country to country and from town to town?'

वेँ ओक्‌रा चाकर के देखल्‌कै ऐ *wẽ ŏk'rá chákar ke dĕkhal'kai ai?* 'Has he (my humble friend) seen his servant?' (Here both subject and object are non-honorific.)

देख्‌लऽ मुर्‌ता नेना के कहिन चाट खीँच के मारल्‌कै *dĕkh'la Mur'tá nená ke kahin cháṭ khích kĕ máral'kai?* 'Did you see how Mur'tá gave a severe slap to the child?' (Here the object, 'the child,' is inferior.)

ओते से गिरा दिहैन *ŏte se girá dihain*, 'Let your honour throw it down from there.'

इहाँ हम्‌रा नेना के देख्‌लोँ छै *ihã ham'rá nená ke dĕkh'lõ chhai*, 'Has your honour seen my child?' (Here the first person of the verb is used honorifically instead of the second person, and no special reference being made to the person of and respect due to the object, the form देख्‌लिऐ *dĕkh'liai* is not used.)

रे छौँड़ा, हम्मर बही देख्‌लेँ छै? *re chhaũṛá, hammar bahi dĕkh'lẽ chhai?* 'Ho! you boy, there, have you seen my book?' (Here the subject is non-honorific, and there is no reference to the object.)

हो काका, देख्‌लऽ मोहन के बौह केहन डाक्‌लक *ho káká, dĕkh'la Mohan kĕ bauh kĕhan ḍák'lak?* 'Hallo, uncle, did you see how Mohan's wife called me?' (Here no special reference is made to the honour of the object.)

CHAPTER V.

AUXILIARY VERBS.

§ 47. There are two classes of auxiliary verbs—the *defective* and the *complete*.

§ 48. There are three *defective auxiliary verbs* in use in this dialect.

(*a*) The first of these is formed from the √ अछ *achh*. It is used only in the present and preterite tenses, and always loses its initial vowel, except in one form of the third singular present. It has in the present tense two forms,—a weak, *e.g.* छै *chhai*, 'he is,' and a strong, *e.g.* छिकै *chhikai*, 'he is.' In the preterite tense it is used only in the weak form, *e.g.* छल *chhal*, 'he was.' I shall call it the *first defective auxiliary verb.*

(*b*) The next of these is formed from the √ अह *ah*, and is very irregular. It exists only in the future tense, and in the third person singular of the present. I shall call it the *second defective auxiliary verb.*

(*c*) The next is formed from the √ रह *rah*, 'remain,' and is used in the present tense in a preterite sense, *e.g.* रहै *rahai*, 'he was' I shall call it the *third defective auxiliary verb.*

§ 49. The complete auxiliary verb is formed from the √ हो *ho*, 'become,' which is conjugated through all moods and tenses. Its preterite is irregular, and is never used as an auxiliary, but only as a verb substantive, meaning 'I became.'

§ 50. First Defective Auxiliary Verb.

√ अछ *achh*, 'be.'

Present : '*I am*,' *&c.*

In this tense an old form of the 3rd plural has survived, and is still used.

WEAK FORM.

Person.	Singular.	Plural.
1st	छूँ *chhû.*	छी *chhi*, छिऐ *chhiai*, छिऔ *chhiau.*
2nd	छेँ *chhẽ.*	छऽ *chha* or (irregular) छौ *chhau.*
3rd	छे *chhe*, छै *chhai*, छौ *chhau.* अछ *achh.*	छत *chhat*, छौन *chhaun.*

STRONG FORM.

Person.	Singular.	Plural.
1st	छिकूँ *chhikû*, छिकोँ *chhikõ*, छिकौँ *chhikaũ*, छिकाँ *chhikā̃.*	छिकी, छिकिऐ, छिकिऔ. *chhiki*, *chhikiai*, *chhikiau.*
2nd	छिका *chhiká*, छिके *chhike*, छिकेँ *chhikẽ*, छिकैँ *chhikaĩ.*	छिकऽ, छिकऽहक. *chhika*, *chhik'hak.*
3rd	छिके, छिकै, छिकैक, *chhike*, *chhikai*, *chhikaik*, छिकौ *chhikau*, छिकौक *chhikauk*, छिक *chhik.*	*Not used.*

Preterite : '*I was*,' *&c.*

Person.	Singular.	Plural.
1st	छलूँ, छलोँ, छलौँ, छलाँ. *chhalū̃*,* *chhalõ*, *chhalaũ*, *chhalā̃*.	छली, छलिऐ, छलिऔ. *chhalī*, *chhaliai*, *chhaliau*
2nd	छला *chhalá*, छले *chhale*, छलेँ *chhalẽ*, छलैँ *chhalaĩ*.	छलऽ, छलहक, *chhala*, *chhalahak*.
3rd	छल *chhal*. छलै, छलैक, छलौ, छलौक, *chhalai*, *chhalaik*, *chhalàu*, *chhalauk*.	*Not used.*

* Or (especially in Central Puraniyá) छिलूँ *chhilū̃* or छेलूँ *chhĕlū̃*, and so throughout.

§ 51. Second Defective Auxiliary Verb.

√ अह *ah*, 'be.'

Present, '*He is.*'

Person.	Singular.	Plural.
1st	*Not used.*	*Not used*
2nd	*Not used.*	*Not used.*
3rd	ऐ *ai.*	*Not used.*

Future, *'I shall be,' &c.*

Person.	Singular.	Plural.
1st	हैबै *haibai*, हैबौ *haibau*, हैबोँ *haibõ*, हैबौँ *haibaũ*.	हैब *haib*, हैबी *haibi*.
2nd	हैबा *haibá*, हैबे *haibe*, हैबेँ *haibẽ*, हैबैँ *hailaĩ*, हैभेँ *haibhẽ*, हैमेँ *haimẽ*.	हैबऽ *haiba*, हैबहक *haebahak*.
3rd	हैत *hait*, हैतै *haitai*, हैतौ *haitau*.	*Not used.*

§ 52. Third Defective Auxiliary Verb.

√रह *rah*, 'be.'

Present *(used in a preterite sense)* :- *'I was,' &c.*

Person.	Singular	Plural.
1st	*Not used.*	रही *rahi*, रहिऐ *rahiai*, रहिऔ *rahiau*.
2nd	रहा *rahá*, रहे *rahe*, रहेँ *rahẽ*, रहैँ *rahaĩ*.	रहऽ *raha*, रहन्हक *rah'hak*.
3rd	रहे *rahe*, रहै *rahai*, रहैक *rahaik*, रहौ *rahau*, रहौक *rahauk*.	*Not used.*

§ 53. The Complete Auxiliary Verb.

√ हो *ho*, 'be,' 'become.'

INDICATIVE MOOD.

(*a*)—Preterite: '*I became*,' *&c.*

NOTE.—This tense is never used as an auxiliary, छलूँ *chhalū́* or रही *rahī* (see above) being used instead. It has two forms, a regular and an irregular.

REGULAR FORM.

Person.	Singular.	Plural.
1st	होलूँ *holū́.*	होली *holí.*
2nd	होला *holá.*	होलह *hola.*
3rd	होल *hol.*	*Not used.*

Optional forms as in छलूँ *chhalū́.*

IRREGULAR FORM.

Person.	Singular.	Plural.
1st	भेलूँ *bhelū́.*	भेली *bhelí.*
2nd	भेला *bhelá.*	भेलह *bhela.*
3rd	भेल *bhel.*	*Not used.*

Optional forms as in छलूँ *chhalū́.* भैल *bhail* may be used instead of भेल *bhel* throughout.

§ 54. (*b*)—Future : '*I shall be*,' *&c.*

Person.	Singular.	Plural.
1st	होबै *hobai*, होबौ *hobau*, होबौँ *hobõ*, होबौँ *hobaũ*.	होब *hob*, होबी *hobí*.
2nd	होबा *hobá*, होबे *hobe*, होबेँ *hobẽ*, होबैँ *hobai*, होभेँ *hobhẽ*, होमेँ *homẽ*.	होबठ *hoba*, होबहक *hŏbahak*.
3rd	होत *hot*, होतै *hotai*, होतौ *hotau*.	*Not used.*

Many people say होअबै *hoabai*, or होइबै *hoibai*, or होएबै *hoëbai*, instead of होबै *hobai*, and so throughout.

CONJUNCTIVE MOOD.

§ 55. (*c*)—Present : '*(If) I be*,' *&c.*

Person.	Singular.	Plural.
1st.	होऊँ *hoú*, होओँ *hoõ*, होऔँ *hoaũ*, होआँ *hoá*.	होई *hoí*, होइऐ *hoïai*, होइऔ *hoïau*.
2nd	होआ *hoá*, होए *hoe*, होएँ *hoẽ*, होऐँ *hoaĩ*.	होअ *hoa*.
	हो *ho*.	होहू *hohú*, होहो *hoho*, होहैन *hohain*.
3rd	हो *ho*.	*Not used.*
	होए *hoë*, होऐ *hoai*, होऐक *hoaik*.	
	होऔ *hoau*, होऔक *hoauk*.	

§ 56. (*d*)—Preterite: '*(If) I had been,*' *&c.*

FORM I.

Person.	Singular.	Plural.
1st	होतूँ *hotū̃*,* होतों *hotõ*, होतौं *hotaũ*, होताँ *hotā̃*.	होती *hotí*, होतिऐ *hŏtiai*, होतिऔ *hŏtiau*.
2nd	होता *hotá*, होते *hote*, होतेँ *hotẽ*, होतैँ *hotãi*.	होतऽ *hota*, होतहक *hŏtahak*.
3rd	होएत *hoait* or होत *hot*, होतै *hotai*, होतैक *hotaik*, होतौ *hotau*, होतौक *hotauk*.	*Not used.*

* Or होअतूँ *hoatū̃*, and so throughout.

FORM II.

Person.	Singular.	Plural.
1st	होतिहूँ *hŏtihū̃*, होतिहोँ *hŏtihõ*, होतिहौँ *hŏtihaũ*, होतिहाँ *hŏtihā̃*.	होतिही *hŏtihí*. होतिहैँ *hŏtihãi*, होतिहैन *hŏtihain*.
2nd	होतिहा *hŏtihá*, होतिहे *hŏtihe*, होतिहेँ *hŏtihẽ*, होतिहैँ *hŏtihãi*.	होतिहऽ *hŏtiha*.
3rd	होतिहै *hŏtihai*, होतिहैक *hŏtihaik*, होतिहौ *hŏtihau*, होतिहौक *hŏtihauk* होतिहा *hŏtihá*.	*Not used.*

Periphrastic form for 3rd present, होबे हैत *hole hait*,—see § 64.

§ 57. Imperative Mood.

Present : '*Let me see,*' *&c.*

The same as the present conjunctive.

Precative Forms.

होउ *hoú*, होएत *noĕt*, हेाइअ *hoïa*, 'be good enough to be.'

The periphrastic tenses are quite regular, and need not be given.

§ 58. Present Participle, '*being.*'

Singular and Plural.

होत *hot* or होइत *hoït.*

Past Participle, '*been.*'

होल *hol* or भेल *bhel.*

Conjunctive Participle, '*having been.*'

भे के *bhe kĕ*, भै के *bhai kĕ*, हो के *ho kĕ*, or होइ के *hoï kĕ.*

Infinitive, '*to be.*'

होब *hob.*

CHAPTER VI.

THE REGULAR ACTIVE VERB.

§ 59. There is only one conjugation of active verbs, if we except a few irregular verbs to be noted further on. The conjugation of neuter verbs differs from that of active verbs only in certain of the past tenses, and these will be treated of in a future page. Verbs whose roots end in vowels also exhibit slight variations, which will be explained at the proper place. For the sake of uniformity the tenses are given in the same order, and under the same names as those in Dr. Hoernle's grammar.

Reference is again made to General Introduction, §§ 34 to 36, with regard to the changes of the root-vowel.

§ 60. √देख *dekh*, 'see.'

PRESENT PARTICIPLE: देखैत *dekhait.*

PAST PARTICIPLE: देखल *dekhal.*

Simple Tenses.

INDICATIVE MOOD.

§ 61. (*a*)—Preterite: '*I saw,*' *&c.*

Person.	Singular.	Plural.
1st	देखःलूँ *děkh'lú*,* देखःलों *děkh'lõ*, देखःलौँ *děkh'laũ*.	देखःली *děkh'lí*.
	देखःलाँ *děkh'lã*.	देखःलिऐ *děkh'liai*, देखःलिऔ *děkh'liau*.
2nd	देखःला *děkh'lá*, देखःले *děkh'le*, देखःलेँ *děkh'lẽ*.	देखःलह *děkh'la*. देखःलहक *děkh'lahak*.
	देखःलैँ *děkh'laĩ*.	
3rd	देखःलै *děkh'lai*, देखःलैक *děkh'laik*, देखःलौ *děkh'lau*, देखःलौक *děkh'lauk*, देखलःकै *děkhal'kai*, देखलःकैक *děkhal'kaik*, देखलःकौ *děkhal'kau*, देखलःकौक *děkhal'kauk*, देखःलक *děkh'lak*.	-*Not used*.

* Or (in Central Puraniyá) देखिलूँ *děkhilú*, and so throughout.

§ 62. (*b*)—Future: '*I shall see,*' *&c.*

Person.	Singular.	Plural.
1st	देख॰बै *dĕkh'bai*,* देख॰बौ *dĕkh'bau*. देख॰बोँ *dĕkh'bõ*, देख॰बौँ *dĕkh'baũ*.	देखब *dekhab*, देख॰बी *dĕkh'bí*.
2nd	देख॰बा *dĕkh'bá*, देख॰बे *dĕkh'be*, देख॰बेँ *dĕkh'bẽ*. देख॰बैँ *dĕkh'baĩ*. देख॰भेँ *dĕkh'bhẽ*, देख॰मेँ *dĕkh'mẽ*.	देख॰बह *dĕkh'ba*, देख॰बहक *dĕkh'bahak*. देखीहक *dĕkhíhak*. देखीहहक *dekhíhahak*.
3rd	देखत *dekhat*. देख॰तै *dĕkh'tai*. देख॰तौ *dĕkh'tau*. Or— देखित *dekhit*. देखितै *dĕkhitai*. देखितौ *dĕkhitau*.	*Not used.*

* Or देखिबै *dĕkhibai*, and so throughout.

CONJUNCTIVE (CONDITIONAL) MOOD.

§ 63. (*c*)—**Present**: '*(If) I see;*' rarely '*I see,*' or '*I shall see,*' *&c.*

Person.	Singular.	Plural.
1st	देखूँ *dekhū́*. देखों *dekhõ*, देखौँ *dekhaũ*, देखाँ *dekhā́*.	देखी *dekhi*, देखिऐ *děkhiai*, देखिऔ *děkhiau*.
2nd	देखा *dekhá*, देखे *dekhe*, देखेँ *dekhẽ*, देखैँ *dekhãĩ*. देख *dekh*.	देखठ *dekha*, देख्हक *děkh'hak*, देख्हैन *děkh'hain*.
3rd	देखै *dekhai*, देखैक *dekhaik*, देखौ *dekhau*, देखौक *dekhauk*, देखे *dekhe*, देख *dekh*.	*Not used.*

§ 64. (*d*)—**Preterite**: '(*If*) *I had seen,*' *&c.*

(FORM I.)

Person.	Singular.	Plural.
1st	देख्तूँ *děkh'tū́*, देख्तों *děkh'tõ*, देख्तौँ *děkh'taũ*, देख्ताँ *děkh'tā́*.	देख्ती *děkh'ti*. देख्तिऐ *děkh'tiai*, देख्तिऔ *děkh'tiau*, देख्तिहैँ *děkh'tihãĩ*, देख्तिहैन्ह *děkh'tihainh*.
2nd	देख्ता *děkh'tá*, देख्ते *děkh'te*, देख्तेँ *dekh'tẽ*. देख्तैँ *dekh'tãĩ*.	देख्तठ *děkh'ta*. देख्तहक *děkh'tahak*.
3rd	देखैत *dekhait*. देख्तै *děkh'tai*, देख्तैक *děkh'taik*, देख्तौ *děkh'tau*, देख्तौक *děkh'tauk*.	*Not used.*

(FORM II.)

Person.	Singular.	Plural.
1st	देखऽतिहूँ *dĕkh'tihū̃*,* देखऽतिहोँ *dĕkh'tihõ*, देखऽतिहौँ *dĕkh'tihaũ*, देखऽतिहाँ *dĕkh'tihā̃*.	देखऽतिही *dĕkh'tihī*, देखऽतिहैँ *dĕkh'tihaĩ*, देखऽतिहैन *dekk'tihain*.
2nd	देखऽतिहा *dĕkh'tihá*, देखऽतिहे *dĕkh'tihe*, देखऽतिहेँ *dĕkh'tihẽ*, देखऽतिहैँ *dĕkh'tihaĩ*.	देखऽतिहऽ *dĕkh'tiha*.
3rd	देखऽतिहै *dĕkh'tihai*, देखऽतिहैक *dĕkh'tihaik*, देखऽतिहौ *dĕkh'tihau*, देखऽतिहौक *dĕkh'tihauk*, देखऽतिहा *dĕkh'tihá*.	*Not used.*

* Or देखऽतिऊँ *dĕkh'tiū̃*, and so throughout.

This tense also forms its third person periphrastically by adding the 3rd person preterite of the verb to the third person future of the second auxiliary verb : thus देखलऽकै हैत *dĕkhal'kai hait*. I have also come across a peculiar form for the same person which I am not able to explain satisfactorily, viz. देखऽतिहैत *dĕkh'tihait*.

IMPERATIVE MOOD.

§ 65. (*e*)—**Present.**—Same as present conjunctive.

Precative Forms.

2nd person : देखी *dekhī*, देखत *dĕkhat*, देखिअ *dĕkhia*, 'be pleased to see.'

(B)—Periphrastic Tenses.

INDICATIVE MOOD.

§ 66. In the following paradigms the optional forms and dialectic forms of the auxiliary verbs will not all be given, as taking up too much valuable space.

§ 67. (*g*)—Definite Present: '*I am seeing,*' &c.

Person.	Singular.	Plural.
1st	देखैछूँ *dekhaichhũ.*	देखैछी *dekhaichhî.*
2nd	देखैछैँ *dekhaichhẽ.*	देखैछऽ *dekhaichhŏ*
3rd	देखैछै *dekhaichhai* or देखैऐ *dekhaiai.*	*Not used.*

Any optional form of the present of the defective auxiliary verb may be used; also the strong form of the defective auxiliary verb. Thus, first plural देखैछिऐ *dekhaichhiai* or देखैछिकी *dekhaichhikî.* The word देखै *dekhai* is only the present participle देखैत *dekhait* with the final त *t* dropped. देखैऐ *dekhaiai* is sometimes used for the first person, meaning 'I am seeing.'

§ 68. (*i*)—imperfect: '*I was seeing.*'

Person.	Singular.	Plural.
1st	देखैछलाँ *dekhaichhalã.*	देखैछली *dekhaichhalî.*
2nd	देखैछलैँ *dekhaichhalẽ.*	देखैछलऽ *dekhaichhala.*
3rd	देखैछल *dekhaichhal.*	*Not used.*

Any optional form of the preterite oı the defective auxiliary verb may be used. In Central Puraniyá the form देखैछिलाँ *dĕkhaichhilã* is preferred.

§ 69. (*j*)—Durative Future: '*I shall be seeing,*' *&c.*

Person.	Singular.	Plural.
1st	देखैहोबै *dekhaihobai.*	देखैहोब *dekhaihob.*
2nd	देखैहोबैँ *dekhaihobẽ.*	देखैहोबऽ *dekhaihoba.*
3rd	देखैहोत *dekhaihot.*	*Not used.*

Any optional form of the future of the complete auxiliary verb may be used throughout.

§ 70. (*k*)—Perfect: '*I have seen,*' *&c.*

This tense has two forms of conjugation, used with equal frequency.

FORM I.

Person.	Singular.	Plural.
1st	देखलौँ ऐ *dĕkh'lŏ ai.*	देखली ऐ *dĕkh'lí ai.*
2nd	देखलैँ ऐ *dĕkh'lẽ ai.*	देखलऽ ऐ *dĕkh'la ai.*
3rd	देखलक ऐ *dĕkh'lak ai.*	*Not used.*

Any optional form of the preterite may be used, and छै *chhai* may be used instead of ऐ *ai.* In Central Puraniyá देखिलौँ *dĕkhilŏ*, &c., is preferred to देखलौँ *dĕkh'lŏ*, &c.

FORM II.

Person.	Singular.	Plural.
1st	देखल छूँ *dekhal chhû.*	देखल छी *dekhal chhî.*
2nd	देखल छेँ *dekhal chhẽ.*	देखल छ *dekhal chha.*
3rd	*Not used.*	*Not used.*

As in the definite present, any optional form of the present of the defective auxiliary verb may be used, and also the strong form of the defective auxiliary verb: thus, first plural देखल छिऐ *dekhal chhiai*, देखल छिकी *dekhal chhikî*, and so on. In Central Puraniyá देखिल *dekhil* is preferred to देखल *dekhal*.

§ 71. (*l*)—Pluperfect: '*I had seen*,' *&c.*

This also, like the perfect, has two forms of conjugation.

FORM I.

Person.	Singular.	Plural.
1st	देखल्लौँ रहे *děkh'lõ rahe.*	देखल्ली रहे *děkh'lî rahe.*
2nd	देखल्लैँ रहे *děkh'lẽ rahe.*	देखल्लठ रहे *děkh'la rahe.*
3rd	देखल्लक रहे *děkh'lak rahe.*	*Not used.*

Any of the other forms of the preterite may be used throughout. In Central Puraniyá देखिलौँ *děkhilõ*, &c., is preferred to देखल्लौँ *děkh'lõ*, &c.

FORM II.

Person.	Singular.	Plural.
1st	देखल छलाँ *dekhal chhalā̆.*	देखल छली *dekhal chhalī̆.*
2nd	देखल छलैँ *dekhal chhalĕ̃.*	देखल छलऽ *dekhal chhala.*
3rd	*Not used.*	*Not used.*

Any optional form of the preterite of the defective auxiliary verb may be used. Also रही *rahī̆*, रहैँ *rahĕ̃*, &c., may be used as the auxiliary In Central Puraniyá the form देखिल छिलाँ *dekhil chhilā̆* is preferred.

§ 72. (*m*)—**Future Exact**: '*I shall have seen,*' '*I may have seen,*' *&c.*

This tense also has two forms of conjugation.

FORM I.

Person.	Singular.	Plural.
1st	देखन्लोँ होत *dĕkh'lŏ̃ hot.*	देखन्ली होत *dĕkh'lī̆ hot.*
2nd	देखन्लैँ होत *dĕkh'lĕ̃ hot.*	देखन्लऽ होत *dĕkh'la hot.*
3rd	देखन्लक होत *dĕkh'lak hot.*	*Not used.*

Any other forms of the preterite may be used throughout. In Centra Puraniyá देखिलोँ *dekhilŏ̃*, &c., is preferred to देखन्लोँ *dĕkh'lŏ̃*.

FORM II.

Person.	Singular.	Plural.
1st	देखल होबै *dekhal hobai.*	देखल होब *dekhal hob.*
2nd	देखल होबँ *dekhal hobã.*	देखल होब॰ *dekhal hoba.*
3rd	*Not used.*	*Not used.*

Any other form of the future of the complete auxiliary verb may be used instead throughout. In Central Puraniyá the form देखिल *dekhil* is preferred to देखल *dekhal.*

CONJUNCTIVE (CONDITIONAL) MOOD.

§ **73.** (*n*) —**Future Conditional** : '(*If*) *I be seeing,' &c.*

Person.	Singular.	Plural.
1st	देखैहोऊँ *dekhaihoũ.*	देखैहोइ *dekhaihoi.*
2nd	देखैहोआ *dekhaihoá.*	देखैहोअ *dekhaihoa.*
3rd	देखैहोऐ *dekhaihoai.*	*Not used.*

Any other form of the present conjunctive of the complete auxiliary verb may be used instead throughout.

§ 74. (*o*)—**Durative Present Conditional**: '*(If) I were seeing,*' *&c.*

Person.	Singular.	Plural.
1st	देखैहोतूँ *dekhaihotû.*	देखैहोती *dekhaihotî.*
2nd	देखैहोता *dekhaihotá.*	देखैहोतऽ *dekhaihota.*
3rd	देखैहोऐत *dekhaihoait.*	*Not used.*

Any other form of the preterite conditional of the complete auxiliary verb may be used instead throughout. So also होतिहुँ *hŏtihû,* &c.

§ 75. (*p*)—**Future Exact Conditional**: '*(If) I have seen,*' *&c.*

This tense also has two forms of conjugation.

Form I.

Person.	Singular.	Plural.
1st	देखऽलौं होऐ *dĕkh'lõ hoai.*	देखऽली होऐ *dĕkh'lî hoai.*
2nd	देखऽलेँ होऐ *dĕkh'le hoai.*	देखलऽ होऐ *dĕkh'la hoai.*
3rd	देखऽलक होऐ *dĕkh'lak hoai.*	*Not used.*

Any other form of the preterite may be used througheut. In Central Puraniyá देखिलौं *dĕkhilõ,* &c., is preferred to देखऽलौं *dĕkh'lõ,* &c.

FORM II.

Person.	Singular.	Plural.
1st	देखल होऊँ *dekhal hoû.*	देखल होइ *dekhal hoi.*
2nd	देखल होआ *dekhal hoá.*	देखल होअ *dekhal hoa.*
3rd	*Not used.*	*Not used.*

Any other form of the present conjunctive of the complete auxiliary verb may be used instead throughout. In Central Puraniyá the form देखिल *dekhil* is preferred to देखल *dekhal.*

§ 76. (*q*)—Preterite Conditional: '(*If*) *I had seen,*' *&c.*

This tense also has two forms of conjugation.

FORM I.

Person.	Singular.	Plural.
1st	देखऽलौं होएत *dĕkh'lõ hoait.*	देखऽली होएत *dĕkh'lì hoait.*
2nd	देखऽलैं होएत *dĕkh'lẽ hoait.*	देखऽलऽ होएत *dĕkh'la hoait.*
3rd	देखऽलक होएत *dĕkh'lak hoait.*	*Not used.*

Any other form of the preterite may be used. In Central Puraniyá देखिलौं *dĕkhilõ*, &c., is preferred to देखऽलौं *dĕkh'lõ*, &c.

FORM II.

Person.	Singular.	Plural.
1st	देखल होतूँ *dekhal hotû.*	देखल होती *dekhal hotî.*
2nd	देखल होता *dekhal hotá.*	देखल होतह *dekhal hota.*
3rd	*Not used.*	*Not used.*

Any other form of the preterite conditional of the complete auxiliary verb may be used instead throughout. In Central Puraniyá the form देखिल *dekhil* is preferred to देखल *dekhal.*

§ 77. Participles.

ADJECTIVAL.

Present, 'seeing' . . . { देखैत *dekhait,* देखित *dekhit,* or देखत *dekhat ; obl.,* देखितेँ *dĕkhitĕ̃* or देखन्तेँ *dĕkh'tĕ̃.*

Past, 'seen' . . . . . देखल *dekhal* or देखिल *dekhil : obl.* देखल्ला *dekh'lá.*

CONJUNCTIVE.

'Having seen' . . . . { देख* के *dekh kĕ,* देख कै *dekh kaĭ,* देखि के *dekhi kĕ,* देखि कै *dekhi kaĭ.*

§ 78. Infinitives or Verbal Nouns, *'to see,' 'the act of seeing.'*

Nominative.	Oblique.
देख *dekh,** देखि *dekhi.*	देखे *dekhĕ* or देखै *dekhaĭ.*
देखल *dekhal.*	देखल्ला *dĕkh'lá.*
देखब *dekhab.*	*Wanting.*

§ 79. Noun of Agency, *'one who sees.'*

देखनिहार *dĕkh'nihár,* देखेवाला *dĕkhĕwálá,* or देखवैया *dĕkh'waiyá.*

* This form of the verbal noun is always the same as the root. So also in the conjunctive participle.

CHAPTER VII.

THE REGULAR NEUTER VERB.

§ 80. This verb differs from the active verb only in the formation of certain of its past tenses. The three more usual past tenses are here given; the conjugation of the rest of the verb can be learnt from the conjugation of the √ देख *dekh*.

§ 81. √ गिर *gir*, 'fall.'

Past Participle: गिरल *giral* or गिरिल *giril*.

Indicative Mood.

§ 82. (*a*)—Preterite: '*I fell*,' *&c.*

Person.	Singular.	Plural.
1st	गिरऽलूँ *gir'lú*,* गिरऽलोँ *gir'lõ*, गिरलौँ *gir'laũ*. गिरलाँ *gir'lã́*.	गिरऽली *gir'lí*. गिरऽलिऐ *gir'liai*, गिरऽलियौ *gir'liau*.
2nd	गिरऽला *gir'lá*, गिरऽले *gir'le*, गिरऽलेँ *gir'lẽ*, गिरऽलैँ *gir'laĩ*.	गिरऽलह *gir'la*, गिरऽलहक *gir'lahak*.
3rd	गिरऽलै *gir'lai*, गिरऽलैक *gir'laik*, गिरऽलौ *gir'lau*, गिरऽलौक *gir'lauk*, गिरलऽकै, गिरलऽकैक, *giral'kai*, *giral'kaik*, गिरलऽकौ, गिरलऽकौक *giral'kau*, *giral'kauk*, गिरल *giral*, (fem. गिरलि *girali*). गिरलऽका *giral'ká*.	*Not used.*

* Or (especially in Central Puraniyá) गिरिलूँ *girilú*, and so throughout.

§ 83. (*k*)—Perfect : '*I have fallen,*' *&c.*

FORM I.

Person.	Singular.	Plural.
1st	गिर॰लौँ ऐ *gir'lõ ai.*	गिर॰ली ऐ *gir'li ai.*
2nd	गिर॰लैँ ऐ *gir'lẽ ai.*	गिर॰लऽ ऐ *gir'la ai.*
3rd	गिरल ऐ *giral ai.*	*Not used.*

Any of the other forms of the preterite may be used throughout. Also छै *chhai* may be used instead of ऐ *ai.* In Central Puraniyá गिरिलौँ *girilõ*, &c., is preferred to गिर॰लौँ *gir'lõ*, &c.

FORM II.

This form means, '*I am fallen,*' rather than '*I have fallen.*'

Person.	Singular.	Plural.
1st	गिरल छूँ *giral chhũ.*	गिरल छी *giral chhí.*
2nd	गिरल छैँ *giral chhẽ.*	गिरल छऽ *giral chha.*
3rd	*Not used.*	*Not used.*

Any optional form of the present of the defective auxiliary verb may be used, and the strong form of the defective auxiliary verb: thus, गिरल छिऐ *giral chhiai*, गिरल छिकी *giral chhiki*, *&c.* In Central Puraniyá गिरिल *giril* is preferred to गिरल *giral.*

§ 84. (*l*)—Pluperfect: '*I had fallen,*' *&c.*

Form I.

Person.	Singular.	Plural.
1st	गिर॰लोँ रहे *gir'lõ rahe.*	गिर॰ली रहे *gir'lí rahe.*
2nd	गिर॰लेँ रहे *gir'lẽ rahe.*	गिर॰लह रहे *gir'la rahe.*
3rd	गिरल रहे *giral rahe.*	*Not used*

Any of the other forms of the preterite may be used throughout. In Central Puraniyá गिरिलोँ *girilõ*, &c., is preferred to गिर॰लोँ *gir'lõ*, &c.

Form II.

This form means '*I was fallen,*' rather than '*I had fallen.*'

Person.	Singular.	Plural.
1st	गिरल छलाँ *giral chhalã́.*	गिरल छली *giral chhalí.*
2nd	गिरल छलेँ *giral chhalẽ.*	गिरल छलह *giral chhala.*
3rd	*Not used.*	*Not used.*

Any optional form of the preterite of the second auxiliary verb may be used. Also रही *rahí*, रहेँ *rahẽ*, &c., may be used as the auxiliary. In Central Puraniyá the form गिरिल छिलाँ *giril chhilã́* is preferred.

CHAPTER VIII.

VOCALIC ROOTS.

§ 85. Many verbs have roots ending in vowels, and the junction of the root with the termination frequently causes some slight apparent irregularity.

For this reason the following examples are given of the conjugation of verbs having roots ending in vowels. They are here conjugated in the masculine gender, and through the four radical and participial tenses. From these the periphrastic tenses can easily be formed. It has not been thought necessary to give the conjugation in full for each person.

With regard to the shortening of the root-vowel, see General Introduction, § 36.

§ 86. Example of a verb whose root ends in आ *á* :—

The conjugation of these verbs should be carefully studied, as a large class of active and causal verbs follows it.

In the preterite indicative these verbs insert a junction vowel between the root and the ल *l* of the termination : thus ख* + ए + लोँ *kha* + *ĕ* + *lŏ*, or खैलोँ *khailŏ*, 'I ate,' and प* + ए + लोँ *pa* + *ĕ* + *lŏ*, or पैलोँ *pailŏ*, 'I got,' where ए *ĕ* is the junction vowel. As will be subsequently seen, the same peculiarity exists in other tenses besides the preterite.

All verbs which take ए *ĕ* in the preterite indicative insert ए *e* or इ *i* in the future, in the past participle, and in that form of the 3rd singular preterite which is the same as the past participle.

---

* With regard to the shortening of the root-vowel and contraction of concurrent vowels, see General Introduction, §§ 34, 36.

§ 87. The first verbal noun, or root, of these verbs sometimes ends in आब *áb* or आव *áw*, and sometimes in आ *á*, according to the following rule :—

1) All active (including causal) roots end in आब *áb* : thus पाब *páb* or पाव *páw*, 'obtain;' obl. पाबे *pábĕ* or पावे *páwĕ*.

   Exception.—The √ खा *khá*, 'eat,' although active, ends in आ *á*.

2) All neuter roots end in आ : thus अघा *aghá*, 'satiate;' obl. अघाए *agháĕ*.

   Exceptions.—The √गाब *gáb*, 'sing,' and the √आब *áb*, 'come,' though neuter, end in आब *áb*.

Verbs whose roots end in आब *áb* may optionally insert a ब *b* or व *w* in the present conjunctive and in the present participle, but not those whose roots end in आ *á*.

Note also that all verbs whose roots end in आब *áb* may drop the ब *b* and be conjugated like simple verbs in आ *á*.

§ 88. √पा *pa*, 'get.'

INFINITIVE (1ST FORM) : पाइ *páï*, पा *pá*, पै *pai*, पाब *páb*, or पाव *páw* ; obl. पाबे *pábĕ* or पाए *páĕ*, पै *pai* or पा *pá*.*

,, (2ND FORM) : पाएल *páĕl*, पाइल *páïl*, or पैल *païl*.

PRES. PART. पाबैत *pábait*, पाएत *páĕt*, पाइत *páït*, or पैत *pait*.†

---

* But from √खा *khá*; *Dir.* only खाइ *kháï*, खा *khá*, or खै *khai*. *Obl.* only खाए *kháĕ*, खै *khai*, or खा *khá*.

† But from √खा *khá*, only खाइत *kháït* or खात *khát*.

INDICATIVE MOOD.

Person.	PRETERITE. (See remarks above.)		FUTURE.	
	Singular.	Plural.	Singular.	Plural.
1st	पैलौं *pailā̃.*	पैली *pailī.*	पैबै *paibai.*	पाएब *páĕb* or पैब *paib.*
2nd	पैलैं *pailẽ.*	पैलऽ *paila.*	पैबैं *paibẽ.*	पैबऽ *paiba.*
3rd	पैलन्कै *pail'kai.*	*Not used.*	पैत *paitai.*	*Not used.*

IRREGULAR 2ND PLURAL IMPERATIVE : पो *po.*

CONDITIONAL MOOD.

Person.	PRESENT.		PRETERITE.	
	Singular.	Plural.	Singular.	Plural.
1st	पाऊँ *páū̃** or [पाबौं *pábõ.*	पाई *pái,* पइऐ *païai,* or पैऐ *paiai,* or [पाबी *pábi.*	पैतौं *paitõ.* पैतिहाँ *paitihā̃.*	पैती *paiti,* पैतिहैं *paitihaĩ.*
2nd	पाएँ *páẽ* or पाबैं [*pábẽ.*	पाअ *páa* or [पाबऽ *pába.*	पैतैं *paitẽ,* पैतिहैं *paitihẽ.*	पैतऽ *paita,* पैतिहऽ *paitiha.*
3rd	पाऐ *páai* or पाबै [*pábai.*	*Not used.*	पाबैत *pábait* or पाइत [*páït.*† पैतिहै *păitihai.*	*Not used.*

* From √ खा *khá,* and other roots ending in आ *á,* the forms are only—

Sing.—(1) खाऊँ *kháū̃,* (2) खाएँ *khaẽ,* (3) खाऐ *kháai.*

Plur.—(1) खाई *khái,* (2) खाअ *kháa,* and not खाबौं *khábõ,* &c.

† But from √ खा *khá* only खाइत *kháït,* and not खाबैत *khábait.* It may be noted here that the 3rd sing. pret. conj. is always the same as the present participle in al its various forms.

§ 89. Example of a verb whose root ends in ई í:—

√पी pí, 'drink.'

INFINITIVE
- (1ST FORM) : पी *pí* ; obl. पीए *píĕ*.
- (2ND FORM) : पीअल *píal* or पील *píl*.
- (3RD FORM) : पीअब *píab* or पीब *píb*.

PRES. PART. पीत *pít*.

INDICATIVE MOOD.

Person.	Preterite.		Future.	
	Singular.	Plural.	Singular.	Plural.
1st	पीलाँ *pílá̃*.*	पीली *pílí*.	पीबै *píbai*.	पीअब *píab* or पीब *píb*.
2nd	पीलेँ *pílĕ̃*.	पीलऽ *píla*.	पीबेँ *píbĕ̃*.	पीबऽ *píba*.
3rd	पिलकै *pil'kai*.	*Not used.*	पीतै *pítai*.	*Not used.*

* Or पीअलाँ *píalá̃*, and so throughout.

CONDITIONAL MOOD.

Person.	Present.		Preterite.	
	Singular.	Plural.	Singular.	Plural.
1st	पीऊँ *píú̃*.	पीइ *píi*.	पीताँ *pítŏ̃*.*	पीती *píti*.
2nd	पीएँ *píĕ̃*.	पीअ *pía*.	पीतेँ *pítĕ̃*.	पीतऽ *píta*.
3rd	पीऐन्ह *píai*.	*Not used.*	पीत *pít*.	*Not used.*

* Or पितिहाँ *pitihá̃*, &c.

§ 90. Example of a verb whose root ends in ऊ *ú* :—

√चू *chú*, 'drip.'

INFINITIVE (1ST FORM) : चू *chú ;* obl. चूए *chúĕ.*
(2ND FORM) : चूअल *chúal* or चूल *chúl*, 'to drip.'
(3RD FORM) : चूअब *chúab* or चूब *chúb.*

PRES. PART. चूत *chút.*

INDICATIVE MOOD.

Person.	PRETERITE.		FUTURE.	
	Singular.	Plural.	Singular.	Plural.
1st	चूलाँ * *chúlā̃.*	चूली *chúlī.*	चूबै *chúbai.*	चूअब *chúab* or चूब *chúb.*
2nd	चूलेँ *chúlẽ.*	चूलह *chúla.*	चूबेँ *chúbẽ.*	चूबह *chúba.*
3rd	चूल *chúl.*	*Not used.*	चूतै *chútai.*	*Not used.*

* Or चूअलाँ *chúalā̃*, and so throughout.

CONDITIONAL MOOD.

Person.	PRESENT.		PRETERITE.	
	Singular.	Plural.	Singular.	Plural.
1st	चूऊँ *chúū̃.*	चूईं *chúī̃.*	चूतों* *chútõ.*	चूती *chútī.*
2nd	चूएँ *chúẽ.*	चूअ *chúa.*	चूतेँ *chútẽ.*	चूतह *chúta.*
3rd	चूऐ *chúai.*	*Not used.*	चूत *chút.*	*Not used.*

* Or चुतिहाँ *chutihā̃*, &c.

§ 91. Example of a verb whose root ends in ओ *o*:—

√ धो *dho*, 'wash.'

INFINITIVE { (1ST FORM): धो *dho*; obl. धोए *dhoë*.
(2ND FORM): धोअल *dhoal* or धोल *dhol*.
(3RD FORM): धोअब *dhoab* or धोब *dhob*. }

PRES. PART. धोत *dhot*.

INDICATIVE MOOD.

Person.	PRETERITE.		FUTURE.	
	Singular.	Plural.	Singular.	Plural.
1st	धोअलाँ *dhoälā̃*.*	धोअली *dhoäli*.	धोबै *dhobai*.	धोअब *dhoäb* or धोब *dhob*.
2nd	धोअलेँ *dhoälẽ*.	धोअलह *dhoäla*.	धोबेँ *dhobẽ*.	धोबह *dhoba*.
3rd	धोअल *dhoäl*.	*Not used.*	धोतै *dhotai*.	*Not used.*

* Or धोलाँ *dholā̃*, and so throughout.

CONDITIONAL MOOD.

Person.	PRESENT.		PRETERITE.	
	Singular.	Plural.	Singular.	Plural.
1st	धोऊँ *dhoū̃*.	धोइ *dhoi*.	धोताँ *dhotŏ̃*.*	धोती *dhoti*.
2nd	धोएँ *dhoẽ*.	धोअ *dhoa*.	धोतेँ *dhotẽ*.	धोतह *dhota*.
3rd	धोऐ *dhoai*.	*Not used.*	धोत *dhot*.	*Not used.*

* Or धोतिहाँ *dhŏtihā̃*, &c.

For further examples of verbs of this class, see conjugation of √ हो *ho*, § 53 & ff. The root √ रो *ro*, 'weep,' which is the verb conjugated in the other grammars of this series, is not used in Púr'niyá, hence √ धो *dho* is substituted.

CHAPTER IX.

IRREGULAR VERBS.

§ 92. The verbs √ कर *kar*, 'do;' √ धर *dhar*, 'seize' or 'place;' √ मर *mar*, 'die;' and √ हो *ho*, 'become,' are irregular in their preterite tense indicative. The conjugation of √ कर *kar* is therefore given in that tense only. √ धर *dhar* and √ मर *mar* are conjugated exactly like √ कर *kar*, and are therefore not given. Besides the irregular forms, √ कर *kar*, √ धर *dhar*, and √ मर *mar*, have also each a regular form of the preterite indicative.

The conjugation of √ हो *ho* has been already given in § 53 and ff., and is not given here.

The verb √ जा *já*, 'go,' is irregular in the preterite indicative and in the present conjunctive, and is therefore given in those tenses.

The verbs √ दे *de*, 'give,' and √ ले *le*, 'take,' are more or less irregular throughout all the tenses. The verb √ दे *de* is therefore given conjugated throughout the four radical and participial tenses. The verb √ ले *le* is conjugated precisely like the verb √ दे *de*.

§ 93. √ कर *kar*, 'do.'

INFINITIVE (2ND FORM): करल *karal* or कैल *kail*.

PRES. PART. करैत *karait*.

PAST. PART. करल *karal* or कैल *kail*.

√धर *dhar*, 'seize,' 'place.'

INFINITIVE (2ND FORM) : धरल *dharal* or धैल *dhail.*

PRES. PART. धरैत *dharait.*

PAST PART. धरल *dharal* or धैल *dhail.*

INDICATIVE MOOD.

Person.	Irregular Preterite.		Regular Preterite.	
	Singular.	Plural.	Singular.	Plural.
1st	कैलौं *kailā̃.*	कैली *kailī̃.*	करलौं *kar'lā̃.*	करली *kar'lī̃.*
2nd	कैलें *kailẽ.*	कैलह *kaila.*	करलें *kar'lẽ.*	करलह *kar'la.*
3rd	कैलक *kailak.*	*Not used.*	करलकै *karal'kai.*	*Not used.*

Similarly is conjugated √ धर *dhar* (धैलौं *dhailā̃*, धरलौं *dhar'lā̃*, &c.).

§ 94. Sq also is conjugated the √ मर *mar*, 'die' (मैलौं *mailā̃*, मरलौं *mar'lā̃*, &c.). √ मर *mar* being an intransitive verb, the 3rd person may be मैल *mail* or मरल *maral*.

§ 95. √जा *já*, 'go.'

This root is conjugated like √खा *khá* in all tenses but the preterite indicative and present conjunctive, which are therefore here given. (See § 87 and ff.)

VERBAL NOUN { (1ST FORM): जा *já*; obl. जाए *jáĕ*.
(2ND FORM): जाएल *jáĕl*, जैल *jail*, गैल *gail*, *or* गेल *gel*.
(3RD FORM): जाएब *jáĕb* or जैब *jaib*.

PRES. PAST. जाइत *jáït* or जैत *jait*. PAST PART. गैल *gail* or गेल *gel*.

Person.	PRETERITE INDICATIVE.		PRESENT CONJUNCTIVE.	
	Singular.	Plural.	Singular.	Plural.
1st	गेलौं *gelaũ* or गैलौं *gailaũ*.	गेली *geli* or गैली *gaili*.	जाऊँ *jaũ*.	जैऐ *jaiai*.
2nd	गेलें *gelẽ* or गैलें *gailẽ*.	गेलह *gela* or गैलह *gaila*.	जैए *jaie*.	जैअ *jaia*.
3rd	गेल *gel* or गैल *gail*.	*Not used.*	जै *jai*.	*Not used.*

IRREGULAR 2ND PLURAL IMPERATIVE: जो *jo*.

§ 96. √दे *de*, 'give.'

VERBAL NOUN { 1ST FORM: दअ *da*, दे *de*, or दै *dai*; obl. देए *deĕ* or देबे *debĕ*.
2ND FORM: देल *del*, 'to give.'

PRES. PART. देत *det*.

PAST PART. देल *del*.

INDICATIVE MOOD.

Person.	PRETERITE.		FUTURE.	
	Singular.	Plural.	Singular.	Plural.
1st	देलौं *delấ.*	देली *delî.*	देबै *debai.*	देब *deb.*
2nd	देलेँ *delẽ.*	देलह *dela.*	देबेँ *debẽ.*	देबह *deba.*
3rd	देलन्कै *dĕl'kai.*	*Not used.*	देतै *detai.*	*Not used.*

CONDITIONAL MOOD.

Person.	PRESENT.		PRETERITE.	
	Singular.	Plural.	Singular.	Plural.
1st	दौँ *daũ*, देऊँ *deű*, or दीयौँ *díõ.*	दी *dí.*	देतौँ *detõ.**	देती *detî.*
2nd	दे *de*, देँ *dẽ*, दैँ *daĩ.*	दह *da.*	देतेँ *detẽ.*	देतह *deta.*
3rd	दे *de*, दै *dai*, दीयै *dîai.*	*Not used.*	देत *det.*	*Not used.*

* Or देतिहाँ *dĕtihấ*, &c.

PRECATIVE: दीय *día.*

IRREGULAR 2ND PLURAL IMPERATIVE: दहिन *dahin* or दिहैन *dihain.*

Similarly is conjugated the √ ले *le*, 'take,' the letter ल *la* being substituted for the letter द *da* throughout.

CHAPTER X.

THE PASSIVE VERB.

§ 97. The passive verb is formed by conjugating the verbal noun ending in अल *al* with the verb √ जा *já*, 'go:' thus देखल जाएल *dekhal jáĕl*, 'to be seen.' This verbal noun is not altered for gender, number, person, or tense, only the verb जाएल *jáĕl* being conjugated. Thus—

Indicative Preterite Masculine: *'I was seen,' &c.*

Person.	Singular.	Plural.
1st	देखल गेलौँ *dekhal gelā̃.*	देखल गेली *dekhal gelí.*
2nd	देखल गेलेँ *dekhal gelẽ.*	देखल गेलह *dekhal gela.*
3rd	देखल गेल *dekhal gel.*	*Not used.*

§ 98. This verbal noun in अल *al* must be carefully distinguished from the past participle having the same termination. The former even in irregular verbs is sometimes quite regular, so that we have verbal nouns such as जैल *jail,* besides past participles like गेल *gel.* At the same time it must be remembered that the verbal noun can also take the form of the past participle as well as its proper form: so that we may have गेल *gel* as a verbal noun as well as जैल *jail.* An example of an irregular passive verb is जैल जैछै *jail jaichhai* (impersonal), 'it is gone'—*itum est;* but, used in the sense of the potential, 'it can go.' When neuter verbs are used in the passive voice, they are always used in an impersonal potential sense: thus हमरा से चलल नहीँ जैछै *ham'rá se chalal nahí jaichhai,* 'by me it cannot be gone,' *i.e.* 'I cannot go.'

§ 99. Another common form of the passive is made by adding to the direct form of the first variety of the verbal noun (which is the same in form as the root) the verb परब *parab*, 'to fall;' the whole then forms an intensive compound. (See § 114.)

An example of this form is—

> कुछु कुछु जानि परैछै *kuchhu kuchhu jánı paraichhai*, 'a little is known,' *i.e.*, 'it is slightly visible.'

§ 100. The Potential Passive Voice.

This voice is formed in the same manner as the causal verb (see § 103). It has a potential force, intimating not so much that a thing *is* done as that it *can be* done. Examples of its use are—

> कुछु नहीं निकसल देखाइ दैछै *kuchhu nahí nik'sal dĕkhäï daichhai*, 'it cannot be seen to be at all swollen.'

> ई तऽ कोइ अजब रङ्ग कर अदिमी देखाइ दैछै *í ta koï ajab rang kar adimí dĕkhäï daichhai*, 'this (fellow) appears to be a man of strange kind.'

§ 101. The Periphrastic Passive Voice.

A very common kind of passive voice is formed by placing the verb √ आ *á* after the first or shortest form of a verbal noun in the locative case: thus देखे में आएब *dekhĕ mẽ áĕb*, 'the coming into seeing,' *i.e.* 'to be seen.' The person by whom the action is done is put in the oblique genitive form of the noun or pronoun when there is one: thus तों हमरा देखे में ऐलऽ *tõ ham'rá dekhĕ mẽ aila*, 'you came into my seeing,' 'you were seen by me.' The following example shows a verb in this voice conjugated in the preterite indicative masculine:—

Singular.	Plural.
1. देखे में एलों *dekhĕ mẽ ailõ.*	1. देखे में ऐली *dekhĕ mẽ ailí.*
2. देखे में ऐलें *dekhĕ mẽ ailẽ.*	2. देखे में ऐलऽ *dekhĕ mẽ aila.*
3. देखे में आएल *dekhĕ mẽ áĕl.*	3. *Not used.*

EXAMPLE.—हम सब तोरा देखे में ऐलियै *ham sab torá dekhĕ mẽ aĭliai*, 'we were seen by you.'

CHAPTER XI.

CAUSAL VERBS.

§ 102. A causal verb is formed by adding आ *á* to the root of the simple verb, and a double causal by adding वा *wá*. The stems thus formed are conjugated exactly like verbs whose roots end in आ *á* (see § 87)—that is, like the √ पा *pá*, taking आब *áb* or आव *áw* in the first verbal noun, the present conjunctive, and present participle. (See § 88.)

Simple Verb.	Causal.	Double Causal.
√ उठ *uṭh*, 'rise.'	उठा *uṭhá*, 'raise.'	उठ॰वा *uṭh'wa*, 'cause [to raise.'
√ कह *kah*, 'say.'	कहा *kahá*, 'cause [to speak.'	कह॰वा *kah'wá*, 'cause [to cause to speak.'
√ नुक *nuk*, 'be hidden.'	नुका *nuká*, 'hide.'	नुक॰वा *nuk'wá*, 'cause [to hide.'
√ पक *pak*, 'be cooked.'	पका *paká*, 'cook.'	पक॰वा *pak'wá*, 'cause [to cook.'
√ मिल *mil*, 'meet.'	मिला *milá*, 'mix.'	मिल॰वा *mil'wá*, ['cause to mix.'
√ सुन *sun*, 'hear.'	सुना *suná*, 'tell.'	सुन॰वा *sun'wá*, 'cause [to tell.'

§ 103. If the simple root contains a long vowel it is shortened, viz. आ *á* to अ *a*, ई *í* to इ *i*, ऊ *ú* to उ *u*, ए *e* to ऎ *ĕ*, ओ *o* to ऒ *ŏ*, ऐ *ai* to ऐ *ăi*, and औ *au* to औ *ău*.

Similarly, if a root ends in a double consonant, it is made single : thus—

Simple Verb.	Causal.	Double Causal.
√ जाग *jág*, 'be awake.'	जगा *jagá*, 'awaken.'	जग॰वा *jag'wá*, 'cause to awake.'
√ पाक *pák*, 'be cooked.'	पका *paká*, 'cook.'	पक॰वा *pak'wá*, 'cause to cook.'
√ जीत *jít*, 'conquer.'	जिता *jitá*, 'cause to conquer.'	जित॰वा *jit'wá*, 'cause to cause to conquer.'
√ सीख *síkh*, 'learn.'	सिखा *sikhá*, 'teach.'	सिख॰वा *sikh'wá*, 'cause to teach.'
√ पी *pí*, 'drink.'	पिआ *piá*, 'cause to drink.'	पिअवा *piawá*, 'cause to cause to drink.'
√ भीज *bhíj*, 'wet.'	भिगा *bhigá*, 'moisten.'	भिग॰वा *bhig'wá*, 'cause to moisten.'
√ घूम *ghúm*, 'be turned.'	घुमा *ghumá*, 'turn.'	घुम॰वा *ghum'wá*, 'cause to turn.'
√ बूड़ *búṛ*, 'sink.'	बुड़ा *buṛá*, 'immerse.'	बुड़॰वा *buṛ'wá*, 'cause to immerse.'
√ सूत *sút*, 'sleep.'	सुता *sutá*, 'put to sleep.'	सुत॰वा *sut'wá*, 'cause to put to sleep.'
√ देख *dekh*, 'see.'	देखा *dĕkhá*, 'show.'	देख॰वा *dĕkh'wá*, 'cause to show.'
√ हेल *hel*, 'swim.'	हेला *hĕlá*, 'cause to swim.'	हेल॰वा *hĕl'wá*, 'cause to cause to swim.'
√ बैस *bais*, 'sit.'	बैसा *baĭsá*, 'seat.'	बैस॰वा *baĭs'wá*, 'cause to sit.'
√ दौर *daur*, 'run.'	दौरा *daŭrá*, 'cause to run.'	दौर॰वा *daŭr'wá*, 'cause to cause to run.'
√ नुक्क *nukk*, 'be hidden.'	नुका *nuká*, 'hide.'	नुक॰वा *nuk'wá*, 'cause to hide.'

Note in connection with the above:—

Simple Verb.	Causal.
√ कह *kah*, 'speak'	कह्ला *kah'lá*, also regular.
√ खा *khá*, 'eat'	खिआ *khiá*.
√ पी *pí*, 'drink'	पिला *pilá*, also regular.

§ 104. Some primitive neuter verbs having a monosyllabic root enclosing a short vowel form the first causal by simply lengthening that vowel. The double causal is formed in the usual way, *e.g.*—

Simple Verb.	Causal.
√ कट *kaṭ*, 'be cut'	काट *káṭ*, 'cut.'
√ बन्ध *bandh*, 'be tied'	बाँध *bā̃dh*, 'tie.'
√ लद *lad*, 'be loaded'	लाद *lád*, 'load.'
√ घिंच *ghiṅch*, 'be dragged'	घीँच * *ghĩch*, 'drag.'

§ 105. Sometimes a cognate diphthong is substituted for the long vowel, *e.g.*—

खुल *khul*, 'be open.' — खोल *khol*, 'open.'

घुर *ghur*, 'melt.' (*Neut.*) — घोर *ghor*, 'melt.' (*Act.*)

§ 106. The verb √ निकल *nikal* or निकस *nikas*, 'come out,' makes its causal निकाल *nikál* or निकास *nikás*, 'take out,' on the analogy of the above. So also √ पसर *pasar*, 'be scattered,' makes पसार *pasár*, 'scatter,' 'extend;' √ ससर *sasar*, 'slip,' ससार *sasár*, 'cause to slip;' √ उपर *upar*, 'be rooted up,' उपार *upár*, 'root up;' and √ उखर *ukhar*, 'be rooted up,' उखार *ukhár* 'root up.'

---

* When the vowel is lengthened, *anuswár* becomes *anunásik*. (Compare General Introduction, § 28.)

§ 107. The following are irregular :—

Simple Verb.	Causal.	Double Causal.
√ अड *aṭ*, 'be stopped.'	आर *ár*, 'stop.'	अरा *ará.*
√ फड *phaṭ* or फाड *pháṭ*, ['be torn.'	फार *phár*, 'tear,'	फरा *phará.*
√ छूड *chhúṭ*, 'be separ- [ated.'	छोर *chhor* or छार *chhár*, ['separate.	छोरा *chhŏrá.*
√ जूड *júṭ*, 'be joined.'	जोर *jor*, 'join.'	जोरा *jŏrá.*
√ टूड *ṭúṭ*, 'be broken.'	तोर *tor*, 'break.'	तोरा *tŏrá.*
√ फूड *phúṭ*, 'be burst.'	फोर *phor*, 'burst.'	फोरा *phŏrá.*
√ बिक्ख *bikk*, 'be sold.'	बेँच *bĕ̃ch* or बिका *biká*, ['sell.'	बेँचा *bĕ̃chá.*
√ रह *rah*, 'remain.'	राख *rákh* or रक्ख *rakkh*, ['place.'	रखा *rakhá.*
√ मर *mar*, 'die.'	मार *már* or मुआ *muá*, ['cause to die.'	

CHAPTER XII.

COMPOUND VERBS.

§ 108. Compound verbs are either intensives, potentials, completives, frequentatives, desideratives, continuatives, staticals, inceptives, permissives, or acquisitives.

§ 109. Compound verbs may be classed as—(1) those formed with the verbal noun, and (2) those formed with the participles.

(1) Those formed with the verbal noun are—

a) Intensives.
b) Potentials.
c) Completives.
d) Frequentatives.
e) Desideratives.
f) Inceptives.
g) Permissives.
h) Acquisitives.

(2) Those formed with the participles—

a) Continuatives.
b) Staticals.

Class I.—Compounds formed with the Verbal Noun.*

§ 110. There are three varieties of the verbal noun—

a) In अ *a* (silent) or इ *i*, oblique form ए *ĕ* or ऐ *aĭ*; as देख *dekh* or देखि *dekhi*, obl. देखे *dekhĕ* or देखै *dekhaĭ*.

b) In अल *al*, oblique form ल्ला *'lá*; as देखल *dekhal*, obl. देखल्ला *dĕkh'lá*.

c) In अब *ab*; as देखब *dekhab*.

The direct first form in अ *a* (silent) is always the same as the root. The last has, in this dialect, no oblique form.

Compound verbs are either formed with the direct form of the first or second variety of the verbal noun, or with the oblique form of the first variety.

---

* Much of the succeeding matter is based on Kellogg's Hindí Grammar.

§ 111. *Intensives* and *Completives* are always, and *Potentials* are generally, formed with the direct form of the first variety; *Frequentatives* are always, and *Desideratives* are sometimes, formed with the direct form of the second variety; *Inceptives, Permissives,* and *Acquisitives,* are always formed with the oblique form of the first variety.

§ 112. *Intensive* compounds intensify or otherwise modify the meaning of the verb whose root stands first in the compound. They are formed by adding to a verbal noun of the first variety in the direct form one of certain other verbs, which latter verb in conjunction with the verbal noun is then conjugated as usual. This second conjugated member does not, however, retain its separate character and significance, but only modifies, in accordance with the general idea which it embodies, the meaning of the unconjugated verbal noun to which it is annexed. Examples are—

फेँकब *phẽkab*, 'to throw.'	**फेँक** (or **फेँकि**) **देब** *phẽk* (or *phẽki*) *deb*, 'to throw away.'
तोरब *torab*, 'to break.'	**तोर डालब** *tor ḍálab*, 'to break in pieces.'
बनब *banab*, 'to be made.'	**बन आएब** *ban áĕb* or **बन जाएब** *ban jáĕb*, 'to be completed.'
खाएब *kháĕb*, 'to eat.'	**खा जाएब** *khá jáĕb*, 'to eat up.'
बोलब *bolab*, 'to speak.'	**बोल उठब** *bol uṭhab*, 'to speak suddenly.'
काटब *káṭab*, 'to cut.'	**काट लेब** *káṭ leb*, 'to cut for oneself.'
राखब *rákhab*, 'to place.'	**राख लेब** *rákh leb*, 'to lay by.'

§ 113. The auxiliary verbs usually employed to form intensives are—

देब *deb*,	'to give,'	implying	*intensity.*
डालब *ḍálab*,	'to throw,'	"	*violence.*
आएब *áĕb*,	'to come,'	"	*completion.*
जाएब *jáĕb*,	'to go,'	"	*completion.*
परब *parab*,	'to fall,'	"	*chance.*
उठब *uṭhab*,	'to rise,'	"	*suddenness.*
लेब *leb*,	'to take,'	"	*reflexiveness.*

परब *parab* is also used in intensive compounds to form passives of transitive verbs. (See § 100.)

§ 114. *Potentials* are formed by adding to the direct form of the first verbal noun of any verb the verb सकब *sakab*, 'to be able,' which may then be conjugated throughout. Examples are—

बोलि सकब *boli sakab*, 'to be able to speak.'

ऊ दौर सकै ऐ *ú daur sakai ai*, 'he can run.'

हम जा सकब *ham já sakab*, 'I shall be able to go.'

जौँ ओकऱरा आर आ सकत *jaũ ŏk'rá ár á sakat*, 'if they are able to come.'

हम नहीँ जै सकैछी *ham nahí jai sakaichhí*, 'I cannot go.'

Frequently, however, especially in Central Púr'níyá, potential compounds are formed with the oblique instead of with the direct form of the verbal noun: thus—

बोलेँ सकब *bolĕ sakab*, ऊ दौरेँ सकैछै *ú daurĕ sakai chhai*, and so on.

§ 115. *Completives* are formed by adding to the same form of the verbal noun of a verb the verb चुकब *chukab*, 'to be finished,' which may then be conjugated throughout. This compound denotes the *completion* of the act denoted by the primary member of the compound. Examples are—

वेँ खा चुकऱलै *wĕ khá chuk'lai*, 'he has done eating.'

जब ऊ खा चुकऱतै *jab ú khá chuk'tai*, 'when he shall have eaten.'

ऊ त० जा चुकल ऐ *ú ta já chukal ai*, 'he is indeed already gone.'

§ 116. *Frequentatives* are formed by affixing to the direct form of the second variety of the verbal noun of any verb the verb करब *karab*, 'to do,' which may then be used in any tense. Examples are—

आएल कर० *ăĕl kara*, 'come often,' *lit.* 'do the act of coming.'

हम शास्त्र के पढ़ल करैछी *ham sástr ke paṛhal karaichhí*, 'I am in the habit of reading the shástras.'

तोँ हमर बात मानल कर० *tŏ hamar bát mánal kara*, 'always obey my words.'

तोँ कहिने रंग करल करैछ० *tŏ kahine traṅg karal karaichha*, 'why do you always do so?'

ऊ जैल करैछै *ú jail karaichhai*, 'he often goes.'

§ 117. ***Desideratives*** are formed, like frequentatives, with the direct form of the verbal noun in अल *al*, substituting the verb चाहब *cháhab*, 'to wish,' for करब *karab* as the second or conjugated member. They denote primarily *desire* to do the action expressed of the principal member; secondarily, the *immediate futurity* of that action. An example is—

ऊ बोलल चाहैअछ *ú bolal cháhaiachh*, 'he wishes to speak.'

Sometimes the principal verb is put in the oblique form of the first variety of the verbal noun. Examples are—

ऊ बोलें चाहै ऐ *ú bolě cháhai ai*, 'he wishes to speak.'

घड़ी बाजें चाहैछलै *ghaṛí bájě cháhaichhalai*, 'the clock was on the point of striking.'

ऊ जाए चाहैछै *ú jáě cháhaichhai*, 'he wishes to go.'

ऊ मरें चाहैछै *ú marǎ̃ cháhaichhai*, 'he is about to die.'

The desiderative compound in the precative form is idiomatically used to express obligation or duty. Examples are—

ई पोथिया के पढ़ल चाही *í pŏthiyá ke paṛhal cháhí*, '(one) ought to read this book.' (*lit.* 'be good enough to wish to read').

ओते जाए चाहिअ *ŏte jáě cháhia*, 'it is right for you (*i.e.* you ought) to go there.'

§ 118. ***Inceptives*** are formed by using the inflected form of the first variety of the verbal noun in construction with the verb लागब *lágab*, 'to be joined,' 'to begin,' and denote the action of the verbal noun as *beginning*. Examples are—

ऊ कहें लगन्लै *ú kahě lag'lai*, 'he began to say.'

ऊँ मारें लागल *uẽ márǎ̃ lágal*, 'he began to beat.'

बाघ खाए लगन्ला *bágh kháě lag'lá*, 'the tiger began to eat.'

§ 119. *Permissives* are formed by combining the same form of the verbal noun with the verb देब *deb*, 'to give,' and express *permission* to do the act denoted by the verbal noun. Examples are—

हम॰रा जाए दीअ *ham'rá jáĕ día*, 'let me go.'

हम॰रा बोलॆ दीअ *ham'rá bolĕ día*, 'be good enough to let me speak.'

वँ ओक॰रा खाए देल॰कै *wẽ ŏk'rá kháĕ dĕl'kai*, 'he allowed him to eat.'

§ 120. *Acquisitives* are the exact converse of the preceding, and are formed in the same way, substituting पाएब *páĕb*, 'to get,' for देब *deb*. Examples are—

तोह॰रा ओते जाए नहीँ पैबऽ *tŏh'rá ŏte jáĕ nahí paiba*, 'you will not obtain permission to go there.'

हम बैसॆ नहीँ पैलाँ *ham baisĕ nahí pailā̃*, 'I was not allowed to sit.'

Class II.—Compounds formed from the Participles.

§ 121. *Continuatives* are formed by combining the direct or oblique form of the present participle of any verb with the verbs जाएब *jáĕb*, 'to go,' or रहब *rahab*, 'to remain.'

The compound with जाएब *jáĕb* expresses *steady progression*, and with रहब *rahab* the *continuance* of a complete action. Examples :—

वँ लिखैत जैछै *wẽ likhait jaichhai*, 'he is going on writing.'

छौँरी सब पढ़॰तँ जैछिलै *chhaũri sab paṛh'tẽ jaichhilai*, 'those girls were going on reading.'

पनिया बहैत जैछै *paniyá bahait jaichhai*, 'the water keeps flowing away.'

वँ गैतँ रहैछै *wẽ gaitẽ rahaichhai*, 'she continues singing.'

लदी कर धार बहितँ रहैछै *ladí kar dhár bahitẽ rahaichhai*, 'the stream of the river keeps flowing on.'

तोँ कहिने हंस॰तँ रहैछँ *tõ kahine has'tẽ rahaichhã̃*, 'why do you keep laughing?'

Closely connected with the above is a common combination in which the past participle in its direct form takes the first place and a verb of motion the second place. Examples are—

> एक बाघ परल फिरैछै *ěk bágh paral phiraichhai,* 'a tiger is prowling about.'
>
> नौँड़ी चलल जैछिलै *naũrí chalal jaichhilai,* 'the slave-girl was going along.'

§ 122. *Staticals* denote motion in a state of doing anything. They are formed by combining a verb of motion with a present participle in its direct or oblique form. Examples are—

> ऊ कानन्तँ (or कानैत) आबैछै *ú kán'tẽ* (or *kánait*) *ábaichhai,* 'he comes weeping.'
>
> एगो मौगी गैतँ आबैछिलै *ego maugi gaitẽ ábaichhilai,* 'a woman was coming singing.'

DIVISION III.

INDECLINABLES.

§ 123. See General Introduction.

APPENDIX.

THE following selections are in the dialect of the *sadr* (or central) sub-division of Puraniyá. The conversation and fables were translated for me by Kumár Chand, Chief Guru in that subdivision. An English translation of them, and of the conversation, will be found in the General Introduction.

SELECTIONS IN THE CENTRAL PURANIYÁ DIALECT.

CONVERSATION BETWEEN TWO VILLAGERS.

१ प्रश्न। कहऽ भै, कते से आबैछैं।

उत्तर। परसिया गाम सँ आबैछी॥

२ प्र.। ओते से कखे चलल छिलैं।

उ.। भोर हीं चलल रही॥

३ प्र.। कथी ले ओते गेल छिलैं।

उ.। ओते हमर खेत छै, वहाय देखे गेल छिलाँ॥

४ प्र.। ओकरा मेँ की बुनल छैँ।

उ.। खाली रहार बुनल गेल छै॥

५ प्र.। कहऽ भै, इबरक फसिल कर की रङ्ग छै।

उ.। ई फसिल कर हाल की पुछैछऽ, पनिया के नहीँ परे सँ बड़ खराबी होलै॥

६ प्र.। ऐज काल तोर भै नहीँ देखै* इ छौन।

उ.। हमर भ ऐज काल किला मेँ नौकर छ, इन्हें बहुत कम आबैछै॥

७ प्र। इहाँ कर बड़ा गै कर की हाल छै।

ऊ.। ऊ ऐज काल गाभीन छै, परन्तु घारा नहीँ मिले सँ टूटि गेल छै॥

८ प्र। कै महिना से गाभीन छै।

उ.। होलै तऽ आठ महिना, मगर ओकर पेट कुछु नहीँ निकसल देखाइ दैछ॥

---

* For देखाइ, 1st verbal noun of the potential passive of √देख. Compare No. 8 below.

९ प्र। नमावै छै नहीं।

उ। हँ, कुछ कुछ जानि परै छै॥

१० प्र। ई कौथा बियान छिकै, आरो केतऽवे दूध दै छै।

उ। ई आठों बियान छिकै, दुइ अढ़ै सेर दूध बखत में करै छै॥

११ प्र। हमऽरा एक बकऽरी लेबे छै, इहाँ कर गाम में मिलऽतै।

उ। हमऽर गाम में बकऽरी आवै छै, मगर दाम बड़ा छै॥

१२ प्र। इहाँ कर बकऽरी की भेल।

उ। हम्मे चरै कर वास्ते गाम है पर छोड़ि रहल छी॥

१३ प्र। कुछ दूध दै छै।

उ। छौंरा सिबी कर खे भरी हो जै छै॥

१४ प्र। अबऽरी केतारी बुनल छैं की नहीं।

उ। केतारी तऽ बुनल छी, परन्तु ओकऽरा में कुछ फैदा नहीं छै॥

१५ प्र। इहाँ कने सँ कूआँ कर रस्सी मँगऽनी मिलै सकै छै।

उ। कहिने नहीं, पड़ौन होला पर ले लीहऽ॥

१६ प्र। इहाँ कने सँ केतऽवे मोट हलै छै।

उ। तीन टा मोट नाधै छै॥

१७ प्र। इहाँ कर आम कर बाड़ी कुछ फरै छै की नहीं।

उ। ई बेर तऽ गाछ सिबी में लही लागि गेलै, नहीं तऽ बहुत होयछिलै॥

१८ प्र। थोड़े आम हमरऽहो* अँवार कर वास्ते देबऽ।

उ। जबे अहाँ कर मन माने, तोरऽवा लीअ॥

१९ प्र। अहाँ कर लरिका कुछ पढ़ै छै।

उ। हँ, गुरू हाँ जै छै। अच्छर तऽ चीन्हि गेल छै, ऐज काल पहाड़ा पढ़ै छै॥

२० प्र। इस्कोल कहिने नहीं भेजै छऽ।

उ। कुछ सिखि लै, तऽ भेजि दियै॥

२१ प्र। हम्मुहो † आपन छौंरा के इस्कोल में भेजे चहै छी॥

उ। अच्छा, हमर छौंरा कर सङ्गे ओकरऽहो ‡ भेजि दीहऽ॥

---

* Emphatic for हमऽरा, 'to me also.'

† Emphatic for हम्मे, 'I also.'

‡ Emphatic for ओकऽरा, 'him also.'

FABLES.

॥ १ बात ॥

॥ मुबगा आर मोती कर दाना ॥

एक मुबगा गोबर कर ढेरी के चङ्गुल से खिटि रहिल छिलै। अचोका ओकरा से बड़ सन मोती निकसि ऐलै। मुबगा बोलल्लै, आहा, कौरङ्ग रङ्ग रूप आरो चमक दमक छै। जौहरी एकरा पैतिहैंत, फुलल नहीँ समैतिहै। परन्तु हमर पेट कर आगीन एकरा सँ नहीँ बुझतै। हँ, एक चौर कर दाना हमर हाथ लगतिहा, तऽ सऽ मोती से बढ़ि के छिलै। साँच छिके

॥ जे आपन काम नहीँ आवे, ज चुल्हा भनसार मैँ जाय ॥

॥ २ बात ॥

॥ कङ्गाल कर पूछब आरो फकीर कर जबाब देब ॥

एक कङ्गाल कोइ पहुँचल फकीर से पुछलकै कि, हम्मे तऽ भूखैँ मरी, आरो हमर पड़ोसी गद्दी तकिया पर परल लेटे। राति दिन चैन करे। ओकरा मैँ कोन अहिन गुन छै जे भगवान ओकरा निहाल करके, आरो हमरा कङ्गाल करकै। ई सुनि के फकीर कहिलकै, बाबा, ई तोँ नहीँ सुनल छँ।

राम जी झरोखा पर बैसि के सभै कर मुजरा लेवै।
जेकर जहिन नौकरी, ओहिनैँ भरि देवै॥

॥ ३ बात॥

॥ देस बिदेस फिरै कर लाभ ॥

कोइ भल मानुस एक गोसैँ सैँ पुछलकै कि महाराज, देस देस आरो गाँ गाँ फिरे से की लाभ छौन। एक जगह रहि के प्रमेसर मैँ लौ कहिने नहीँ लगावैछ, आरो कोइ मठ मैँ बैसि के भगवान कर गुन कहिने नहीँ गावैछऽ। जोगी जी कहलकै। बाबा, ई सब साँच छै, पर तोँ ई कथा नहीँ सुनल छँ,

बहत पानी निरमल, बान्हल गन्ना होइछै।
साधु जन फिरला भल कि कोइ दोख नहीँ लगावै॥

॥ ४ बात ॥

एक दिन जाड़ा कर दिन मेँ कोइ बड़ अदमी कर घर मेँ आगीन लग॰ले। सभ चीज बस्तु जरि के छौर हो गेलै। ऊ बाहर मेँ ठाढ़, हाथ मलि रहिल छिलै। कि एक गरीब परोसी जाड़ा कर ठक॰रल, थर थर काँपतेँ घर से निकधि ऐलै, आरो हाथ सेके लग॰लै। तबे ऊ मातब्बर बोल॰ले, बाह बाह, केक॰रो घर जरै, आरो कोइ तापै॥

॥ ५ बात ॥

॥ बान्हल लक॰री सब आरो छिरिऐल लक॰री सब ॥

एक गिरहस्तक बेटा अप॰ना मेँ बहुत लड़े झगड़ा करैछिलै। ओकर बाप ओक॰रा सब के बात से बहुत समुझैल॰कै, परन्तु कोइ कुछु नहीँ मनल॰कै। तबे गिर॰हस्त आपन मन मेँ कहिलक कि, जौँ एक॰रा सभी के कुछु करि देखैऐ, तबे एक॰रा सभी समुझि जाय। एक दिन ऊ किसान आपन बेटा सिबी के बजा के कहिल॰कै कि, थोड़े सन लक॰री हमर साम॰ने लानँ। तबे ऊ किसान ऊ सब लक॰री के एकट्ठा सुत॰री से कसि के बान्ह॰कै, आरो एकाँ एकी के कहिल॰कै कि, रस्सी मतु खोलँ, आरो लक॰री सिबी के तोरी डालँ। तबे एकाँ एकी ऊ लकरी पर झूकि पर॰ले, पर ओक॰रा सिबी से कुछु नहीँ भेलै। फिनु किसान एक एक टा लक॰री देल॰कै। तबे ओक॰रा सभी ऊ लक॰री के जल॰दी तोरि देल॰कै। तबे ओकर बाप कहिल॰कै कि, बेटा, जौँ तोँ बान्हल लक॰री कर तौर से अप॰न्हँ मेँ मेल करि रहिबँ, त॰ सभे बेरी कर दाँत खट्टा कर॰भँ, आरो जभी छिरिऐलँ, त॰ जानँ कि बिग॰रलँ।

॥ छिरिऐल से बिग॰रल ॥

॥ ६ बात ॥

॥ ऊँड़ार आरो भेँड़ा सिबी कर मिलाप ॥

एक बेर ऊँड़ार सब भेँड़ा सिबी कहा पठैल॰कै कि, आवँ, हम्मे तोँ अप॰ने मेँ मिलाप करि लौँ। कहिने अप॰ना मेँ लड़ौँ, आरो एक दोसर कर लौह कर पियासल रहौँ। ई पाजी कुत्ता कुल लड़े कर जड़ छिकै। अहिनँ रोज भूकि भूकि के हम॰रा भड़॰कावैछै। आरो हम॰रा तोरा सी लड़ावैछै। एक॰रा हमर पास भेजि दहिन, फिनु तोरा आरो हम॰रा से कियो कर झगड़ा छै। हम॰रा तोरा मेँ रोजे मेल भाव रहित, त॰ तोर एको बाल टेढ़

नहीं होतौ। भेँड़ा सब ई लटन्खल ऊँड़ार कर बात मानि के, कुत्ता के ओकर पास भेजि देलन्है। पहिनेँ तऽ ऊँड़ार कुत्ता के खे गेलै। पिछु से भेँड़ा सिबौ पर हाथ बढ़ावे लगन्हे आरो थोड़े दिन मेँ सब भेँड़ा के खाय गेलै। साँच छिकै,—

॥ बैरी रोजे धोखा देहे, ऊ बड़ा गँवार हे, जे बैरी के सच्चा समुझे ॥

॥ ७ बात ॥

॥ बाघ ऊँड़ार आरो चीता ॥

एक बेर बाघ ऊँड़ार आरो चीता अपन्ना मेँ ई ठहन्रैलक कि, सब कोइ मिलि के सिकार मारौँ। फिनु अपन्ना मेँ बाँटि लौँ। ई ठानि के जङ्गल मेँ कूद फान करे लागल, आरो जबे करिया तथ हरिन मारक, तबे बाघ बजन्लै कि, लानँ, एकन्रा बखन्रा करौँ। आरो जलन्दी सन ओकर तीन बखन्रा करन्कै। आरो बाघ गरजि के बजन्लै कि पहिन्क बखन्रा हम्हे लेब, कहिने कि हम्मे जङ्गल कर राजा छिकाँ। आरो दोसन्रो हमी * लेब, कहिने कि एकन्रा मारै मेँ बहुत दौर धूप करल छी। आरो तेसर बखन्रा ई धरल हे, देखौँ केकर मुँह परैहे, जे हमर सामन्ने से उठा के ले जाय ई सुनि के चीता आरो ऊँड़ार नाँगर सटन्का के भागि गेलै; आरो बाघ हरिन के अकन्सरे खाय गेलै। ई कथा साँच छिकै,—

॥ जेकर लाठी तेकर भैँस ॥

॥ ८ बात ॥

॥ माटी आरो पीतर कर बरिया कर बातन्चीत ॥

एक बेर कतन्हौँ नदी बढ़न्लै, कि एक पीतर कर बरिया आरो एक माटी कर बरिया भँसि चलन्लै। पीतर कर बरिया माटी कर बरिया से कहिलन्कै कि, हमर सङ्गे भीड़ल चलँ, तऽ हम्मे तोरा बचा लेबौँ। माटी कर बरिया बोलन्लै कि, इहाँ अच्छा बात कहिलाँ।† हम्मेँ अहाँ कर भला मानब आरो रोजे गुन गैब। परन्तु साँच पूछऽ, तऽ हमन्रा ई डर हे कि, कतन्ऊँ पानीक हिलोरा कर धक्का से अहाँ कर पास नहीँ जाय रही। कहिने कि

---

* Emphatic for दोसर हम्मे, 'the second also I alone (will take).'

† First person used politely instead of the second person.

औँ अहाँ से फरक रहिआँ, तऽ अहिने छिलऽतँ डोलऽतँ कतऽहौँ कच्छा मँ जा के लागब। परन्तु औँ अहाँ से भँट भेल, आरो कतऽहौँ भूल से ठोकर लागि गेल, तऽ हमर पेट फाडि जैत। साँच छिकै,—

॥ बड़ से आस रखिअ, पर पास नहीँ जेअ ॥

॥ ९ बात ॥

एक टा मुन्सी हाट मँ बैसि के चिट्ठी लिखि रहल छिलै। एक टा परऽदेसी ऐलै, आरो पुछलऽकै कि, मुन्सी जी, की लिखैछऽ। मुन्सी कहिलऽकै कि, भै, चिट्ठी लिखंछी। कहिलऽकै कि, हमऽरो * सलाम लिखि दऽ। मुन्सी जी कहिलऽकै कि, नहीँ जी, अऽरऽओ लिखैछी। वँ कहिलऽकै कि, हमऽरो * सही करि दऽ। मुन्सी औकऽता के बोलऽलै कि, ठीक लिखैछी। वँ कहिलऽकै कि, हमरो * गभै लिखि दऽ। मुन्सी सोचलऽकै कि, ई तऽ कोइ अजब रङ्ग कर अदिमी देखाइ दैछै, पुछलऽकै कि, तोर नाम की। वँ हँसऽलै, आरो बजऽलै कि, हमर नाम छिक,—

॥ मान कि नहीँ मान, हम्मे तोर मेजऽमान ॥

॥ १० बात ॥

एक बड़ अदिमी कर घर मँ रातिक समै मँ आगीन लागि गेलै। ज तऽ आपन बाल बच्चा समेत निकसि के भागल, आरो नौकर के हुकुम देलऽकै कि, चीज वस्तु निकालँ। एतऽवे मँ आगीन बहुत छिरिया गेलै। नौकर बजऽलै कि, जी, हम्मे की की निकासिऐ। तबे ज बड़ अदिमी ठण्ढा साँस भरि के बोलऽलै कि, बाबा,

॥ आगीन लागल झोँपड़ी मँ, जे निकऽसे से लाभ ॥

॥ ११ बात ॥

॥ गमारिन गोरऽनिया ॥

एक गमारिन गोरऽनिया माथा पर दहीक बरऽतन राखि के चलि जैछिलै। जेतैँ जेतैँ ओकर मन मँ ऐन्ह उमग उठऽलै कि, ई दही के बैँचब, आरो पैसा से आम मोल लेब। कुछु आम हमर सङ्ग छे। सभै मिला के तीन सऽ से कुछु बैसी हो जैतै। आरो एकऽरा

* Emphatic for हमर, 'of me also.'

मेँ से कुछु सड़ि पचि जैत, तैयो अदे सऽ बचि रहित। आरो ओकरा मेँ सँ जे बचि निकलत, ओकर अच्छा दाम उठत। तबे दिवाली मेँ एक हरा रङ्ग कर साड़ी लेब, आरो ओकरा पेन्हि के सारथ जेब। आरो खूब ऐँठि जूठि के आपन गहना कपड़ा कर पहिनावा आरो हुँह कर चमक दमक देखैब, आरो चाल चाल मेँ सठ बल खैब। ई सोँच बिचार मेँ ऊ गमारिन गोरऽनिया चमकि ठमकि के टेढ़ी चाल चलऽली। त्योँ दहिया कर बरतन माथा पर से गिरि के चूर चूर भे गेलै, आरो कुल बतल बतैल घर बिगरि गेलै ॥

॥ १२ बात ॥

॥ चिल्हा आरो कौआ ॥

एक चिल्हा कर ठोर मेँ एक डोका छिलै। केतऽन्हीँ धरती पर धरि धरि पटऽकलऽकै पर डोका नहीँ टुटऽलै। तबे कौआ ई राह बतैलऽकै कि, ई डोका के ठोर मेँ ले करि के बहुत ऊपर उड़ि जो, आरो ओते से गिरा दिहैन, तेवे डोका टूटि जैतौ। चिल्हा कहिलऽकै कि, ई बहुत अच्छा बात छिकै। आरो डोका के ले करि के उड़ऽलै, आरो ऊपर जा करि के छाड़ि देलऽकै। जौँ डोका धरती पर गिरऽलै, कि टुकऽड़ा टुकऽड़ा हो गेलै, आरो कौआ ओकर गुद्दा चाखि गेलै। थोड़े देरी बाद चिल्हा नीचेँ उतरऽलै, तऽ बोखऽला छाड़ि आर कुछु नहीँ पैलक ॥

॥ १३ बात ॥

॥ खट्टा अँगूर ॥

एक खिखिर कोइ बाड़ी मेँ जा पहुँचऽलै। देखलऽकै कि अँगूर कर थौक टट्टी मेँ लटकि रहिल छै कि, जेकऽरा से रस टपकि परैछै, आरो कोइ रखऽवारो नहीँ छै। ई देखि ओकर मुँह मेँ पानि भरि ऐलै। बहुत तरह उछऽली कुदऽली परन्तु अँगूर कर थौक तक नहीँ पहुँचे सकऽली। जबे कोनोँ रकऽमेँ दा नहीँ लगऽलै, तबे ईरङ्ग बड़ऽबड़ैतेँ ओते से चलऽली कि, खट्टा अँगूर के खाय।

॥ १४ बात ॥

॥ रसैनी ॥

एक रसैनी कोइ अदिमी से कहिलऽकै कि, जौँ तोँ कुछु चानीँ हमर पास ले आवँ, तऽ हम्मे अहिन जड़ि गारिबै, कि तुरन्ते ऊ चानीँ कर सोना भे जाय। ऊ सोझ सिधङ्ग अदिमी ओकर दमऽपड़ी मेँ आबि गेलै; आरो कतऽन्हीँ सँ दुख सुख सहि के

दो सऽ टाका, कर अंगौं उ रसैनी के लानि देलऽकै। वहाय राति के बिछौना उठा के कन्हौ चल गेल। अबे उ बेचारा दुख कर मारल लटऽखट रसैनी कर खोज मेँ दौर धूप करे लागल। जङ्गले जङ्गले छावऽलक, परन्तु उ रसैनी कर पता कतऽहौँ नहीँ पैलक। एकऽरा ईरङ्ग घबऽरैल देखि के, एक अदिमी कहिलऽकै कि, तोरा से ई चूकत भेलौ, कि उ लटऽकट फकीर कर फन मेँ फँसि गेलैँ। अबे पछऽतैलैँ आरो ओकर खोज मेँ दौर धूप कैला से कुछु नहीँ होतौ। ई बात पर हम्मे एक बात तोरा सुनाबैछियौ, जेकऽरा हृदा फम राखे चहिय।

॥ १५ बात ॥

एक चिरई कोइ गिरऽहस्त कर बाड़ी मेँ जा करि के काँचा पाकल फर सभे कर सभे काटि जैल करैछिलै। गिरऽहस्त ओकर रोजे खोज मेँ छेल। एक दिन अँगूर कर टट्टी पर जाल लगा के पकऽड़लऽकै, आरो मारे चहिलऽकै। चिड़िया गिरऽहस्त के कहिलऽकै कि, जौँ तोँ हमऽरा छाड़ि देबऽ, हम्मे इ भलै कर बदऽली मेँ तोरा कै टा बात बटै देबौँ, जेकऽरा सँ बड़ा नफा होतौ। गिरऽहस्त कहिलऽकै कि तोँ पहिनैँ बता दे, तऽ हम्मे तोरा छाड़ि देबौँ। चिरई ओकऽरा तीन बात कहिलऽकै। एक तऽ ई कि बैरी जौँ आपन बस मेँ आबि जाय, तऽ छाड़े नहीँ चहिय। दोसर, जे बात ध्यान मेँ नहीँ आबे, ओकऽरा माने नहीँ चहिय। तेसर, गेल चीज कर वास्ते पछऽतावे नहीँ चहिय। आरो चौठ एक बात आरो छै, कि जबे तोँ हमऽरा छाड़ी देमेँ, तबे कहिबौँ। गिरऽहस्त ई सब बात सुनि के जेरङ्ग कहिलक छिलै, सेरङ्ग करऽलक, आरो वँ उ चिरई के छाड़ि देलऽकै। तबे चिरई छत पर बैसि के कहिलऽकै कि, हमर पेट मेँ मुरगी कर अन्ना से ओ बड़ मोती छेल। जौँ तोँ हमऽरा नहीँ छाड़ऽतिहँ, आरो मारि डालऽतिहँ, तऽ उ मोती तोर हाथ लगऽतिहौ। गिरऽहस्त पछऽतावे लागल। वँ कहिलऽकै, हे गमार तोँ हमर तीनो बात एखनिहँ बिसरि गेलँ। कहिने कि हम्मे तोर बैरी छिलूँ। जबे पकऽड़ल छिलँ तऽ छाड़ऽला की छिलौ। आरो मुरगी कर अन्ना कर बराबर तऽ हम्मे अपऽने हो नहीँ छी, फिनु मुरगी कर अन्ना से बढ़ि के मोती हमर पेट मेँ होएब कहिया ध्यान मेँ आबै सकैछौ। पर तोँ ई बात पर भरोसा कैलँ। आरो अबे जौँ हम्मे तोर हाथ सँ निकसि गेलाँ, तऽ पछऽतैला से की होइछै। एकऽरा सँ ई फल निकऽसैछै, कि पहिने से हर एक काम के सोँचि बिचारि के करै चहिय, आरो जबे कोइ काम बिगरि जाए तऽ पछऽतावे नहीँ चहिय।

॥ १६ बात ॥

कोइ मातऽबर के दो बेटा छिलै। जबे ओकर बाप मरि गेलै तबे दुओ भै ओकर धन अपना मेँ बाँटि लेलऽकै। बड़ऽका भै ओकर आपन टाका पैसा सुख चैन आरो खेल तमासा मेँ उड़ाबे लगऽलै, आरो छोटऽका भै बड़ा ततऽबीर सेँ बनिज बेपार करै लगऽलै। एक दिन बड़ भै छोट भै के उलहन दे के कहिलऽकै कि, भै, कहिने दिन भर अनाज तौलल करैछँ। हमर सङ्गे रहँ, खो, पीयँ, चैन करँ। बहुत दिन पिछु जबे छोट भै लेन देन करि के बहुत टाका जमा करऽलक, तबे ओकर बड़ऽका भै, जे राग रङ्ग आरो खेल तमासा मेँ आपन सब धन उड़ा के भिखारी हो गेल छिलै, ओकर डौढ़ी पर आबि के कहै लगऽलै कि, भै, हम्मे तोरा पहिनेँ ठट्ठा मेँ उड़ैल छिलौँ। परन्तु जौँ हम्मे ओ तोर तरह से बनिज बेपार करऽतिहा, आरो अनाज तौलऽतिहाँ, तऽ ऐज के पा भरि दाना इम्मे उम्मे से माँगि के नहीँ खैतिहाँ। साँच छिकै।

॥ आलस ईरङ्ग हो कीड़ा छै, कि धन के धूरा करि दैछै ॥

॥ १७ बात ॥

॥ लालऽची कुत्ता ॥

कोइ कुत्ता नदी कर कछ्छा मेँ एक हड्डी पैलऽकै आरो मुँह मेँ लेलऽकै। जौँ छैयाँ ओकर पानि मेँ देखलऽकै समुझऽलक कि दोसर हड्डी छिकै। मारे लालच कर मुँह खोलक, कि ओकरऽहौ* पानि से निकासे। ऊ हड्डी जे मुँह मेँ छेलै, सेहौ खोयलक। साँच छिकै।

माछी दूध पर बैठऽलै, आरो पाँख लटऽपटा गेलै। हाथ मलै आरो माथ धूनै कि लालच बुरा बलाय ॥

---

* Emphatic for ओकऽरा, 'it also.'

REVIEWS OF THIS SERIES OF GRAMMAR.

"THE INDIAN CHRONICLE."

7th April 1884.

Mr. Grierson's Grammars.—It is impossible not to admire the amount of energy possessed by the educated European: and the legion of useful channels into which it flows in the pursuit of science or literature is equalled only by the effect and rapidity of the flow. People in this country and other countries "where the climate is sultry" are not capable of regular, sustained mental labour to such an extent as is possible in colder latitudes. The amount of work which an ordinary English or German student goes through daily, without in the least feeling fagged, is many times more than what we go through in forty-eight hours; and the fact is due both to climatic and constitutional defects, for we see that the climate alone of India—said to be the home of lassitude and the liver—has not affected the energy of Mr. Grierson. Now, it is not our intention to bespatter Mr. Grierson with fulsome flattery. But when we know that the duties of a civil servant in charge of an important district are multifarious and engrossing, and that a single moment of that precious commodity—spare time—is to him almost a forbidden luxury, we cannot certainly but admire Mr. Grierson for his *Seven Grammars of the Dialects and Subdialects of the Behári Languages*, of which the first three parts have just been published by the Bengal Government. To understand the difficulty of his task we must place ourselves in his position and suppose that we are called upon to write, within a stated period, and probably for the best part of that period away from a library, grammars of the unwritten dialects of Yorkshire or the Highlands, and yet our task would not be half so heavy as that of Mr. Grierson, for we have been familiarised with the English language from early infancy and gone through a regular and long course of school and collegiate instruction in that language, while Mr. Grierson's acquaintance with Sanskrit or Hindi must have been picked up during the odds and ends of spare time between one official work and another. The object of these grammars, Mr. Grierson says, is to make many Behar officials understand "the *ganwari boli* of the witnesses who come into their courts;" and notwithstanding the extreme modesty and limitedness of this object, we are not prepared to say that it would be entirely served out by Mr. Grierson's very laborious work. Unless these Behar officials, for whom Mr. Grierson has toiled so heartily and so well, have his patience and perseverance, we think it is scarcely possible for them to understand the language of our "roughs" even with the help of these grammars. The fact is that many of these Behar officials are in search of a royal road to a knowledge of the dialects of Behar; and they will be certainly disappointed to find no indication of such a road in Mr. Grierson's book. To those who don't scorn the weary way of schooling one's self by regular study, Mr. Grierson's book will be most certainly a very useful help. But a higher and better object than the one mentioned by Mr. Grierson will be served out by his grammars, which possess exceptional philological and literary interest. They make the regeneration of the dialects treated by them a matter of near possibility. The dialects of Mithila or Bhojpore, though they will never supersede Hindustani as the common or standard language of Hindi-speaking India, they may become, now that they have got their grammars, written languages current within limited local areas, with more or less refinement according to the measure of progress. Whether these dialects are the dialects, technically so called, of any language that ever was or is now current in India, is a matter of pure philological speculation; but that they will remain in a subordinate position to what is now called the Hindustani language, is a fact which cannot be now doubted. Mr. Grierson, however, would leave a name behind him in India should his grammars, as we think they would, be the means of imparting to these dialects some sort of literary pomp and refinement even in the subordinate position they are to occupy. So much for the usefulness of these grammars. As to their intrinsic merit, it is simply sufficient to say that we have no particular grounds of complaint. Excepting occasional slips in the fables, slips which it is impossible for a foreigner, however careful, to avoid, and the unpopular character of some of the songs quoted as being popular songs, these grammars are highly satisfactory productions; and, considering the immense amount of labour they must have cost, and to which we have alluded before, these little mistakes are not at all detractory in their character, and naturally dwindle out of consideration. On the other hand, Mr. Grierson's method of treating his subject is that of a practised grammarian: the explanations, where necessary, are full and lucid; the introduction in itself is a piece of rare merit; and the charts highly elucidatory. The Government of Bengal could not have entrusted the task to a better hand.

"THE INDIGO AND TEA PLANTERS' GAZETTE."

8th April 1884.

Mr. George A. Grierson's Seven Grammars of the Dialects and Subdialects of the Bihari Language.

In our issue of the 7th June 1882 we noticed shortly Part I, the Grammar of the Maithili language by Mr. Grierson, and on the 15th March of the following year we drew attention to the same author's Part II, the "Chrestomathy and Vocabulary." On the present occasion we have much pleasure in saying a few words regarding Mr. Grierson's Grammars of the Bíhári language, which have just been completed. The work which Mr. Grierson has effected in these volumes is one of which men whose names are much better known amongst philologists and scholars might well be proud. To gather together a language of varying dialects, with no literary standard, almost without a literary existence, from the tongues of the people, and to construct grammars of the dialects for the use of students and scholars, so that future work in the same field may be rendered comparatively easy, is a task of no ordinary magnitude; and when a piece of such notable work as that under notice has been effected amid the discharge of onerous duties in the plains of India, under difficulties and deterrents of no ordinary kind, the work is all the more praiseworthy. It would be presumption on our part to attempt to criticise the grammars of Mr. Grierson, for the simple reason that his books are the only ones in existence which deal so fully with the dialects of Behár, and no person, either in India or out of it, knows more of the dialects treated of than Mr. Grierson himself. To officials, planters, and others whose duties call them to mingle much with the people of Behár and the districts covered by the dialects dealt with, Mr. Grierson's grammars will be simply invaluable; while the philologist will find the work well worth his study. General readers do not as a rule turn to such works as those under notice either for relaxation or amusement, but it is nevertheless true that the study of a language reveals a storehouse of facts regarding the people using it which would quite surprise the majority of readers unaccustomed to attach little importance to the speech of the common folk. Among a people without a literature, or what amounts to no literature, the wisdom of gathered years is crystallised into proverbs: their emotions and deeper feelings find vent in song; and under the guise of fable a master-mind here and there gathers up much which give colouring and life to a dead past or a prosy present—pathos, humour, shrewd practical wisdom, and homely details which otherwise would perish. On a previous occasion we reproduced a few proverbs, and we venture now to present our readers with a song or two which may give some idea of the topics dealt with by the local verse-makers, and their treatment so far as a literal translation will admit. Here is a song sung by women in Shahabad district:—

See how this black-faced one beats me, abuses me, beats me.
I cleaned up the courtyard and brought water, and still he chides me.
Thus does he regard, O mother, my co-wife, while he makes out evil against me.
I am not thief nor a glutton, still he reproaches me falsely.
He beats me like seven donkeys and drags me about as if I were a pig.
See, O my neighbours! how he abuses me for no fault.
My stupid husband does not understand what I say, and keeps trying to set water on fire.
O Ambika! understand that he is blaming me openly.

The refrain of the following is "Ah Ram!"

In my sister-in-law's yard is there a sandal-tree, and upon it sits and caws a forest crow.
I will give thee, O crow! a morsel of milk and rice if thou wilt give me news about my love.
Sweetheart of thy beloved! say not beloved, beloved, for thy beloved also hath fallen captive to a young *tamorin*.
Alas! what is that country and that land like, and what the young *tamorin*.

Her body is delicate and her face is fair, and humble bees keep humming round her hair (so sweet is it).

Poison will I pound and venom will I eat, for he hath set that wanton before me.

Das Bulaki sang this ghato at a fit season, saying it, singing it, and her freinds consoled the deserted one.

The following fable is a fair sample of those given in Part I:—

Once upon a time somewhere a river rose and an earthen pitcher and a brass one were floated away. The brass pitcher said to the earthen, "Come along close by me and I'll take care of you." The earthen said, "The words which you have spoken are excellent, and I shall always be grateful to you and sing your praises for them; but, if you ask the truth, (I must confess to) this fear, that from the motion of the wave I may perchance be knocked against you. Now if I remain apart from you, while I am thus washed hither and thither, I will reach the bank somewhere; but if I meet you and anywhere accidentally knock against you, my belly will be burst." True it is:—

Hope in the great, but go not near them.

"THE ENGLISHMAN."

11*th April* 1884.

MR. G. A. GRIERSON, of the Civil Service, has completed the work which he began so well, many months ago, of trying to formalise the Bihari language as spoken by the people in Bihar in general into a language that could be used in the courts and understanded of the people by publishing grammars of the dialects and subdialects of that language. These grammars will appear in seven parts, of which we have at present received three. The advantage of the system adopted by Mr. Grierson is that not only does he fully show, in the different numbers of his grammars, the variations of the dialects of the different tribes inhabiting various parts of Bihar, but by neatly executed maps he shows in different colours the localities in which the dialects are used. Some years ago Mr. Beames, who was then employed in Bihar, published a grammar of the Bhojpuri dialect, but this is now out of print, so Mr. Grierson's grammar would have to be accepted as the authentic source of information regarding the language. Although the different dialects may not differ very much in their spoken form, there is sufficient difference to establish the fact that they are not one and the same. This distinction without a difference Mr. Grierson's grammars fully point out, and there can be no doubt that they will be found most useful by all officers employed in Bihar. The scope of the work is, the author tells us, so arranged that the grammar of each dialect or subdialect shall be, so far as is possible, uniform with the others. The series consists of seven grammars, arranged as follows :—

(1) No. 1 refers to the Bhojpuri dialect of Shahabad, Saran, Champaran, and North Mazaffarpur.

(2) No. 2 refers to the Magadhi dialect of Gaya and South Patna.

(3) No. 3 refers to the South Maithili dialect, mixed with Bhojpuri, of Central and South Mazaffarpur.

(4) No. 4 refers to the South Maithili dialect of South Darbhanga, North Munger, and the Madhepura subdivision of Bhagalpur.

(5) No. 5 refers to the South Maithili dialect affected by the Magadhi of South Munger.

(6) No. 6 refers to the Maithili-Bangali of South Bhagalpur.

(7) No. 7 refers to the Maithili-Bangali of Central and Western Purniya. In Eastern Purniya a dialect of Bangali is spoken which is not represented in these grammars.

Mr. Grierson, whose work, beyond the cost of printing, has not cost the Government a single pice, is well deserving of some particular recognition for his philological services.

"THE BEHAR HERALD."

22nd April 1884.

THE LANGUAGE OF BEHAR AND NORTHERN INDIA.

WE owe an apology to Mr. Grierson for not being able to notice earlier the first three parts of his "Seven Grammars of the Dialects and Subdialects of the Bihari Language" which we have received. The first part contains a general introduction to the whole series. Part II treats of the Bhojpuri dialect of Shahabad, Sarun, Champarun, North Mozufferpore, and the eastern portion of the North-Western Provinces, and Part III of the Magadhi dialect of South Patna and Gaya. In the historical sketch prefixed to the book, Mr. Grierson finds objections to the use of the word "dialect" in its popular acceptation to the various forms of speech spoken of above. He says:—"There is this other grave objection against the use of the term 'dialect' that this term, as popularly (though not scientifically) accepted, necessarily presupposes the existence of some one closely connected form of speech to which the dialects can be referred as a standard." With all our respect for Mr. Grierson's scholarship in Hindi, we cannot bring ourselves to agree with him on this point. We are of opinion that all the various forms of speech prevalent in different parts of Behar and the North-Western Provinces are but dialects of one language, and can be referred to literary Hindi as a standard. This literary Hindi may not be very rich in its literature, but it exists all the same and furnishes the common standard by the light of which all of them are to be viewed and examined. The Ramayan of Toolsidas and the school-books taught in the educational institutions of the country supply instances of this literary tongue. The language of the Muggerpal ryot or the Shahabad shopkeeper may be as different from that of the *Ramayan* as the language of Sam Weller from that of *The Pickwick Papers* or of Dandie Dinmont from that of the *Guy Mannering*. But this we think is hardly a reason to consider that the *Ramayan* typifies a language entirely distinct from that of Monair or Bhabuah. Our own view on this subject is that the colloquial forms of speech treated of in Mr. Grierson's grammar, as also those which he calls "the Hindi dialects," are all but different varieties of the same language. The dialect of Dorset differs in many particulars from that of York, some of them as material as those in which the Behari and Hindi disagree. The language of common parlance being more subject, from the very conditions under which it exists, to phonetic decay and dialectic regeneration, is far less inflexible in its character than the literary dialect, which in time is stereotyped from the fact of its being reduced into writing. And where the geographical area over which it extends is considerable, differences spring up much sooner and are more numerous than in comparatively shorter tracts of country. It will be as reasonable to say that because a Shahabad cultivator would use the provincialism "ghor'wa" for "ghora" (horse) or pronounce the Hindi word "langoti" as "nangot," the Magadhi and Hindi are not dialects of the same language, as it would be to hold that because a low-Londoner would pronounce *horse* and *education* as *orse* and *heddication* that they are not speaking English. Similar provincialisms are to be found in all languages. They occur in the Bengali. As an instance of the difference in pronunciation between the Behari and Hindi languages, Mr. Grierson cites the verb पड़ब, meaning "to fall," and says that Behari has often र where Hindi has ड़. This word, he points out, is pronounced as परब "parab" in the Behari, while the र is changed into ड़ in Hindi. The self-same divergence, however, is to be found in different parts of Bengal. Some of the Eastern districts invariably pronounce the letter ড় of the literary Bengali as র. We are not sure, however, whether the same invariability is observed in the pronunciation of this letter in all the dialects of Behar. In Patna, at any rate, the word "parab" is always pronounced as पड़ब as in the Hindi. Another very frequent provincialism met with in various parts of Bengal is to be found in the interchange of ন (N) into ল (L) and *vice versâ*, the word নৌকা being pronounced by the common people as লৌকা and নব্বুই as লব্বুই। Such discrepant pronunciation therefore can hardly be considered as a well-defined characteristic demarcating one language from another. More curious changes of pronunciation than any pointed out by Mr. Grierson are known to take place in the Bengali as we pass from one district to another. In some parts of East Bengal the dental স (S) is changed into the aspirate হ (H) as the Sanscrit স is changed into হ in Zend and the modern Persian—*Sindhia* (from *Sindhoo*) being changed into *Hindia*, the primitive form of the modern *India*, by the followers of Zoaraster, and the Sanscrit *Saptam* into the Persian *haptam* by their descendants. Another interesting illustration of this peculiarity is to be noticed in the derivation of the word "Ormuzd" as given by Professor Max Müller. He says that it is a contraction of a form of *Ahura mazdao* to be found in the cuneiform inscriptions of the age of Darius and Xerxes, which latter phrase is itself traceable to the Sanscrit *Asura medhas* (the Wise Spirit). But we are digressing. Under the head of *Derivation* the book before us, in noticing the peculiarities which, according to the differentiate Hindi, from the cognate dialects of Behar, says "the singular possessive (or genitive) of the personal pronouns has in Behari a medial *o*, but in Hindi *e* or *á*: thus Behari *mor*, 'my,' but Hindi *merau* or *marau*. Compare the Bengali *mor*." But this Bengali *mor* should have suggested to the learned author that the example he has cited does not indicate any material diversity of character of the dialects referred to. *Mor* in Bengali is simply a contraction of the more generally prevalent word *ámár*, and is only used by the vulgar in some parts of the country. In Behar, moreover, the word *mor* is not at all of general application. In Patna the word is very seldom if at all used even by the common people. As this review has already run to the length of an average newspaper article, we stop here for the present.

"THE SATURDAY REVIEW."

Dialects of Hindi.*

2nd May 1885.

Just thirty years ago the late Mr H. H. Wilson, in the Preface to his Glossary of Revenue, Judicial, and Useful Terms, remarked that the peculiarities of the Hindi dialects had never been investigated, and that we only had a grammar of one of them, the Braj, which was somewhat meagre. He also

---

* *Seven Grammars of the Dialects and Subdialects of the Bihárí Language spoken in the Provinces of Behar, in the Eastern Portion of the North-Western Provinces, and in the Northern Portion of the Central Provinces.* In Four Parts. Compiled, under the orders of the Government of Bengal, by George A. Grierson, B.C.S., Officiating Joint-Magistrate of Patna. Calcutta: Bengal Secretariat Press.

said that "each province may be said to have its own form of Hindi, and in Behar, Bhojpur, Benares, Brindaban, Delhi, various shades of it are known under the appellations of Magadhi, the dialect of Magadha or South Behar; Maithili, that of North Behar or Purnea, and Tirhut; Bhojpuri, that of Bhojpur; Purbi, Eastern; Braj Bhakhá, or the speech of Braj, and others." A more recent and high authority declares that it is not very easy to define the exact limits of Hindi. It is said roughly to be spoken by eighty millions of people, and to extend over nearly 250,000 square miles. Its boundary on one side may be given as Nepal and the Terai. On the other the Hindi crosses the river Nerbudda, enters the country of the aboriginal Gonds, and touches on the Uriya and the Marathi languages. It is difficult to draw a line or prescribe a limit. Orientalists differ considerably as to its schools, standards, and divisions or subdialects. All that can be laid down for certain is, that there is a Hindi literature of some extent, including such old works as the Ramayana of Tulsi Dass and the Mahabharata of Gokulnath; that the character most in use is the Nagari or Sanskrit, written from left to right; that, if we include the semi-Dravidian and semi-Kolarian dialects we may count fifty variations; and that any scholar with a fair stock of Sanskrit will be able at once to master the most common forms of Hindi, and with a little pains its grammatical and linguistic vagaries. Residence in a district or Division, combined with a quick ear for pronunciation, can alone enable an Englishman to understand the rustic speech of a Kurmi or an Ahir.

To a scientific investigation of the parent languages of India as well as of their offshoots, Englishmen and some natives have both contributed. Such works as the late Raja Radhakant's Sanskrit Dictionary and the Bengali Dictionary of Ram Kamal Sen are well known. But the most prominent class of explorers have been missionaries and members of the Civil and Military services of the Government. Their labours have been most serviceable in what we may call the jungles and bypaths of oriental dialects. Strange local terms, quaint sayings, current satirical songs, weights, measurements, customs, have been collected, sifted, and compared by officials as a mild sort of recreation after the real work of the day, or at scattered intervals of leisure. The native student is a lukewarm Gallio in these things. No doubt much has been familiar to him from his childhood. But the high-born Pundit scorns the coarse language of the villager, and though under the direction of an Englishman his intimate knowledge of Hindu life can be turned to a profitable account, it is to Englishmen that we owe most of the collections, vocabularies, and elementary works that bring home to the average student the vast and comparatively untrodden field of exploration that still lies before him in India.

Mr. Grierson, the compiler of the four little grammars before us, has not been many years in the service; for he has not yet attained to that enviable position, the charge of a district, with its two or three magisterial sub-divisions, its million or two of Hindus and Mahommedans, and its multifarious duties. But he has certainly made a very good use of his time. To some evident acquaintance with one of the classic languages of the East and the more correct forms of the vernacular and spoken dialects, he adds a mastery over the rude language of the agriculturist and an ability to superintend the labours of Pundits and Inspectors of Schools. We are by no means satisfied that Mr. Grierson's nomenclature is happy or likely to be permanent. He argues apparently that there is no universal or paramount standard of Hindi to which every offshoot or dialectic variety can be referred, and that the term Hindi ought not to be applied to that form of the language which is spoken in Behar. We fear that this attempt to expel Hindi with a pitchfork will end like many others. "Bihari" may be defensible on philological grounds. It might have been adopted by Imperial edict some time before the reign of Akbar, had Mr Grierson been then consulted, or had he filled the post of one of that emperor's lieutenants. But it will be long before Bihari finds its way into popular acceptation. The Mahommedans of Lower Bengal obstinately persist to this day in applying the term *Farsi* or Persian to the diluted Hindustani which they are in the habit of writing and reading. Moreover, as Mr. Grierson subdivides his new language into many branches, and does not, so far as we make out, set up any one high standard of "Bihari," there was every reason why he should have contented himself with an original, a well-understood, and a by-no-means inaccurate philological term, Hindi. His inquiries into the Hindi language as spoken in various districts of the great Behar province have led him to the conclusion that it was divisible into seven branches, of which he now gives us three—Bhojpuri, Magadhi, and Maithili or Maithil-Bhojpuri. The first term includes nearly all the Behar districts north and east of the Ganges, and that of Shahabad.

The second comprises South Patna and Gya; the third a part of Mozuffarpur, formerly known as Tirhut. We presume that he will eventually give us other grammars for Hindi as spoken in Bhaugulpore and Monghir, which he calls Munger, and some day, perhaps, for Hazaribagh and the districts of the South-West Frontier Agency. It is true that Mr. Grierson argues for some radical distinctions between the real Hindi or Braj Bhakha and his new bantling the Bihari. He lays stress on pronunciation, on the declensions and participles, and on the use or omission of the particle *ne*, on the conjugation of verbs, on construction, and on the vocabulary. Pronunciation is surely a weak argument. Every scholar of modern languages knows how differently Italian is pronounced at Venice, Siena, and Naples; French in Provence or Picardy; and German in Hanover or Switzerland. Need we mention the difference in speech between a Somersetshire and a Northumbrian peasant? Or, to take an illustration from another part of India not so remote from Behar, has Mr. Grierson ever compared the speech of a boatman from Noacolly or Sylhet with that of a Kaibarto from Beerbhum? He may rely on it that he will be startled by the way in which one of these two speakers of one common language, the Bengali, elides or alters consonants, and plays havoc with verbs, moods, and tenses. Neither do peculiarities in the use of nouns and verbs and their terminations seem to us sufficient to make out his case. Differences between weak forms and strong forms, long vowels and short vowels, verbal nouns and postpositions, between one future tense which ends in *ab* and another which ends in *as*, omissions and redundancies of tenses, peculiarities in the formation of causal verbs and other queer metamorphoses, merely show to our thinking that Hindi has more dialects or subdialects, and branches out into more channels, than Orientalists had fully recognised. Constructions and vocabularies may differ, but on analysing some of the compiler's specimens we find them to differ more in appearance than reality. All the same these commentaries with grammars and vocabularies will be serviceable to juniors when shifted suddenly from Sasseeram and its soap manufacture on the Grand Trunk Road to the subdivision of Kishengunge in Poornea, under that useful and inexorable formula of the Secretariat,—“the exigencies of the public service.”

In the general student not expected to trouble himself too much about the varying termination of the Hindi verbs, to remember all about vocalic roots and periphrastic tenses, and to say exactly where the Bhojpuri slides into the Maithili dialect, more interest will be awakened by the specimens of conversation between two villagers, the fables, and the songs sung at marriages and other festive occasions. If not real gems and treasures, they are lively, original, and illustrative of agricultural life. Some of them are familiar enough. The dog with a piece of meat or bone in his mouth of which he sees the reflection in the water; the tiger that divides the stricken deer into three parts and takes all three for himself; the milkmaid indulging in visions of wealth, who smashes her pot of curds to atoms; the rich man who has one idle and one industrious son; the farmer who, by the illustration of a faggot, impressed on his children the fact that union is strength, and divers others, are well known from Æsop's time in the nurseries and schools of the East and the West. But some of the songs may be as new to many as the minstrelsy of the border was when first discovered by Walter Scott. We select specimens. The successive ceremonies of a marriage, the arrival of the bridegroom at the bride's house, the scattering of rice, and the introduction of the barber who cuts the nails of the happy pair, are well described in a blessing sung at marriages. The bride is naturally compared to Sita. Gauri, the wife of Shiva, and Ganesa, are duly invoked, and jests are passed round, not of the most delicate kind. The poet invokes all manner of happiness on the couple and takes care that his own name shall not be forgotten. In a climate where health, life, and comfort depend on the regularity of the seasons, songs of the whole year and of particular months have a peculiar significance. Asarh (June–July) is a happy month as the beginning of the rains; that the next month, Sawan, should be "a fire of exceeding sorrow" has no meaning unless we infer a failure of rain. It is everywhere in Northern and Central India, and in Bengal Proper, the wettest month of the year. Kartik (October–November) is distinguished by bathing in the Ganges; Pus or Pos (December–January) by excessive cold and well-wadded quilts; Phalgun (February and March), by the Holi and its repulsive red powder; and Jeth (May and June) by a hot wind that roars and howls and turns the atmosphere into a furnace. The month of Chait (March and April) has several songs of its own. It is an auspicious month for marriages. The hot season has set in, and it is the time for Krishna to sport with the milkmaids in the woods of Brindaban and Mathura. A young woman asks a crow for news of her beloved, and is told that he has been captivated by another young woman who sells betel-leaves, whereupon she threatens her rival with poison. Another wife, not so ill-fated, watches anxiously for her lord and promises a golden bracelet in return for good news of him. A third is very properly apprehensive lest her faithless husband should be caught in the rain and get wet through. A fourth boasts that the turban of her husband will shine in the assembly of men like a sword in battle or the *chulhwa* fish in the lake, which is rather an anticlimax.

Another song of the seasons makes the east wind to blow in Sawan, as it often does; the lakes and ponds to be filled with water in Bhadon, and the cold season to be felt in Kartik, which it would be in any part of Upper India as far down as Behar. A song in which one Churila is asked by a wife to play the flute, and having first excused himself for fear of the dogs and the watchman, at last yields to her importunities, would hardly commend itself to an Inspector of Schools. The sequel is not decent, as the minstrel, whom the frail one believes to be a prince, turns out to be a low-caste Dosadh. A divided household is illustrated by one wife who complains that she has to sweep the courtyard, draw water, and endure blows and abuse, as if she were seven donkeys, while all the honour is paid by the husband to her co-wife. Another faithful wife dressed herself in red and sought in vain for her husband at Gokul, Brindaban, and Benares, in the jungle and in the mountains, and found him not, because all the time he was in his own house. One young wife gets much abuse from her mother-in-law for her clumsiness in breaking the broom with which she is sweeping the courtyard, and invokes the aid of her elder brother, who is supposed to have a cooly with a load of new brooms ready to hand. The nectar or drink of Rama is so powerful in one ditty that ordinary men become deaf or die when they drink it. Only saints like Durab, Pahlad, and Mirabai can swallow it; and Kabir Das, whom we take to be the poet himself, will have to leave the world if he drinks more of it. There is a flavour of antiquity about some of the above songs. Others clearly show that village bards are not extinct, and that new songs are made regarding social and political changes. The Maharaja of Domraon is a personage of consequence in the district of Shahabad. He maintains, we find from Mr. W. Hunter, a dispensary in his native town at his own cost, and owns many villages. But when Koer Sing, described in the song as the Babu, went a-hunting, or, as would have been said in Scotland, was "out" in the year 1857, and had a fight with the English at Hetampur, the Maharaja did not come to his assistance, whereat the hinds of the forest wept. A more recent song commemorates the linguistic revolution accomplished, if we mistake not, by Sir G. Campbell when Lieutenant-Governor of Bengal. The member for the Kirkaldy Boroughs, with a benovolent despotism which his constituents may scarcely credit, abolished the Urdu language and the Persian character in which it is written by a stroke of the pen. We are sorry to say that in two songs commemorative of his masterly stroke of business Sir George's name is not actually mentioned. He is, however, introduced as the Lord Sahib to whom the case was represented by Baboo Bhuban Deb Mukerji, a Kulin Brahman of Bengal, Inspector of Schools, and now a Companion of the Indian Empire. The consequence of his interview or correspondence with the Lieutenant-Governor, for we are not told which, was that the language of the Javans or Mahomedans was banished. The Nagari character was restored. Persian books were to be sent to the spice-seller—*in vicum vendentem thus et odores*; forgeries, hitherto common in the Persian character, were prophetically to cease when the Hindu could write in Kaithi or Nagari; and all men were invited to sing the praises of her Majesty the Queen by the poet Ambika, who adds a prayer that her reign may last as long as the sun and the moon.

In Part III of the Seven Grammars Mr. Grierson gives us some fifteen pages of a vocabulary of the Magadhi dialect as spoken in Gaya and the south of Patna. Many of the terms are expressive of agricultural customs, rude domestic implements, garments, ornaments, insects, and articles of food. The compiler is justified in saying that few of them will be found in any Hindi dictionary. We can assure him that we have looked in vain for a good many in the new and copious dictionary of Mr. Platts. There are words which express the ox nearest the post in a threshing-floor, or the animal on the right hand of the pair attached to a harrow. The word *bes*, which Mr. Grierson thinks to be Hindi and translates as "all right," strikes us as a mere corruption of the Persian *besh*, "capital," "excellent." In this sense we have known it constantly used. *Galu* in the vocabulary is "false;" in Mr. Platts's, it is "boastful." *Tapawan*, similarly, is "wine."

Mr. Platts interprets it as "a libation." There is perhaps not much difference between the two. *Chev*, 'to cut,' we should derive from the verb *chedna* and not from *katna*, as Mr. Grierson does. He gives a number of meanings to the word *majha*. It is the angle on which the front of a cart rests; ground-bait for fishes ; and a plaster of powdered glass applied to kite strings by a kite-flier who wishes to cut his rival's kite. Mr. Platts gives the last meaning only. *Dah* with Mr. Grierson is a ditch ; with Mr. Platts and with other experts it is an abyss or pit. *Nara* is interpreted as straw. More correctly it is the stubble which remains on the field after the crop has been cut by the sickle and carried away. The common word for straw is *bichali*. We have no doubt that the grammars of the remaining dialects will be marked by the same diligence, accuracy, and method. But we must warn Mr. Grierson against the snare of a captivating theory or the discovery of a new language. We have compared his translated fable with the original in different dialects, and his new classification of verbs, potentials, completives, frequentatives, and desideratives, which, however ingenious, are merely old acquaintances under new aspects; as well as the vagaries of verbal nouns and grammatical forms, and we see no reason to think they are other than mere dialectic varieties of Hindi, mainly due to circumstances and places. But he has made a valuable contribution to Hindi literature, the more remarkable because makers of dictionaries have too often been unacquainted with village life ; and the district officer, who knows that life thoroughly, has had no time to compile even a vocabulary. Mr. Grierson is one who can get at the speech of rustics and can put it into a shape for which scholars and pundits may be thankful.

"THE INDIAN ANTIQUARY."

1st *July* 1885.

Seven Grammars of the Dialects and Subdialects of the Bihari Language. By G. A. Grierson, B.C.S.—Calcutta, Bengal Secretariat Press, 1883.

These little volumes, four only of which have as yet appeared, show the immense progress that has been made in the study of Indian dialects since

I published my article on the Bhojpurî dialect, seventeen years ago, in the *Journal of the Royal Asiatic Society* (Vol. III, 1868). In the first place, it is now clearly recognised that the term Hindî, as used by Europeans, is merely a vague expression for so many of the Aryan dialects as have not been distinguished by territorial names. I had partially grasped this fact, though not fully, when I wrote the remarks on p. 31 *et seq*. of Vol. 1 of my *Comparative Grammar of the Modern Aryan Languages of India* in 1872. All round the outer edge of Aryan India is a circle of kingdoms or provinces; Bengal, Orissa, Mahârâshtra, Gujarât, Sindh, Pañjâb, Nepâl; and the "Indian," or, as the Muhammadans called it, the Hindî, spoken in each of these places came by degrees to be called Bengâlî, Oriya, Marâthî, and so on.

But in the centre there remained a vast area for which no special name was found: it was merely Hindî, and its language or languages were all merely Hindî. It has long been known that under this general term were included forms of speech differing very widely from each other, and it only remained for some scholar to enquire into the subject and classify these various forms, referring them to their proper relationships. Mr. Grierson has done this for the Eastern part of the hitherto undefined area, and he has therefore a perfect right to give a name to the form of speech whose independence he has successfully established. Indeed, it is highly probable that had the province of Bihâr, like the neighbouring province of Bengal, maintained itself in independence of the crown of Delhî for any length of time, its language would have been called Bihârî many centuries ago.

In the second place, the researches of Dr. Hoernle into the obscure subject of the Prâkrit dialects have placed it beyond a doubt that these forms of speech fall into two groups, called respectively Mâgadhî and Saurasênî ; the former being the elder of the two and at one time probably the only language of Northern India, the latter and younger having gradually extended from the west eastwards and pushed the older language before it, till the domain of Mâgadhî lay entirely to the east of a line drawn north and south through Benares, though its influence on the Saurasênî resulted in the growth of a mixed dialect called Arddha-Mâgadhî, which seems to have extended far to the west. At a later period Mâgadhî pushed to the south-west through the Marâthâ country, but in the valley of the Ganges it never seems to have got much further west than the longitude of Benares. From this it follows that the dialects spoken in Bihâr have very much less connexion with those spoken in the western parts of the loosely-defined and misleadingly-designated "Hindî" area than they have with the other speech forms of Mâgadhî origin, such as Bangâlî and Oriya.

While, however, I fully agree with Mr. Grierson in separating Bihârî from the so-called Hindî, I feel a little difficulty in following him when he divides his newly-discovered language into so many as *seven* dialects. Indeed, he himself seems rather doubtful on this point, for he admits on p. 15 of the Introduction that there are in reality only *three* dialects—Bhojpurî, Maithilî, and Mâgadhî, and his seven grammars are, or are to be, made up by giving, in addition to these three, four mixed forms, such as Maithilî affected by Mâgadhí, Maithilî-Bangâlî, and so on. All this extremely fine classification and subdivision, though it entitles Mr. Grierson to high rank among scientific philologists, is rather out of place in hand-books intended to teach officials the patois of their districts.

When one comes to look even at the three leading dialects, one finds them so very much alike that a grammar of any one of them would almost be a sufficient guide to the whole group. Take for instance the pronouns. That of the first person may be summarised as follows :—

	Nominative.		Oblique.	
	Short form.	*Long form.*	*Short form.*	*Long form.*
Singular, "I" . .	meṅ.	ham.	morâ.	hamrâ.
Plural, "we" . .	hamanî,	hamrani.	hamanî	hamranî.

The only deviations from this scheme are that *men* is not used in Magadhî or South Maithilî; that North Maithilî uses *moh* as well as *morâ*; that Bhojpuri adds *kâ* to *hamanî*, and all the dialects use also *ham sabh* and *hamrâ sabh* for the nom. and obl. plural respectively. The same close similarity runs through all the parts of speech. Apart from this defect of over-refining and over-classifying, which is a defect only in so far as it tends to embarrass the practical student, these little grammars are as complete and perfect as can be desired. The arrangement is admirable, being both scientific and simple. The rules are clear and not too numerous, and the examples well chosen and carefully worked out. As none of these languages possesses any literature (with the exception of Maithilî, which has a little poetry), there is no recognised standard of speech for any of them, and it is therefore inevitable that there should be many varying forms for every person of every tense. Mr. Grierson's trained musical ear has enabled him to detect a very large number of these variations,—very many more, in fact, than are apparent to the ordinary observer; and all of these are very fully given. It would have been well if some effort had been made to select for each person or tense one form, to be considered as the standard form, from which the others should be held to be deviations. By this means the vagaries of rustic pronunciation might by degrees be reduced into manageable limits.

Specially noteworthy is the attempt to indicate several fine distinctions in vowel sounds by signs borrowed from the Gurmukhi character—a measure in which Dr. Hoernle took the lead, and which, it may be hoped, will become general.

JOHN BEAMES.

"THE ATHENÆUM."

25th July 1885.

SEVEN GRAMMARS OF THE DIALECTS AND SUBDIALECTS OF THE BIHÁRI LANGUAGE. BY G. A. GRIERSON. Parts I—IV.

THE enthusiastic Professor Garcin de Tassy close upon sixty years ago laid down a broad distinction between Hindí and Hindúí, comprising under the latter denomination the more archaic literary forms of the Hindí language in which the poems of Chand, Súrdás, Tulsídas, and others, and the hymns of the mediæval reformers were composed. It is only within the last fifteen years that, upon a better acquaintance with the numerous varieties of Hindí speech, that distinction has been abandoned, and the various languages, dialects, and subdialects spoken within the Hindí area have gradually been classed according to a more scientific arrangement. The investigations of Dr. Trumpp ('Sindhi Grammar,' 1872), Dr. Hoernle ('Essays on the Gau*d*ian Languages,' 1872-74), and the Rev. S. H. Kellogg ('Hindí Grammar,' 1876), and his own continued labours in this field, enabled Mr. Beames to work up in the latter part of his 'Comparative Grammar' (1872-79) a mass of fresh material, while Dr. Hoernle's 'Gau*d*ian Grammar' (1880) laid a solid foundation for all subsequent researches on the dialects of Eastern Hindi, and pointed out the wide gulf which separates them from those of the Western Hindí group. Mr. G. A. Grierson, aided by Dr. Hoernle, has since devoted his studies exclusively to the Eastern Hindí dialects, which are spoken by some fifty to sixty millions, over an area extending west to east from Benares to Purníyá and north to south from the Himálayas to Jabalpúr. These dialects are comprised by him under the general name of Bihárí, and embrace the Maithilí, Bhojpúrí, and Mágadhí, each again with various local subdialects. The Asiatic Society of Bengal a few years ago published his grammar, chrestomathy, and vocabulary of Northern Maithilí; and the Government of Bengal subsequently commissioned him to compile for the use of the Bihár officials a series of grammatical manuals of the other local dialects spoken throughout those parts, which differ from one another far more in grammar than in vocabulary. The first half of this series, consisting of an introduction and grammars of the Bhojpúrí, Mágadhí, and South Maithilí dialects, is now before us. Of these the first-named covers the largest extent of country, running from the Himálayas down to Jabalpúr in the Central Provinces; it has few local varieties, and possesses no literature; neither does Mágadhí, which is spoken throughout the south of the Patna district, the whole of Gayâ, and the north of Chutiá Nágpúr. None of its peculiarities appears to point to its descent from the Mágadhí of the Southern Buddhists or the scenic Prakrit of that name. Maithilí, spoken in its greatest purity in the northern half of the Darbhangá district and in the Supaul subdivision of North Bhágalpúr, is the least developed of the Bihárí dialects; and as "it still retains many old forms which have been lost by the two other more advanced dialects," it is specially worthy of the attention of philologists, "as offering a key to a number of grammatical puzzles which would otherwise remain unsolved." We may well say that these valuable monographs mark altogether a new departure in modern Indian philology, and we are glad to have received within the last week or two the first instalment of the great Bihárí Dictionary which Mr. Grierson and Dr. Hoernle have had in hand for some years.

THE "LITERARY WORLD."

22nd January 1886.

The Bihari Language.*

Dialects of what has been conveniently called the Bihari language are spoken in the province of Behar, in the eastern portion of the North-Western Provinces, and in the northern portion of the Central Provinces of India. These districts all lie along the Ganges and its affluents. They are administered by British officials, who are supposed to be sufficiently qualified as regards matters linguistic when they have passed an examination or two in Hindustani or Bengali, according as they belong to the Local Government of Upper or Lower Bengal. But when these officials come to have dealings with the natives they are, at first, at a loss how to address the latter, who, apparently, speak neither language. For many years past Mr. George A. Grierson, of the Bengal Civil Service, has devoted his leisure to the study of these local dialects and subdialects. The importance of the subject led the Bengal Government in 1881 to depute Mr. Grierson to compile a series of Bihari grammars, and the first part of these was published in 1883. Since then four other parts have been issued, and two more—making seven parts in all—are to come. Each part, in reality, represents a separate grammar, the method adopted differing from that used in Dr. Hoernle's "Comparative Grammar of the Gaudian Languages," which was the first attempt at reducing them to rules. The historical introduction with which Mr. Grierson commences the series is a valuable contribution to Oriental philology. He traces back the numberless dialects now existing in Northern India to two Prakrit languages which divided that immense area between them, and both of which could boast of possessing literatures. One of these, the Sauraseni language, is preserved for us in the Sanscrit plays, and Magadhi, the other, is also found in them, although to a lesser extent. The two differed as much as do French and Italian. Some useful maps are given to illustrate the origin, and also the present distribution of languages and dialects.

---

* Seven Grammars of the Dialects and Subdialects of the Bihari language. Parts I—V. By George A. Grierson, B.C.S. Trübner and Company. 2*s.* 6*d.* each Part.